# Visual Basic® Developer's Guide to ASP and IIS

A. Russell Jones

SYBEX®

San Francisco • Paris • Düsseldorf • Soest • London

Associate Publisher: Richard Mills
Contracts and Licensing Manager: Kristine O'Callaghan
Acquisitions & Developmental Editor: Denise Santoro
Editor: Sharon Wilkey
Project Editor: Colleen Strand
Technical Editor: Greg Guntle
Book Designer: Kris Warrenburg
Graphic Illustrator: Jerry Williams
Electronic Publishing Specialist: Grey Magauran
Project Team Leader: Shannon Murphy
Proofreaders: Kathy Drasky, Catherine Morris,
Laura Schattschneider
Indexer: Nancy Guenther
Cover Designer: Design Site
Cover Illustrator/Photographer: Jack D. Myers

SYBEX is a registered trademark of SYBEX Inc.

Developer's Handbook is a trademark of SYBEX Inc.

Screen reproductions produced with Collage Complete.
Collage Complete is a trademark of Inner Media Inc.

TRADEMARKS: SYBEX has attempted throughout this book to distinguish proprietary trademarks from descriptive terms by following the capitalization style used by the manufacturer.

The author and publisher have made their best efforts to prepare this book, and the content is based upon final release software whenever possible. Portions of the manuscript may be based upon pre-release versions supplied by software manufacturer(s). The author and the publisher make no representation or warranties of any kind with regard to the completeness or accuracy of the contents herein and accept no liability of any kind including but not limited to performance, merchantability, fitness for any particular purpose, or any losses or damages of any kind caused or alleged to be caused directly or indirectly from this book.

Copyright ©1999 SYBEX Inc., 1151 Marina Village Parkway, Alameda, CA 94501. World rights reserved. The authors created reusable code in this publication expressly for reuse by readers. Sybex grants readers limited permission to reuse the code found in this publication or its accompanying web site for applications developed or distributed by the reader so long as the author is attributed in any application containing the reusable code and the code itself is never distributed, posted online by electronic transmission, sold or commercially exploited as a stand-alone product. Aside from this specific exception concerning reusable code, no part of this publication may be stored in a retrieval system, transmitted, or reproduced in any way, including but not limited to photocopy, photograph, magnetic or other record, without the prior agreement and written permission of the publisher.

Library of Congress Card Number: 99-65203
ISBN: 0-7821-2557-3

Manufactured in the United States of America

10 9 8 7 6 5 4 3

# Visual Basic® Developer's Guide to ASP and IIS

*I dedicate this book to my parents, Russell and Wanda Jones, whose unflagging support and lifelong love of learning have inspired me and made this book possible, and to my wife, Janet, for listening gracefully whenever I needed a sympathetic ear and for offering sage linguistic advice at opportune moments.*

# FOREWORD

As Visual Basic developers, we have seen a distinct move away from single, monolithic executables to distributed, component-based architectures. With this shift has come the need to think differently. We need to think of applications as a set of components working together to provide the needed solution.

As technology changes, we continue to modify our component architectures to support those changes. With the increased need for the development of Web-based applications, the next step is to combine what we know about component-based development with today's Web-based technologies. Tools such as Hypertext Markup Language (HTML), Active Server Pages (ASP), and Internet Information Server (IIS) applications (also known as WebClasses) must be added to our tool kit.

But how do we fit these tools into what we already know as Visual Basic programmers? Do we need to learn HTML? Can we build components that are then called by ASP? Can we build Web applications by using our favorite tool: Visual Basic?

This book answers these questions. The author, A. Russell Jones, provides a brief introduction to HTML to get us started. He then presents examples of ASP and IIS applications and discusses them in detail to help us get up to speed quickly and keep us in step with today's technologies.

Deborah Kurata

InStep Technologies, Inc. (www.insteptech.com)

Author of *Doing Objects in Visual Basic 6.0*

# ACKNOWLEDGMENTS

I would like to thank Bob Yeager and Margo Pearson at InterCom for letting me play with new technology as a major part of my job. Not everyone (in fact, hardly anyone) gets that kind of opportunity, and I truly appreciate it. I would like to thank Susannah Pfalzer at *Visual Basic Programmer's Journal* for the recommendation that started this book. I would also like to acknowledge the excellent work of the editorial team at Sybex, in particular, Denise Santoro, Colleen Strand, Sharon Wilkey, and Greg Guntle. Their patience and guidance have helped make writing this book an experience to treasure.

Other people have had a large influence on my life and on this book, and I would like to take this opportunity to thank them as well: Donald Pederson, for introducing me to programming; Charles Leonhard and Esther Steinberg, for their wisdom and advice; G. David Peters, for being an example; and David Northington, for teaching me how to practice.

Finally, I would like to thank you for buying this book. I hope you find it useful, that you learn a lot, and that you have as much fun reading it as I had writing it.

A. Russell Jones

arjonesiii@intercom-interactive.com

# CONTENTS AT A GLANCE

| | |
|---|---:|
| *Introduction* | *xiv* |
| Chapter 1: Visual Basic and the Web | 1 |
| Chapter 2: IIS Applications | 9 |
| Chapter 3: Building ASP Applications | 27 |
| Chapter 4: Introduction to WebClasses | 65 |
| Chapter 5: Securing an IIS Application | 87 |
| Chapter 6: WebClass Debugging and Error Handling | 125 |
| Chapter 7: Controlling Program Flow | 157 |
| Chapter 8: Maintaining State in IIS Applications | 191 |
| Chapter 9: Dealing with Multiple Browsers | 235 |
| Chapter 10: Retrieving and Storing Data in Databases | 251 |
| Chapter 11: Using ActiveX DLLs from WebClasses | 279 |
| Chapter 12: IIS Applications and Microsoft Transaction Server | 313 |
| Chapter 13: Deploying WebClass Applications | 339 |
| Chapter 14: What's Next? | 355 |
| *Index* | *368* |

# TABLE OF CONTENTS

| | | |
|---|---|---:|
| | *Introduction* | *xiv* |
| **1** | **Visual Basic and the Web** | **1** |
| | What's a Web Application? | 3 |
| | Why Write a Web Application in VB? | 4 |
| | What's the Difference between IIS and DHTML Applications? | 6 |
| |     This Book Concentrates on IIS Applications | 6 |
| **2** | **IIS Applications** | **9** |
| | How Browsers Request Files | 10 |
| | So Many Requests, So Little Time | 12 |
| | ASP Object Model | 13 |
| |     Server Object | 14 |
| |     Application Object | 15 |
| |     Session Object | 16 |
| |     Request Object | 18 |
| |     Response Object | 19 |
| |     ScriptingContext Object | 21 |
| |     ObjectContext Object | 22 |
| | Web Applications vs. Client-Server Applications | 23 |
| **3** | **Building ASP Applications** | **27** |
| | Understanding the Structure of an ASP Application | 28 |
| | Using Include Files | 30 |
| | Understanding Language Independence | 31 |
| | Using Cookies with ASP | 32 |
| | Using the Scripting.Dictionary Object | 34 |
| | A (Very) Brief Introduction to HTML and Forms | 39 |
| | Creating a Self-Modifying ASP Application | 42 |
| | Tying It All Together—Caching Table Data | 52 |

## 4 Introduction to WebClasses — 65

- Understanding How WebClasses Work — 66
- Understanding HTML Templates — 71
- Writing HTML without Templates — 72
- Exploring the WebClass Event Sequence — 75
- Optimize, Optimize, Optimize — 77
- Comparing the Advantages and Disadvantages of VB/WebClasses vs. ASP — 81

## 5 Securing an IIS Application — 87

- Understand How Security Works — 88
- Create the Project — 88
- Create an HTML Template — 92
- Add a Custom Event — 100
- Add a Custom WebItem — 103
- Test the Security — 113
- Compile the Project — 115
- Improve Site Security — 119
- Take Advantage of NT Security — 120

## 6 WebClass Debugging and Error Handling — 125

- Exploring the WebClass Event Sequence — 126
- Debugging Client-Side Script — 136
- Logging and Displaying Errors — 140
- Trapping Errors — 144
  - Error-Handling Scenario — 146

## 7 Controlling Program Flow — 157

- Understanding Program Flow — 158
- Creating the AccountInfo Project — 159
- Repurposing WebClasses — 170
- Using Multiple WebClasses in an Application — 174

## 8 Maintaining State in IIS Applications — 191

- Selecting a State Maintenance Option — 192
  - Maintaining State with Session Variables — 194
  - Maintaining State with Cookies — 198
  - Maintaining State with QueryString Variables — 201

| | |
|---|---|
| Maintaining State with Hidden Form Variables | 203 |
| Maintaining State in a Database | 204 |
| Summing Up State Maintenance Options | 206 |
| Exploring the State Maintenance Options | 206 |
|     Using Session Variables to Maintain State | 206 |
|     Using Cookies to Maintain State | 208 |
|     Using QueryString/URLData Variables to Maintain State | 208 |
|     Using Form Variables to Maintain State | 209 |
|     Using Database Tables to Maintain State | 210 |
|     Storing State across Sessions | 219 |
|     Eliminating Obsolete Data | 221 |
| Caching Information | 221 |
|     Writing a StoredRecordset Class | 223 |
|     Writing a StoredDictionary Class | 227 |
|     Using the CStoredRecordset and CStoredDictionary Classes | 230 |
| Summing Up State Maintenance | 232 |

## 9   Dealing with Multiple Browsers   235

| | |
|---|---|
| Understanding Differences between Browsers | 236 |
| Determining Browser Type | 238 |
|     Using the Browser Capabilities Component | 241 |
| Writing Browser-Specific Code | 244 |
|     Writing Browser-Specific HTML Templates | 244 |
|     Writing Browser-Specific HTML from a WebClass | 246 |
|     Using Replaceable Markers to Create Browser-Specific Pages | 248 |
| Writing Code with Code | 248 |

## 10   Retrieving and Storing Data in Databases   251

| | |
|---|---|
| Understanding ADO | 252 |
| Introducing the ADO Object Model | 253 |
|     Opening and Closing Connections | 254 |
| Retrieving Data with ADO | 256 |
|     Retrieving Data with the ADO Connection Object | 256 |
|     Using ADO Cursor Types | 256 |
|     Retrieving Data with the Recordset Object | 257 |
|     Using ADO Record-Locking Options | 259 |
|     Understanding ADO's Unfortunate Options Argument | 260 |
|     Retrieving Data with the Command Object | 261 |
|     Investigating Stored Procedures | 265 |

| | Accessing Databases from WebClasses | 273 |
|---|---|---|
| | Get In, Get the Data, Get Out | 274 |
| | Write Functions to Simplify ADO | 276 |
| **11** | **Using ActiveX DLLs from WebClasses** | **279** |
| | Thinking of WebClasses as Glue | 280 |
| | Accessing ActiveX DLLs from WebClasses | 281 |
| | Using the ObjectContext Object with WebClasses | 282 |
| | Testing ActiveX DLLs from a WebClass | 284 |
| | Persisting ActiveX Objects | 290 |
| | Store Object Data, Not Objects | 290 |
| | Automate Object Persistence and Retrieval | 294 |
| | Maintain State via Object Persistence | 296 |
| | Building a Browser-Based Code Repository | 297 |
| | Techniques Included in the CodeRepository Project | 297 |
| **12** | **IIS Applications and Microsoft Transaction Server** | **313** |
| | What Is MTS? | 314 |
| | How Does MTS Fit into the IIS/Web Application Model? | 317 |
| | Using Microsoft Transaction Server Explorer | 317 |
| | How Can MTS Help You? | 320 |
| | When Should You Use MTS? | 321 |
| | How Do You Use MTS Components? | 322 |
| | How Do You Move a Project into MTS? | 328 |
| | Make MTS-Specific Code Changes | 329 |
| | Compile the Project | 329 |
| | Create and Configure an MTS Package | 331 |
| | Run the Project | 333 |
| | Change DCOM Permissions | 334 |
| **13** | **Deploying WebClass Applications** | **339** |
| | Preparing for Deployment | 340 |
| | Clean Up the Code | 341 |
| | Test in Compiled Mode | 342 |
| | Generate Likely Errors | 342 |
| | Deploy to a Test Server | 343 |
| | Beta Test the Application | 343 |
| | Determine the Target Server's Configuration | 344 |
| | Creating an Installation Package | 345 |

| | | |
|---|---|---|
| | Configuring the Target Server | 347 |
| |    Capture the Server Configuration Settings | 348 |
| |    Run the Installation | 348 |
| | Dealing with Permissions Issues | 350 |
| **14** | **What's Next?** | **355** |
| | Where Are Web Applications Headed? | 356 |
| | What about Java and CORBA? | 359 |
| | What about Database Technology? | 361 |
| | What about XML? | 362 |
| | Conclusion | 367 |
| | *Index* | *368* |

# INTRODUCTION

This book shows you how to use Visual Basic (VB) to tap into the Web, a computing model that is rapidly replacing all older models for building programs. It's not replacing the older models because building programs is easier for the Web than for standard networks (although in some ways it is). It's not replacing the older models because the Web is faster (it's not) or more robust (it's less robust—at least so far). No, it's replacing them because it's a better model.

As developers, we'll see some new languages appear that are suited to the new model. In fact we already have—Java is the prime example. We'll see others disappear, because languages rise, conquer, and decline like civilizations. Those languages that still have sufficient vigor will adapt to the new model, just as they have adapted to other model changes in the past.

VB is one of those adaptive languages. Basic has its roots deep in the beginnings of personal computers. It has grown as the PC has grown, gaining speed and power. Basic has been able to evolve by adding new programming paradigms as they became available: features such as named subroutines, functions, structured programming, strong variable typing, long variable names, optional parameters, variants, and objects. When Microsoft released VB in 1990, it quickly became the preferred method for creating Windows programs. Forms, event-driven programming, and, above all, the capability to easily encapsulate useful functionality in easy-to-use and commercially available third-party controls have made VB the most popular programming language in history; and VB isn't through yet.

The latest release of the language, version 6, extends VB into a new realm: Web programming. In the process, Microsoft has provided developers with a way of applying both their expertise and the full development power of VB—including its debugger—to the new computing model.

The scope of programming has been increasing almost as fast as the capabilities of computers themselves. Just a few years ago, developers targeted most programs to run on a single computer; the application's code and data all resided on a hard drive. Most applications fit on just a few floppy disks. To share information, people would copy data files from one computer to another. Almost as soon as this model became common, small networks became ubiquitous. Although their initial usefulness was limited to extending storage, not computing capability, people began to understand how sharing data among many people could improve business responsiveness. This was such an attractive capability that soon most business programs began to provide access to business information from individual PCs.

This central-data-to-client computing model drove the development of early client-server applications. A "fat" client, containing all the user-interface code and all the business rules, could connect to a central data-store to let business people access the corporate data in near real-time. Unfortunately, the model was expensive, because you had to attach the client computers to a private network to use the application. In addition, the network vendors all had different—and proprietary—methods for letting remote clients attach to their networks; in fact, the networks were generally incompatible because computers had no standard way to communicate. The code to access the databases and display information on the computer screen was proprietary. There was no standard interface. Each company and application had different keystroke actions and menu items. Programmers coded every screen differently. There were no standard keys to pull down menus, move a cursor, or cut and paste information. You couldn't cut and paste information between programs at all; instead, you had to export and import information in plain text files. Programs all had proprietary file formats. You couldn't mix and match program components because there was no standard way to communicate between languages. There wasn't even a standard way for a computer to print a file—you had to install a custom printer driver for each program that you used.

Into this Tower of Babel came Windows 3. Despite its sometimes-awkward interface, Windows captured the desktop of almost every computer on the market within two years. DOS was dead; Windows was king. Moreover, with Windows came standards: standard menus; standard windowing interfaces; standard keystrokes; one printer driver per printer rather than one per program; standard network interfaces; the capability to cut and paste not only within, but also between, programs. Command-line interfaces nearly disappeared; the visual interface had won. But behind all this beauty and ease of use was a ferociously complicated programming model, all written in C. As a programmer, if you wanted to tap into the power of Windows, you had to learn C. Fortunately, VB appeared just in time to save us all from going crazy and introduced a new programming paradigm—visual programming. Rather than spending hours calculating pixel values, recompiling, and checking placement of objects on the screen, you could drag and drop the objects into place at design time. Now it's difficult to find a programming environment that doesn't advertise itself as "visual."

Yes, VB spawned a revolution in programming, but the revolution wasn't visual programming, it was code reuse. Programming texts have paid lip service to code reuse for more than 20 years, but it took lowly Basic to make widespread code reuse a reality. VB did this by introducing the VBX-based control. VBX files were special DLLs that had a visual component you could drag and drop onto a form. The functionality these DLLs encapsulated spanned everything from simple text controls to database connectivity to entire word processors, and everything in between. Because VBXs were so powerful, easy to use, and saved so much time, an entire industry grew up around them.

VBXs quickly gave way to OCXs, a better technology but an unfortunate name change that quickly gave way to ActiveX controls. By Visual Basic version 5, you could create your own ActiveX controls. Much more important, by version 5, Microsoft had completely rewritten Visual Basic and added support for classes and interfaces.

Most recently, VB 6 has introduced a special kind of class called a *WebClass* designed to work with Internet Information Server (IIS) and Microsoft's Active Server Pages (ASP) technology. Together with Microsoft Transaction Server (MTS), WebClasses are a powerful tool for building stable and scaleable Web sites.

# Why Am I Writing This Book?

I'm writing this book because I believe that we're in the middle of a computing revolution that in many ways is much more important than the development of the PC. I've been writing computer programs since 1979, when using Apple Basic on an 8K Apple II computer was state-of-the-art program development. I've worked in many languages besides VB (among them C, SmallTalk, and several "authoring" languages such as ToolBook and TenCORE) to develop computer-based training programs and corporate applications. For the past several years I've been writing Internet programs—initially with DOS CGI programs, then VB running through an ISAPI DLL, and finally with Visual InterDev and ASP. I'm excited about VB's new capabilities because I think the language is on track to simplify development of Web applications.

Web application development so far has been, at best, an awkward marriage of formatting code (HTML) and back-end programming. The server and client haven't communicated with each other well, other than for the client to request "pages" of formatted content, and the server to provide them. Although formatted content can be extremely useful, an essential component of computing has been missing—interaction between the user and the computer. Static pages aren't enough. Web development is now at the stage where we can begin to add some of the interactivity back into the client.

In addition, no single environment has emerged that can help develop *all* the components of a complete Web application: the client interface, the business logic, and the data access components. We've had HTML editors such as HotMetal Pro, Hotdog, and FrontPage; CGI-type languages such as Perl; client-side scripting in JavaScript and VBScript; and a number of custom solutions to tie things together, among them Visual InterDev and ColdFusion. Then there's Sun Microsystems, which touts Java as the solution for everything, including running your toaster for you. Java's a great language with an unfortunate syntax. Fortunately, the Visual Basic development team has stepped forward to save us from having to switch languages by providing a unified development environment in which we can connect HTML-based front ends, running in any browser, to a robust set of VB classes and objects running on one or more servers.

# What Should You Expect to Get Out of It?

In the same way that building client-server applications required a different model than building applications for stand-alone computers, building applications for the Web requires yet another model. In some ways, we've gone full circle from the mainframe days, when a "smart" mainframe computer supplied data and formatting to dumb terminals. As the terminals became PCs and got smarter, program designers decentralized the model. They moved processing away from the central computer and onto the client, but the data (which companies needed to share among many people) remained centralized.

Unfortunately, the decentralized, fat-client model had its own set of problems. Clients aren't all the same, so programs often had to be rewritten multiple times so they would run on different client hardware configurations. When Windows became the dominant client platform, it eased this situation a bit by providing a common way for clients to talk to networks and peripherals. However, enough differences remained to make the client-server program a difficult model to maintain.

The Web repopularized the idea of a smart central processing unit—the Web server, connected to remote terminals. The remote terminals, though, are now PCs that—unlike the old dumb terminals—are powerful enough to be efficient at processing graphical displays. The central processing unit no longer needs to be an expensive mainframe; instead, it can be a relatively inexpensive PC server, or better still, a collection of servers linked together to provide information upon request.

In essence, the key to a successful Web application lies in storing information on the server in such a way that retrieving that information and getting it to the client is a smooth and fast operation. If it is not, the server will eventually bog down with unfulfilled requests, the clients will be left waiting, and your application will be unsuccessful. In this book, I'll provide a model that will enable you to build applications that scale from workgroup to enterprise without significant changes in the applications' structure. I'll also help you take advantage of another change in the programming paradigm—one that is not new, but that takes on additional importance in the interconnected world of Web programming—component-based programming.

# Who Should Read This Book?

I've aimed this book at those developers and program designers who are already familiar with VB, and to some degree, with HTML and the Web. This book is not a primer on VB programming, nor will it teach you much about HTML, DHTML, or even about building static Web sites. Instead, it's meant to show you how you can leverage your existing VB skills to create server-based Web applications. The kinds of applications you create with these new tools are up to you.

If you're a VB programmer who wants to move into the world of Internet programming, this book will help you design or redesign your applications so they'll be successful. It won't teach you the low-level details of Winsock programming or the various connectivity protocols, such as HTTP, FTP, or Telnet. But it will show you how to leverage your existing knowledge—the programming language you know (and love) best, VB, and the existing infrastructure—so you can continue to create useful, responsive, and robust programs.

Microsoft uses its Active Server Pages technology to connect VB programs to its Web servers—Internet Information Server (on NT) and Personal Web Server (on

Windows 95/98). You don't have to be an expert ASP programmer to read this book, but if you're already familiar with ASP programming, so much the better—you can skip those parts that discuss the ASP object model. In fact, you'll be impressed at how neatly the ASP model integrates into VB.

## Why Were Certain Projects Selected?

This book contains two types of information:

- Explanations that I hope will provide a framework of knowledge about the Web on which you can build applications in VB or in any language
- Code examples, in the form of projects you'll build in most of the chapters

Many books take the approach of creating a complete application, building small parts of the whole in each chapter. This method can be useful to the writer because it helps to tell a story and keep continuity between chapters. However, I have elected not to take this approach, mostly because I usually find that such projects have little application in my work. Instead, I've opted to provide a series of smaller projects that, while they may have little *direct* application to your projects, contain code and ideas that you may be able to reuse. A few of the projects are included simply to illustrate a point rather than because they're useful in their own right—sometimes it's easier to see the reasoning behind code if you can strip it down to the essentials rather than try to make it do something useful.

This idea of small, reusable bits of code is in many ways central to the process of building Web applications, which consist primarily of small, almost autonomous programs that often stand by themselves.

## What Do You Need to Know Already?

This is not a beginner's book. To get the most out of this book, you must be comfortable with VB. Specifically, you should be an intermediate to advanced VB programmer who is comfortable with class structures, VB's event model, and COM. You do not need to know much about the Internet, although some knowledge of HTML will make it easier to read the code, build the projects, and understand the examples.

You should be familiar with relational databases, either Access or ODBC databases such as SQL Server. You should also be at least minimally familiar with ActiveX Data Objects (ADO); however, if you've worked only with Data Access Objects (DAO) or Remote Data Objects (RDO), you'll have few problems understanding the code.

# What Hardware/Software Is Required?

You will need the following to complete the projects in this book:

- Visual Basic 6, Professional or Enterprise Edition
- Microsoft Access or SQL Server version 6.*x* or higher
- Visual InterDev or another good HTML editor

You'll need Visual Basic 6, Professional or Enterprise Edition, to build these projects. You'll also need either Microsoft Access or (preferably) SQL Server version 6.*x* or higher. In fact, let's get this out of the way right now: If you try to build Web sites with Microsoft Access, you're asking for trouble. I know this will get me into hot water with all the Access fans out there, but there's a simple reason why I make this judgement (well actually, two reasons). First, the Microsoft Access engine is not thread safe; therefore, when you use Microsoft Access as your database with a Web application, you have the potential for trouble. Although you may not have this problem immediately, it will occur if you use Access long enough. Second, I've tried it, several times, and it doesn't work very well. I'll back off on this enough to say that if you want to use Microsoft Access to initially *develop* your applications, OK. Just don't use it to *deliver* applications. By the time you are ready to move your program into beta testing, get it onto Sybase, SQL Server, Oracle—I don't care, just get it out of Access.

Some (only some) of the projects in this book use the Microsoft `pubs` database that comes with SQL Server. If you don't have SQL Server, you can download a Microsoft Access database containing the tables of the `pubs` database from the Sybex Web site.

> **NOTE** To download code, navigate to `http://www.sybex.com`. Click the Catalog button and search for this book's title. Click the Downloads button and accept the licensing agreement. Accepting the agreement grants you access to the downloads page for the book.

You'll also need either Visual InterDev (highly recommended) or an HTML or text editor—I use both the Visual InterDev text editor and Notepad. I've also used and liked Homesite, Hotdog, HotMetal Pro, and several other editors. It doesn't really matter which editor you use as long as you can read and edit HTML with it. You won't need a high-powered visual HTML editor to build the projects in this book. You will need to delve into HTML code a little, but this book will help you do that.

The Web has been primarily a world of text files: text files with markup, text files with code, text files containing XML, etc. The idea is that in a world of standards, everybody can read everybody else's file format. The lowest common denominator has always been the lowly text file, and guess what? It still is, only now the number of text-file-based formats is rising, and they're called "standard," although they're anything but at the moment. Fortunately, you don't have to worry about that too much. As long as you stick to "standard" HTML, *and* you don't use DHTML, *and* you don't use ActiveX controls, almost anything you write will work fine in almost any browser as long as you get the syntax right for that specific browser. Welcome to the cross-platform world. Is that generic enough for you? Don't worry, things are not (quite) as bad as I'm painting them here. In any case, you can now use almost any text editor to edit almost any kind of content: text, formatting, database content, code. The Web has been kind to the makers of text file editors.

# What Kind of Code Is in This Book?

You will see at least three kinds of code in this book: Visual Basic (or Visual Basic for Applications, known as VBA) code, VBScript code, and Access-SQL or Transact-SQL code (although not too much of that). All the example code in this book will be in VBScript when the code is a script in an Active Server Page, in VB/VBA when the code is inside any Visual Basic module or class, and in Access-SQL and Transact-SQL whenever the code applies to a database.

# CHAPTER ONE

# Visual Basic and the Web

- What's a Web Application?

- Why Write a Web Application in VB?

- What's the Difference between IIS and DHTML Applications?

**V**isual Basic was an instant hit in the Windows programming community but so far it hasn't been a major force in the Web programming world, except peripherally, through VBScript. (Microsoft selected Visual Basic's young "challenged" cousin, VBScript, as the default programming language for their Active Server Pages, or ASP, technology.) There are several reasons why VB hasn't been the language of choice for Web programming.

First, Visual Basic runs on only one platform, Windows. Until Microsoft's Web server, called Internet Information Server (IIS), became commonplace (about three years ago, with the introduction of version 3), VB couldn't talk directly to the Web server. This made it tough to use VB for the Web. You could do it, though, and some people did.

Second, VB has a large runtime dynamic-link library (DLL) that gets loaded whenever you run a VB application, even if the compiled application is only a few kilobytes of code. The large runtime made VB programs running on the Web painfully slow. Each time a client browser requested a Web page, the Web server had to dutifully load the runtime DLL, load the application, process the request, and then unload the application and the runtime DLL. Because the Web works on a get-in, get-the-data, get-out-quickly schedule, it's overkill to load a 1MB-plus application-support DLL simply to provide a little marked-up HTML text. Furthermore, because your application "died" after each request, storing data values between requests was difficult—which meant that the approach was primarily useful for formatting simple requests and database reports, not full applications.

In an attempt to alleviate these problems, Microsoft provided an application programming interface (API) called Internet Server API (ISAPI), through which programs could communicate with the Web server. However, the company neglected to provide VB with the means to access the API. Microsoft also "solved" the problem of large support DLLs (after all, Visual C++ has one, too) by letting you load DLLs directly into the Web server's address space. That way, they stay loaded all the time, which dramatically speeds up response time. ISAPI was an instant hit, but you couldn't take advantage of it until Visual Basic 5 provided the capability to create compiled DLLs. Unfortunately, this capability also dramatically decreased the stability of the Web server, because if one of the in-process DLLs crashed, the Web server often went down with it.

Meanwhile, several methods of connecting VB applications to the Web server appeared. A freeware DLL called Object Linking and Embedding Internet Server Application Programming Interface (OLEISAPI and later OLEISAPI2) provided connectivity between VB applications and the Web server. Other, relatively full-featured solutions not only provided connectivity, but also loaded a configurable number of instances of your application, provided load balancing between them, and enabled you to connect one instance to a single user so that programs could keep user-specific data between requests on the server. These solutions also kept program instances alive between client calls to the Web server, so you could store data easily in program variables.

In addition, you could (and still can) program directly to the underlying protocols. Carl Franklin (of Carl and Gary's Visual Basic Home Page) wrote an excellent book called *Visual Basic 4.0 Internet Programming*, in which he discusses Winsock programming, the use of various Internet protocols, and other low-level programming topics for the Internet. All that information is still valid, and if you want to get "under the hood," Carl's book (since updated for VB 6) can do more for you than this one.

Luckily, with VB 6, Microsoft has finally provided Visual Basic with a direct connection to the Web. The method they provide works via Component Object Model (COM) automation through one or more ASP pages. You build a DLL that exposes a WebClass object. The client calls an ASP page that loads a copy of your DLL. From then on, you use the WebClass methods, properties, and events to deliver content from template files and/or created on-the-fly to the client browser.

If you don't understand all of this right now, don't worry—by the end of this book you will. The important point to remember is that WebClasses aren't a brand new technology and they aren't difficult to understand. They don't do anything you can't do with Visual Basic 5 and an ASP page or two—they just do it more easily.

# What's a Web Application?

A Web *application* is different from a Web *site*. A Web site provides information that has been pre-built and can be stored (more or less) in static Hypertext Markup Language (HTML) files. Information in a Web site moves primarily from the server to the client. When the user must enter information, the server provides a generic, canned response. Between requests, the server doesn't care what the client does. The client can skip from one place to another with no effect on the Web site because each page is a stand-alone unit; the Web is composed of discrete groups of hypertext documents. In contrast, a Web application provides information specifically retrieved and formatted for a single user or group of users. Information moves in both directions—the user's input or identity often determines the content that appears on the browser.

A Web application serves dynamic information, not static HTML files. The application extracts content as needed, often from a database server. A Web application not only provides information, but also accepts information from you and responds to your actions with a specific custom response.

A Web application *does* care what you do from one request to another. It needs to track you to serve your needs. You can't always skip around in a Web application the way you can in a Web site. Sometimes, you need to follow a process from start to finish (for example, filling out an online application) or the entire process is suspect and must be discarded.

# Why Write a Web Application in VB?

You can write Web applications in many languages: Perl, Python, Java, C, C++, even QuickBasic or Unix shell scripts. So why would you choose to write a Web application in Visual Basic? Whenever you need to make decisions, it's always good to look at the requirements first. Let's look at the requirements of a Web application and at how well VB meets those requirements. The five major requirements are:

**Database connectivity**   A Web application often accumulates and manages critical information, storing it in a database for future reference. It also uses that information store to provide specific services. Therefore, a Web application language should be good at storing and retrieving information—preferably in databases. Since version 3, VB has had industry-leading database connectivity and it still does.

**Speed**   A Web application must often service many clients. Visual Basic, compiled into native code, is nearly as fast as C.

**String handling**   A Web application must be able to handle string searches, concatenation, and token replacements. Visual Basic has excellent string-handling ability.

**Security**   A Web application must be able to handle security demands. Any compiled language provides greater security than an interpreted language. Visual Basic meets this requirement equally as well as C, and better than Java or a scripting language such as VBScript or JavaScript.

**Transactions**   A Web application often needs to perform several actions that *must* complete successfully for the data to remain valid. When working with a database, you usually wrap such actions in a *transaction*. A transaction is a contract that guarantees that the entire set of operations either will succeed or will fail in such a way that no changes will be made to data. The classic example of a transaction is that of a checking account. When you deposit a check, the bank debits the amount from one account and credits the same amount to another account. Both must succeed, or both must fail. The dual act of debiting one account and crediting another is a transaction. Through Microsoft Transaction Server, you can perform multiple actions in your Web pages, even use multiple objects to accomplish the transaction. Although you don't always need transactions, when you do need them, you need them badly.

In addition to the five major requirements, there are others that are somewhat less important:

**Familiarity**   You write better code faster if you're familiar with the language. Because all of you are Visual Basic programmers, you're ahead of the game here.

**Debugger**   You also write better code if you have a powerful debugger. Here Visual Basic and Visual Studio are leaders. The capability to view and change the contents of variables, rewrite code on-the-fly, move the execution pointer, step through code in DLL projects, step through code in ASP files, and step through code running in the browser—all from your Visual Basic project group—is awesome debugging power. Until Visual Studio 6 was released last year, ASP debugging was done through `Response.Write` statements in concert with `Response.End` statements, which is analogous to working in Visual Basic if the only debugging capabilities you could use were `Debug.Print` and `Stop` statements.

**Code/object reuse**   Sure, you can do this in any language, but I'll bet no other language has as many third-party tools, libraries, and examples available as Visual Basic. I suspect that many of you reading this book also have a large set of routines and objects that you reuse when appropriate. Many of these routines will work just fine in a VB-based Web application, so once again, you're probably ahead of the game here.

As you can see, Visual Basic is as suited for Web application development as it is for any other type of program—it's a general-purpose language and meets these requirements easily.

# What's the Difference between IIS and DHTML Applications?

Visual Basic has two built-in kinds of Web projects:

**IIS applications**   These applications run on the Web server, under Microsoft's Internet Information Server. You can write Web applications for any kind of browser (or even non-browser) client using an IIS project.

**DHTML applications**   These applications run on the client and use the built-in dynamic HTML (DHTML) capabilities of Microsoft's Internet Explorer (IE) browser to provide fast response to user input. These types of applications are well suited to games, simulations, and data-input applications. Unfortunately, they're limited to Internet Explorer version 4 and higher at this time.

If you're going to write games or applications that need fast response time and don't have heavy database requirements, and all your clients are running the IE browser, DHTML applications can be a good choice. But despite their advantages, I'm not going to discuss them much in this book, as I explain in the following section.

## This Book Concentrates on IIS Applications

Let me say that again. This book concentrates *only* on IIS applications. I've chosen to focus on IIS applications for several reasons:

- IIS applications run with multiple browsers and multiple versions of those browsers. You can write an IIS application that will run on anything from version 1*x* browsers all the way to the latest versions, and anything in between. They'll also run on multiple platforms, including the Mac and Unix machines. This makes IIS applications admirably suited for business applications used by clients who may not all be running Windows or have the latest browser.

- IIS applications have a single code base. Because the application resides in its entirety on the Web server, you can update the entire application with a single code change. The advantages of this are hard to beat when you realize how often business rules and database requirements change.
- There are no client-side installation issues. This alone makes IIS applications worth considering. I'm sure your Information Technology (IT) department won't be excited about supporting a new type of application on every computer in the enterprise. There are also no versioning issues, because you control the only public version of the application.
- The application is available from any location. After an IIS application is up and running, any client computer that can connect to the server can run your application. The application may run more slowly over a dial-up connection than over a 100Mbps network connection, but it will run.
- A client isn't bound to one computer. You can use sign-on and password or other security measures to identify clients no matter which computer they're running on. That means, for example, that if you built a training application, a person could sign on to your application and begin a lesson in Des Moines, get called overseas, and finish the application from the Netherlands the next day—all without worrying about saving data or installing anything.
- All the data is centralized. Your clients won't ever lose data when they use your application (assuming you have backup procedures in place on the server). Additionally, you have the ability to prove (or disprove) how useful your application is to the business because you can (and should) track use of the application down to the page level. This kind of tracking capability is priceless when it comes to justifying the cost of an application.

Visual Basic's other type of Web project, DHTML applications, are a completely different sort of animal. They're inextricably bound to the IE browser, version 4 and higher. To try to do justice to both DHTML and IIS applications in the same book would do a disservice to both types. Believe me, you'll have enough to keep you busy with IIS applications alone.

That's probably enough history and introduction, so let's get started. In the next chapter, I'll give you a model so you can see how an IIS application works and how Visual Basic fits into that model.

# CHAPTER TWO

# IIS Applications

- How Browsers Request Files
- So Many Requests, So Little Time
- ASP Object Model
- Web Applications vs. Client-Server Applications

In spite of their graphical power, browsers act more like mainframe terminals than Windows clients in a client-server program. Unless you add client-side script, browsers simply display the information sent by the server. In other words, browsers show a great deal of intelligence about how to display information but little intelligence about content. To write an effective Web application, you need to understand how a browser requests information and how the server responds to each request.

# How Browsers Request Files

When you type a Uniform Resource Locator (URL) into your browser's address field, many things happen. The browser parses the URL, sends a message to a Name server to translate the text name (for example, `microsoft.com`) into an Internet Protocol (IP) address (for example, `207.84.25.32`). The browser then connects to the server with that IP address and requests the file. The server reads the file and sends the contents back to the browser. The browser parses the HTML, using the embedded commands to figure out how to format the file. Most HTML files contain references to graphics. These references are in the form of URLs as well, so the entire process repeats for each graphic reference, sometimes many times for files that contain many graphics or other file references.

So, the process of displaying an HTML file consists of a series of small transactions between the client (the browser) and the server (the Web server).

IIS applications work like the Web—in small transactions. First, a client browser makes a page request to the Web server. The request is always for a specific file. The server's response depends on the type of file requested. If the file is an HTML file (having an .htm or .html extension), the server simply reads the file contents, URL-encodes the content string, and then sends the encoded string back to the requesting browser. The entire process, from request to response, is a *transaction* between a client and a server. The client always initiates the transaction, then waits until the server returns a response, at which time the transaction is complete.

The file request to the Web server is similar to what happens when you double-click a network file in Windows Explorer, with two differences:

- The Web server never lets your local application (the browser) open or write to the requested file; instead, the Web server opens the file and returns the file contents.

- The connection is *transient*. You don't need to assign a drive letter to contact the Web server. After the Web server finishes processing your request, it disconnects.

As soon as the transaction is complete, the Web server forgets all about you. If you immediately click the Refresh button, the Web server simply repeats the transaction—it doesn't remember that you requested the file five seconds ago.

With a standard Hypertext Transfer Protocol (HTTP) connection, most Web files require several such transactions—one for the base HTML file, then one for each referenced graphic in that file. So to display a file with five embedded graphics, the browser makes *six* separate requests to the Web server (see Figure 2.1).

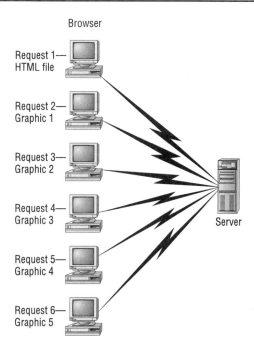

**FIGURE 2.1:**

Browser-server request cycle

Note that in Figure 2.1 the first request is for an HTML file. The next five requests, for the graphics, are for a different file type (often referred to as the MIME type) that contains binary data. For each file type, both the server and the browser can treat the request and response differently. I won't explain all the MIME types right now; it's enough that you realize that browsers and Web servers respond differently to different kinds of files.

File extension associations control how IIS responds to file requests. These associations are stored in the Registry. This is the same method used by Windows Explorer to open the appropriate application when you double-click a file. With browsers, the MIME-type header returned by the server controls how the browser responds to different file types. MIME stands for Multipurpose Internet Mail Extensions. The server returns the file's MIME type with each request. Browsers use the MIME type header to determine how to display the file. In most cases (text/.html files, .gif files, and .jpg files), the browser can display the files directly. For other types, such as .doc and .avi, the browser will find the MIME type in a custom list, then launch the appropriate application to display the file.

**NOTE** If you're interested in knowing more about MIME, you can find a list of all the registered types at `http://www.isi.edu/in-notes/iana/assignments/media-types/media-types`.

# So Many Requests, So Little Time

IIS handles all requests on a time-slice basis. It accepts a request, begins to service that request, and then accepts the next request. It continues to process the pending request during its time slice until that request is complete. Either the server can begin sending a response immediately, or it can cache the response until it has finished processing the entire request and then send the response all at once.

Browsers can request executable file types as well. The generic term for executable files is Common Gateway Interface (CGI) files or programs. As I explained in Chapter 1, "Visual Basic and the Web," you can use Visual Basic to create a CGI program. Here's a pseudocode model:

```
Read any data sent by the browser from StdIn
Process the data
Write the response to StdOut
```

When the requested file is an ASP file, the server handles the request slightly differently. It retrieves the file, either from disk or from the cache, then sends the file contents to the ASP engine.

The ASP engine parses the file to determine which parts are script code (code in ASP files is enclosed in percent signs and brackets, for example, `<% this is code %>`).

At this point, I should warn those who are thinking, "This isn't VB! I don't need to read this part!" that you really *do* need to read this part. VB's connection to the Web server is through the ASP engine. You have to work with the Web server through the objects exposed by ASP. Luckily, a Visual Basic WebClass exposes these ASP objects globally, so you don't have to declare them or receive them from an event call.

Because these objects are so important to Web applications built with Visual Basic, I'm going to explain each object briefly, then go through their properties, methods, and events in some detail, showing you how to use each one.

# ASP Object Model

The ASP object model has changed very little since version 1. The version described here and that you'll work with in this book is ASP 3, but almost everything in the book will work with version 2. For those of you already familiar with ASP 1, the only significant object model changes are that the Application and Session objects expose a `Contents` property and that ASP now exposes a ScriptingContext object. The `Contents` property can be helpful when you need a list of the items stored in the Application or Session objects. Until now, you had to maintain that list yourself.

There are six objects in the ASP type library:

- Server
- Application
- Session
- Request
- Response
- ScriptingContext

Each is described in the following sections.

## Server Object

There's only one Server object for a Web server. All the applications share a single Application object. In an ASP page, you use the Server object to create other object instances—this is equivalent to the Visual Basic command `Set myObject = new someObject`. The Server object also contains methods and properties to map virtual Web paths to physical paths. In other words, if your Web application is located in the `myWeb` virtual directory, you can find out where the files for `myWeb` are physically located. The Server object can also encode and decode string information for transmission to or from the HTTP protocol.

Table 2.1 lists the Server object's properties and methods.

**TABLE 2.1:** The Server Object

| Name | Description |
| --- | --- |
| `CreateObject` method | Returns an object instance. The following example creates a Dictionary object:<br><br>```<br>Dim d<br>Set d = Server.CreateObject("Scripting.Dictionary")<br>```<br><br>The `Server.CreateObject` method is equivalent to the following Visual Basic code:<br><br>```<br>Dim d as Dictionary<br>Set d = new Dictionary<br>```<br><br>You would normally use the `CreateObject` method only from an ASP page. From VB, use the standard syntax to create a new instance of an object. |
| `MapPath` method | Returns the physical path corresponding to the virtual path parameter. Example:<br><br>```<br>MyPhysicalPath = Server.MapPath(myVirtualPath)<br>```<br><br>You use this function to find physical file locations when you know only the virtual path (the URL) for the file. You need physical paths to read and write files. |
| `HTMLEncode` method | Encodes the string parameter in a manner suitable for transmission over HTTP. |

*Continued on next page*

**TABLE 2.1 CONTINUED:** The Server Object

| Name | Description |
| --- | --- |
| URLEncode method | Encodes a string so that the server can transmit it via Transmission Control Protocol/Internet Protocol (TCP/IP) as a valid URL. URL encoding involves replacing non-text and numeric characters with a percent sign and the hex ASCII value of the character. For example, a space (ASCII 32) is equivalent to %20 (hex 32). You need to use this method to build valid URL strings. |
| ScriptTimeout property | Sets or returns an integer value that specifies the number of seconds the server should wait for a specific request to finish executing before it returns a timed out message to the requesting browser. |

## Application Object

There's one Application object for each Web application. An application, to the ASP engine, is the set of all files and subdirectories within a directory that contains a file called global.asa. The .asa extension stands for Active Server Application. The Application object is a container object that can hold other values. In fact, although it's not a Dictionary object, it's easiest to think of the Application object as a Dictionary. Dictionaries, like Visual Basic collections, are lists of key-value pairs.

The name for such pairs is *associations*. The association key is a string value, but the value associated with each key is a variant; therefore, each key can be associated with a value of any variant subtype, including Object and Nothing. You can use the Application object in the same way that you normally use global variables in your application. Tempting as it is, don't use the Application object to store anything except simple data types and arrays. You can't store apartment-threaded objects in the Application object, and there are good reasons not to store anything there if you don't have to. Table 2.2 lists the Application object's properties, collections, methods, and events.

**TABLE 2.2:** The Application Object

| Name | Description |
| --- | --- |
| Contents collection | Returns a collection of key-value associations. Because this is a collection, it also supports the `For Each...Next` syntax, the `Count` and `Item` properties, and the `Remove` method. |
| `Lock` method | Locks the Application object, restricting access to it so that only the current session can use the object. Obviously, you want to minimize the time that any given session locks the Application object. To release the lock, use the `Application.Unlock` method. If you don't release the lock, the ASP engine releases it when the current page ends. |
| `Unlock` method | Unlocks the Application object, freeing it for use by another session. |
| `OnEnd` event | Occurs when the last session for a Web application either times out or is abandoned (see `Session.Timeout` and/or `Session.Abandon in the following section`). You can write code to perform application cleanup in the `Application_OnEnd` event procedure in the `global.asa` file. |
| `OnStart` event | Occurs the first time that any user requests any page in your application. You can write code to perform Application-level variable initializations in the `Application_OnStart` event procedure in the `global.asa` file. |
| StaticObjects collection | Returns a collection of all the objects created with `<object>` tags that have been stored in the Application object. Like other collections, it has a `Count` property and an `Item` property. You can also use `For Each` to iterate through the collection. This is a read-only property. |

## Session Object

Each application may have many sessions, one for each user accessing the application. The Session object is a container object like the Application object. It's also similar to a Dictionary object, with keys and values. The biggest difference is that each user gets a unique Session object, whereas all users of the application share the Application object. Table 2.3 lists the Session object's properties, collections, methods, and events.

**TABLE 2.3:** The Session Object

| Name | Description |
|---|---|
| Contents collection | Returns a collection of key-value associations. Because this is a collection, it also supports the **For Each...Next** syntax, the **Count** and **Item** properties, and the **Remove** method. |
| SessionID property | Returns the ID for the current session. The **SessionID** is a pseudo-random identifier that is generated automatically by the ASP engine the first time a user requests any page in the application. This is a read-only property. |
| Timeout property | Sets or returns an integer value that specifies the number of minutes before a session will expire if no activity occurs. |
| Abandon method | Forces the current session to expire when the current page finishes executing. |
| OnEnd event | Occurs when a session times out or is abandoned. You can write code to perform end-of-session cleanup in the **Session_OnEnd** event procedure in the **global.asa** file. If the current session is the only active session, this event fires immediately before the **Application_OnEnd** event. |
| OnStart event | This event occurs the first time that any user requests any page in your application. You can write code to perform Application-level variable initializations in the **Session_OnStart** event procedure in the **global.asa** file. If the current session is the first active session in the application, this event fires immediately after the **Application_OnStart** event. |
| StaticObjects collection | A collection of all the objects created with **<object>** tags that have been stored in the Session object. Like other collections, it has a **Count** property and an **Item** property. You can also use **For Each** to iterate through the collection. |
| CodePage property | Sets or returns the **CodePage** used for representing characters. |
| LCID property | Sets or returns the **LocaleID** setting for the client machine. |

# What's a Session?

At this point, it may be useful to explain what a *session* is. Unfortunately, this is more complicated than it should be. A session begins when a user requests any file in your Web application *and* that user's browser does *not* send a valid ASP-generated SessionID cookie for that site. That's confusing, I know, but bear with me; I'll explain it shortly.

*Continued on next page*

As soon as the ASP engine sees a request from a browser without a valid SessionID cookie, it creates a new Session object, generates a pseudo-random SessionID value, and sets the cookie. On all subsequent requests from that browser, the ASP engine reads the SessionID cookie and uses the value to match the Session object it generated on the first request to this request. That's how ASP manages to store information about a specific user between page requests.

If the user's browser refuses the cookie (either the browser doesn't support cookies, or the user has opted to refuse them), the ASP SessionID cannot be stored in the browser, and the user will not have a valid Session object.

Note that the request created a Session object although the server can't use that Session object to save data between requests.

Because of the missing cookie value, the ASP engine won't be able to connect subsequent requests to the Session object. When the user's browser refuses the cookie, the ASP engine will create a brand new Session object for each request. Therefore, you can still use the Session object to store values when the user refuses cookies, but you will lose the values after the page is complete. Although you can code around the cookie problem, most ASP sites don't work as intended if the user's browser refuses the cookie.

> **NOTE** Cookies are key-value pairs stored on the client computer, either in memory (transient cookies) or on disk (permanent cookies).

## Request Object

Browsers send a good deal of information to the server for each page request. You don't normally see any of this "header" information when you're browsing a site, but it is available at the server for applications to use. The ASP engine packages this information nicely in an object called the Request object. The Request object contains all this header information as well as information about the specific page request and any form information submitted by a user. You can retrieve the information through the properties and collections of the Request object. Table 2.4 lists the Request object's properties, collections, and methods.

**TABLE 2.4:** The Request Object

| Name | Description |
| --- | --- |
| `BinaryRead` method | Reads binary information from submitted form data. |
| ClientCertificate collection | Returns a collection of client security certificates. You can use this to provide secure services. |
| Cookies collection | Returns a collection of cookies sent by the client. The Request.Cookies collection is read-only. To set, alter, or remove a cookie from the collection, use the Response.Cookies collection instead. |
| Form collection | Returns a collection of form key-value associations sent by the client browser. The collection contains information from the input controls enclosed in a `<form>` tag. The keys are the names or IDs of the controls; the values are the contents. You'll see more about this in Chapter 3, "Building ASP Applications." |
| QueryString collection | Returns a collection of key-value associations from the URL sent by the client browser. For example, if the client browser navigates to the URL `myFile.asp?Action=1&Total=2`, there would be two values in the QueryString collection:<br><br>`Action=1`<br>`Total=2` |
| ServerVariables collection | Returns a collection of header key-value associations sent by the client browser. These variables are sent regardless of the method (`Post` or `Get`) used to request the page. This is a read-only property. |
| `TotalBytes` property | Contains the size of the client form data, in bytes, when the client sends information to the Web server via the `Post` method. This value is empty when the request method is `Get`. This is a read-only property. |

# Response Object

You use the methods of the Response object to send a response to the client browser. The Response object is your primary way to communicate with the client. Table 2.5 lists the object's properties, collections, and methods.

**TABLE 2.5:** The Response Object

| Name | Description |
| --- | --- |
| `AddHeader` method | Adds an HTTP header value to the page. |
| `AppendToLog` method | Logs a message to the Internet server log file. |
| `BinaryWrite` method | Writes binary information (information that should not be HTTP encoded) to the client browser. |
| `Buffer` property | As you process a request, you can either begin returning information immediately, or you can *buffer* the information and begin returning it only after you have completed processing the request. In practice, you will usually buffer the information; otherwise, you cannot add headers or redirect after processing begins. The `Buffer` property sets or returns whether the Response object will buffer information. You can set it to `True` or `False`. |
| `CacheControl` property | Controls how a client proxy server caches the page. The default value is `False`. Setting the value to `True` enables proxy servers to cache the page, which can improve the response time for ASP pages on which the information rarely changes. |
| `Charset` property | Controls which character set the browser will use to display information on the client browser. |
| `Clear` method | Clears all the information from the response buffer. |
| `ContentType` property | Lets you control the contents of the MIME-type header sent to the client browser. |
| `End` method | Ends processing immediately. The server will send any buffered information to the client browser. |
| `Expires` property | Controls how long the information you send to the client remains valid before the client must return to the server to refresh the page. You specify the interval in minutes. A value of 0 tells the browser that the page expires immediately. |
| Cookies collection | Provides access to the browser's cookie collection for this site. You can add and delete cookies from the collection by using the `Append` and `Remove` methods. |
| `ExpiresAbsolute` property | The `Expires` property lets you set the number of minutes until the content in a page is no longer valid. In contrast, the `ExpiresAbsolute` property lets you set a specific date and time when the information will become invalid. |
| `Flush` method | Sends the contents of the response buffer immediately. |

*Continued on next page*

**TABLE 2.5 CONTINUED:** The Response Object

| Name | Description |
| --- | --- |
| IsClientConnected property | Lets you find out whether a specific SessionID is currently connected. Note that this is not a way to determine whether the client browser is still using your program, only whether it is currently requesting a page. |
| PICS property | Adds an HTTP header value containing a Platform for Internet Content Selection (PICS) label. The PICS label contains a rating for the page. Using this system, parents can determine the levels of content that their children can see. For more information, see the PICS specification on the W3C Web site: http://www.w3.org. |
| Redirect method | Sends a redirect header to the client browser specifying a page to which the browser should navigate. When the browser receives a redirect header, it immediately requests the specified page from the server. |
| Status property | Sets the value of the status line returned by the server. You've probably seen this one before: 404 Not Found. You set the Status property to return a specific number and explanation to the browser. |
| Write method | You'll use this method most often. The Response.Write method sends string information to the browser. If buffering is on, the method appends new string information to the string that the server will return. |

## ScriptingContext Object

This is a wrapper object that enables an external ActiveX object to obtain references to the other ASP objects. VB 6 WebClasses provide these references automatically, so the ScriptingContext object is not important. The preferred method for gaining references to the ASP objects from external ActiveX objects is to get a reference to the ObjectContext object by calling the getObjectContext method.

The ScriptingContext object provides a "wrapper" that encloses all the other ASP objects in a single object that can be passed as a parameter. When a page containing ActiveX object references starts, the ASP engine calls the OnStartPage method for each ActiveX object on the page with a ScriptingContext object as a parameter. The ActiveX objects use the ScriptingContext parameter to gain reference pointers to the Server, Application, Session, Request, and Response objects. Following is a list of the ScriptingContext object properties:

- Server

- Application
- Session
- Request
- Response

These five properties return reference pointers to the ASP objects.

**WARNING** Microsoft recommends that you use the `getObjectContext` method rather than the ScriptingContext object. Although the ScriptingContext object still exists for backward compatibility reasons, it is obsolete, and you should no longer use it.

## ObjectContext Object

The ObjectContext object is the communications channel to Microsoft Transaction Server (MTS). Through MTS, you can let ActiveX objects participate in transactions initiated by an ASP page. You can also gain references to the other ASP objects through the ObjectContext object. You'll see more information about this object in Chapter 11, "Using ActiveX DLLs from WebClasses," when you create ActiveX DLLs for use with ASP pages and WebClasses. The ObjectContext object has no properties. Table 2.6 lists its methods and events.

**TABLE 2.6:** The ObjectContext Object

| Name | Description |
| --- | --- |
| `SetComplete` method | Calling the `SetComplete` method tells MTS that, as far as the calling component is concerned, the transaction was a success. MTS declares the transaction successful only when *all* the participating components call `SetComplete`. |
| `SetAbort` method | Calling the `SetAbort` method tells MTS that the transaction was unsuccessful. MTS declares the transaction unsuccessful if *any* participating component calls `SetAbort`. |
| `OnTransactionCommit` event | MTS raises the `OnTransactionCommit` event only if the transaction was successful. You can write code in an `OnTransactionCommit` subroutine to perform specific actions if the transaction is successful. |
| `OnTransactionAbort` event | MTS raises the `OnTransactionAbort` method only if the transaction was unsuccessful. You can write code in an `OnTransactionAbort` subroutine to perform specific actions if the transaction fails. |

# Web Applications vs. Client-Server Applications

Now that you've seen the ASP objects, let's explore a typical Web request. Figure 2.2 shows the entire ASP request cycle from client to server and back.

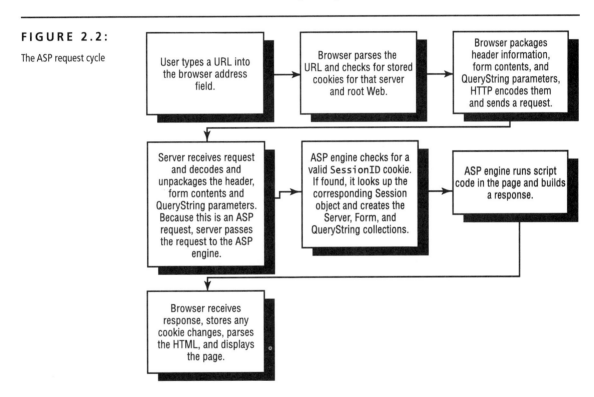

**FIGURE 2.2:**
The ASP request cycle

> **NOTE** I've left out some facts and processes showing how the browser finds the server's IP address and how the Web server and the ASP engine communicate because these processes don't have any immediate bearing on Web application development.

The actions shown in Figure 2.2 occur *every time* the browser sends a request, so there's a lot of work going on behind the scenes. You need to keep the request cycle in mind because it has a direct effect on how well your applications will work and how much of a load you will place on the network and the server. For example, suppose you store 2KB of information in a cookie and update some part of that cookie for each request. Those 2,048 bytes must travel to the server and back for each subsequent request. If you have 10 clients connected, you are responsible for 40KB of network traffic above and beyond the page content, form content, or `QueryString` variables for *each page* those clients request. If you have 100 clients, you've increased network traffic by 4MB for each page.

I'm not advocating that you never use cookies—the problem is just as acute if you use `QueryString` or `Form` variables to maintain state. The point is, you want to minimize your application's footprint on the network and the server so that your application will respond quickly, scale easily, and be a good Net citizen.

Although the ASP request cycle in Figure 2.2 looks similar to a standard client-server application request cycle, it is different in several ways.

First, you need to firmly grasp that the Web server knows nothing about the browser client at the beginning of the request. It has to have the SessionID cookie to be able to look up any information stored on the server for that particular client. The Web server immediately forgets about the client's identity when the request has completed. In a standard client-server application, the server knows when clients attach or detach from the application.

The entire application runs as a series of pages. You can control which pages a client can see and you can control the order of those pages, but you can't control the scope of a client's requests. In a standard client-server application, the application runs as a single entity.

Second, the Web server can't initiate any activity on or communication with the client—the client has to request a page before the server can do anything. In a standard client-server application, the server can initiate actions on the client by sending messages or raising events.

A lot of normally invisible or barely visible information flows back and forth for each request: headers, server (HTTP) variables, form contents, URL or `QueryString` parameters and values, and cookie values. You can take advantage of these values if you're aware of them. There's no need for all this invisible information in a standard client-server application because the connection doesn't disappear; therefore, after either the client or the server transfers information, it's there for the duration of the session.

Third, after completing a request, you never know if or when the client will return. If the client does return, you can't control which page it will request next. You can't guarantee that any IDs you send to the client will be valid the next time the client requests a page, because you have no control over the time between requests. In a standard client-server application, you have some control over what happens next. In any case, you will know if the client disconnects. Because the server portion of the application has only a few entrance and exit points, you don't have problems with the client suddenly requesting unexpected pages.

The point of all this is that you have to plan Web applications differently than you plan standard applications, because you have such little control over the client portion of the application.

As an example, suppose you have built a series of three form pages that a user must fill out to complete a job application. The user completes the first page and posts it to the server. You store the page and return the next page. The second page has a Cancel button, but the user clicks the browser's Back button instead. What should you do? Redisplay the first form empty? Redisplay the first form filled in? Are you going to allow changes on the first page? Suppose the client had completed the form, then clicked back? Would you then allow the client to make changes? Suppose the client bookmarks page 2 of your form, then uses the bookmark a week later. You don't want to display page 2 first. For your application to work correctly, you'll need to plan for and solve all these potential problems.

In contrast, in a standard client-server application, such problems rarely arise because clients don't have a Back button or a bookmarking capability unless you give it to them.

In the next chapter, you'll get a chance to use the ASP objects by building an ASP application.

# CHAPTER THREE

# Building ASP Applications

- Understanding the Structure of an ASP Application
- Using Include Files
- Understanding Language Independence
- Using Cookies with ASP
- Using the Scripting.Dictionary Object
- A (Very) Brief Introduction to HTML and Forms
- Creating a Self-Modifying ASP Application
- Tying It All Together—Caching Table Data

Because WebClass-based applications are closely tied to Microsoft's Active Server Pages (ASP) technology—they are, in fact, essentially compiled ASP applications—you need to thoroughly understand the object model exposed by the ASP engine to make efficient use of WebClasses.

In this chapter, you'll see how to set up an ASP Web site and how IIS maintains user data for an application. You'll also build two projects that illustrate the flexibility and power of ASP development. After you have completed these projects, you'll be ready to move on to WebClass development in Chapter 4, "Introduction to WebClasses."

# Understanding the Structure of an ASP Application

An application, to the ASP engine, is the set of all files and subdirectories within a directory that contains a `global.asa` file. Most ASP applications consist of ASP files and include (.inc) files, both of which can be any mixture of HTML, code, and graphics files; however, you can freely intermix ASP files with HTML files or any other file type that the server understands.

Figure 3.1 shows the directory structure for a typical ASP application.

**FIGURE 3.1:**

A typical ASP application directory structure

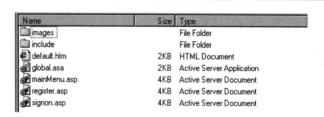

The top-level directory of the structure contains the `global.asa` file. The `global.asa` file defines the root directory for an application. The first time a user requests an ASP file in any directory in the application, the ASP engine traverses the tree upward until it finds a `global.asa` file (or until it reaches the root Web directory). This is important, because if you nest applications, the `global.asa` file that will be run for any particular user's request depends on which file the user requests *first*. Because you can't control a user's first request, don't nest ASP applications unless you have a good reason.

On IIS 4, you need to take an additional step to create a Web application: You must tell IIS that the virtual directory containing the `global.asa` file is the root of a Web application. You'll see more about that later in the section "Creating a Self-Modifying ASP Application."

The `global.asa` file always runs first, regardless of which file was requested. At this point, you can gain control of the request by redirecting the browser to the page of your choice in the `global.asa` file. As people use your application, they're likely to save bookmarks or favorites. These bookmarks may or may not point to the starting file in your application. If your application depends on users starting at a particular point, or if you have security requirements, you should route users to the appropriate page by redirecting them in `global.asa`.

The application shown in Figure 3.1 contains several ASP files as well as two subdirectories, `images` and `include`. No single directory structure fits all applications; you can put all the files in a single directory if you wish. In practice, though, it's much easier to build and maintain the application if you arrange files according to their function.

**NOTE** The virtual Web root and the ASP application root do *not* have to be the same.

For example, you might have a single `global.asa` file that applies to several ASP applications. You could place that `global.asa` file in a directory and then define each subdirectory in that directory as a virtual root, named according to the application. The directory structure in Figure 3.2, for example, contains four applications: 401k, Paycheck, Retirement, and Timesheet.

**FIGURE 3.2:**

Directory structure with a shared `global.asa` file

The highest-level directory, called `HR Applications`, contains the `global.asa` file. Whenever a user attaches to any of the four applications, the ASP engine climbs the directory tree until it reaches the `HR Applications` level, where it finds the `global.asa` file. One reason to set up an application in this manner might be that all four sites share security arrangements. Another reason might be that all four applications share a common database connection or other data, and you want to initialize that information in the `global.asa` file.

# Using Include Files

To reduce the amount of repetitive code or HTML in your ASP pages, you can *include* external files inside your ASP page. An include file is code from an external file that the server places in the ASP page at runtime. Include files have an .inc extension. You control where the server places the content of an include file with an include *directive*. An include directive is formatted as an HTML comment, so servers that don't understand the directive will ignore it, as will browsers. The entire process is exactly the same as if you were to cut and paste the contents of the file into your ASP page. Here's an example of an include directive:

```
<!-- #INCLUDE FILE="c:\ include\myInclude.inc" -->
```

The include directive tells the server to replace the include directive with the contents of the file—in this case, myInclude.inc. There are two forms of include directives: #INCLUDE FILE and #INCLUDE VIRTUAL. The FILE form requires a physical path for the file, whereas the VIRTUAL type references a file in a virtual directory.

Regardless of which form you use, the ASP engine performs all include replacements *before* it processes any code. Therefore, you cannot use code to determine *which* file to include or *whether* to include a file. The following code will not work as intended—the ASP engine will include both files.

```
<%
if myVar=True then
    %>
    <!-- #INCLUDE FILE="c:\include\myInclude.inc" -->
    <%
else
    %>
    <!-- #INCLUDE FILE="c:\include\yourInclude.inc" -->
    <%
end if
```

When the ASP engine parses this file, it will replace the two include directives with the contents of myInclude.inc and yourInclude.inc—and it will make the replacement *before* it runs the code for the if...end if structure. This is a common misconception, so I'll repeat. Once again, with emphasis: *You cannot use code to determine which file to include and you cannot use code to determine whether a file will be included.*

Despite this, with a little planning, you can still take advantage of include files. Using the preceding example, suppose `myInclude.inc` contains the HTML to display the graphic `HappyBirthday.gif` and that `yourInclude.inc` contains HTML to display the graphic `HappyAnniversary.gif`. In this case, the code would work even though the ASP engine replaces both include directives. This time, although the ASP engine inserts the HTML code for both files, the `If…Then` structure ignores one of them, depending on the value of the `myVar` variable. Therefore, only one of the files displays on the browser, which is the intent.

Include files are useful for inserting often-used functions or subroutines into an ASP page. By placing the code in an include file, you can update all pages that reference the code by making changes in only one place. Using include files in this way is like placing your favorite routines in a module in VB.

Include files are not limited to code. I've seen many sites that use them for toolbars, common graphics, common sections of text, etc. You can create include files that are all code, all HTML, or a mixture of both—just like any other ASP page. You can and should use include files to enforce consistency and reuse code in your application.

# Understanding Language Independence

ASP pages can be written in several scripting languages because the ASP engine is a *scripting host*, not a language. Currently, VBScript and JScript (Microsoft's implementation of ECMAscript) are included with the ASP engine installation, but you can also use Practical Extraction and Report Language (Perl), Restructured Extended Executor (REXX), or any language that conforms to the Microsoft debugging protocol. Almost all the code examples in this book use VBScript (this is, after all, a book about VB). However, you will see some JavaScript as well because you're going to write browser-independent applications, and you can't use VBScript for client-side script unless you're running Internet Explorer.

The ASP engine even supports pages written in more than one language. Each ASP page has a primary language, designated by the `<%@ LANGUAGE= %>` directive at the top of each page.

Within a page however, you can use other languages by wrapping the code in `<script></script>` tags, for example:

```
<script language=someLanguage runat=server></script>
```

Each page in an ASP application can set the default language for that page.

If you use multiple languages on a single page, or for any server-side script contained in `<script></script>` tags, remember to include the `runat=server` parameter and value. Otherwise, the parsing engine will think you're writing client-side code. You must always keep in mind whether you're writing code that will execute on the browser or on the server. On the server, you have access to the ASP objects—the Server, Application, Session, Request, and Response objects. On the client, you have access to the document and all its properties and methods.

This can be a tough concept to master, because you probably haven't written code in an environment where you're mixing and matching server-side code, client-side code, and HTML all in a single file.

Always remember:

- Code inside code-delimiter brackets (`<%` and `%>`) runs on the server.
- Code outside the brackets that is wrapped in `<script></script>` tags will run on the client unless the `<script>` tag includes the `runat=server` parameter.
- The ASP engine sends all other text in the page to the browser as part of the response. Usually, this other text consists of HTML tags and content.

# Using Cookies with ASP

The ASP engine maintains Session state with cookies; if the user's browser won't accept cookies, the ASP engine cannot maintain Session state for that user. That's because there has to be some sure method of identifying a particular browser. Given the uniqueness of IP addresses, you'd think that they would be perfect for identifying a particular browser, but no such luck. Multiple users often share an IP address or block of addresses. That's what a proxy server does—it maps the user's "real" IP address to one or more public IP addresses. The proxy then makes the request via the shared address. Therefore, it's perfectly possible for two or more browsers to access your application from the same IP address. Enter the cookie.

Cookies are text strings that a browser sends to a Web site each time it requests a page from that site. You can use HTTP headers to manipulate the contents of cookies directly, although it's much easier to use the Response.Cookies collection methods. Of course, that's all that the Response.Cookies collection does—send HTTP headers to add, alter, or delete cookies.

Basically, there are two kinds of cookies:

>**In-memory cookies**   These are held in memory, which means they disappear when you close the browser.

>**Persistent cookies**   These are persisted to disk, which means they expire when you delete the file or when their expiration date arrives, whichever comes first.

The ASP `SessionID` cookie is an in-memory cookie.

Because some people don't want to accept any information that might identify them to a Web site, browsers generally have a setting that lets you refuse cookies. ASP sites typically don't work well if the browser doesn't accept cookies, because most ASP sites rely on the cookie so they can maintain session information for you.

The ASP engine writes a `SessionID` cookie as soon as the user requests the first file from an ASP application. The ASP `SessionID` cookie is in every way a normal cookie, except that it is usually invisible to your application. If you query the Request object cookie collection, you won't see the ASP `SessionID` cookie. You can prove it by creating the following ASP page script:

```
<%@Language=VBScript%>
<html><head><title>List Cookies</title></head>
<body>
<%
Dim V
If Request.Cookies.Count > 0 then
For each V in Request.Cookies
                Response.Write V & "=" &
     Request.Cookies(V) & "<BR>"
Next
Else
     Response.Write "No Cookies"
End If
%>
</body>
</html>
```

Name the file and place it in a Web site. If you're using Visual InterDev, create a new Web project and call it **ASPProject1**, add a new ASP file, and place the code listing in it. Now use your browser to navigate to the page. You will see the text No Cookies. What happened?

Now, add one more line of code to the file, just before the end-of-script marker—the percent sign and right bracket (%>):

```
Response.Write "HTTP_COOKIE=" &
Request.ServerVariables("HTTP_COOKIE") & "<BR>"
```

This line of code displays the "raw" contents of the HTTP_COOKIE variable, without the filtering and organization applied by the ASP engine for the Request.Cookies collection. Run the file again (by refreshing the page). This time, you'll see No Cookies, and another line as well, that probably looks something like this:

```
HTTP_COOKIE=ASPSESSIONIDGGGQGQYE=DILDAIIBIFLCKEJCBLPCFCNI
```

That's the ASPSESSIONID cookie. It's a meaningless, semi-random ID that is highly likely to be unique. The ASP engine doesn't show it to you because you didn't generate it—the ASP engine did. I guess Microsoft thought it would be confusing to request the cookie count and get a 1 in response before ever setting a cookie yourself.

Consider one more interesting fact before we move on to a larger ASP project. Add this line to the end of the code listing:

```
Response.Write Session.SessionID
```

Refresh the page again. This time, you should see one additional line containing a long integer number like 411057027. The SessionID property doesn't return the SessionID cookie value at all! So will the "real" Session identifier please stand up? It turns out that the real SessionID is the long integer. The ASP engine generates the cookie as a long string of text for security reasons. It's much harder for a hacker to guess the long cookie string value than to guess the long integer value with which the cookie string is associated on the server.

# Using the Scripting.Dictionary Object

A Scripting.Dictionary object is similar to a Visual Basic collection object, but faster and much more flexible. The documentation describes it as similar to a Perl associative array, if that helps you. Both the VB collection object and the Dictionary object have keys, values, and Add, Remove, and Item methods; however, for the

Dictionary Add method you must supply the key first, then the value. The Add method for a VB collection requires the value first, then the key. I find the Dictionary object syntax more natural. In addition, the Dictionary object has methods to get the list of keys or values, and has an `Exists` method, which lets you find out whether a specified key exists.

In VB, to find out whether a Dictionary key exists, you would use code like this:

```
Dim d as new Dictionary
d.Add "Name", "Bill"
Debug.Print d.Exists("Name") ' prints True
```

In contrast, to find out whether a key exists in a VB collection object, you have to use `On Error Resume Next`, attempt to retrieve the value, and check for errors.

```
Sub keyExists(c as Collection, aKey as string) as Boolean
    Dim V as variant
    On Error Resume Next
    V = c(aKey)
    KeyExists = (Err.Number <> 5)
End Sub
```

**NOTE** The preceding code explicitly checks for `Err.Number=5` rather than just checking if any error occurred. This is because if the key exists, but the associated value is an object variable rather than a scalar variable, you will get Error 450 instead of Error 5.

The keys are strings. The values are variants, which means that they can be any data type, including objects. You can imagine that a Dictionary object looks like a table with two columns, as shown in Table 3.1.

**TABLE 3.1:** Dictionary Object Keys and Values Example

| Key | Value |
| --- | --- |
| "FirstName" | "John" |
| "LastName" | "Davis" |
| "City" | "Albuquerque" |
| "State" | "New Mexico" |
| "Address" | "1723 Candelaria" |

*Continued on next page*

**TABLE 3.1 CONTINUED:** Dictionary Object Keys and Values Example

| Key | Value |
| --- | --- |
| "Age" | 42 |
| "Telephones" | (Array) "555-555-5555", "555-555-5556" |

The keys must be unique. Having unique keys enables the Dictionary object to keep a sorted key list so that it can find any specific value with a fast binary lookup. This makes the Dictionary object larger than an array of the same size but much more efficient at finding values quickly.

Several other features of the Scripting.Dictionary object are worth noting. Unlike a VB collection object, you don't have to use the Add method to add new items; if you assign a value to a key that doesn't exist, the Dictionary creates a new key for you.

You can change the values of associations in the Dictionary through simple assignment—you don't have to remove the key and then add it again with a new value. Here's a VBScript example:

```
Dim d
Set d = Server.CreateObject("Scripting.Dictionary")
d("newKey") = "This is a new key"
Response.Write d("newKey") ' displays "This is a new key"
d("newKey") = "This is a changed value"
Response.Write d("newKey") ' displays "This is a changed value"
Response.Write d("NewKey") ' fails to display
```

When this code runs, it creates a new Dictionary object with one key, `newKey`, and one value, the string `"This is a new key"`, which displays in the browser. The code then assigns a new value to the association with the key `newKey`, and displays that. Finally, to show that keys in the Dictionary object are case sensitive by default, the program tries to display the key `NewKey`. That statement fails to display because the Dictionary object can't find the key, but unlike referencing missing keys in a VB Collection object, it doesn't cause a runtime error.

You can control how a Dictionary object treats case sensitivity in keys by using the `CompareMode` property. There are three `CompareMode` constants defined in the Microsoft Scripting Runtime Library: `BinaryCompare`, `TextCompare`, and `DatabaseCompare`, which are equivalent (and equal in value) to the VBScript `CompareMode` constants `vbBinaryCompare`, `vbTextCompare`, and `vbDatabaseCompare`. One restriction: You must set the `CompareMode` property before adding any items to the Dictionary; otherwise, a runtime error occurs. To avoid having to define the Scripting `CompareMode` constants, use the built-in VBScript `CompareMode` constants. Alter the code so it looks like this:

```
Dim d
Set d = Server.CreateObject("Scripting.Dictionary")
d.CompareMode = vbTextCompare
d("newKey") = "This is a new key"
Response.Write d("newKey") ' displays "This is a new key"
d("newKey") = "This is a changed value"
Response.Write d("newKey") ' displays "This is a changed value"
Response.Write d("NewKey") ' displays "This is a changed value"
```

Now, when you browse to the page, the browser displays all three lines.

Although the Object Browser lists the `DatabaseCompare` constant as one of the available `CompareMode` constants, the documentation for the Dictionary object doesn't include it as a valid value. Using it doesn't raise an error, though. As an experiment, set the `CompareMode` property of the Dictionary object to `vbDatabaseCompare` and run the file. Running it the first time appears to cause the Dictionary to treat keys as case insensitive; however, if you refresh the file, the third line disappears. Add a line to display the `CompareMode` property. The first time, the file properly displays 2, the value of the `vbDatabaseCompare` constant. If you run the file again, though, it will display the `CompareMode` property as 0, which corresponds to the `vbBinaryCompare` constant. I don't have a good explanation for this behavior (yet). Don't set the `CompareMode` property to `vbDatabaseCompare`.

Remember that, by default, Dictionary keys are case sensitive. This case sensitivity, coupled with the lack of a runtime error when you reference missing keys, goes against the case-insensitive theme of VB and VBScript and caused me several hours of frustrated debugging before I realized the reason. I don't like using the Dictionary in case-sensitive mode. If you don't either, you can avoid this problem altogether by wrapping the code that creates the Dictionary object in a function:

```
Function newDictionary()
    Set newDictionary = Server.CreateObject _
        ("Scripting.Dictionary")
    newDictionary.CompareMode = vbTextCompare
End Function
```

The function returns a case-insensitive Dictionary object.

> **NOTE**
>
> Like VB, VBScript uses the name of the function to return values; it creates a local variable with the same name as the function. You can often use this feature to make your code more readable, save yourself typing, and avoid the overhead of creating an extra local variable.

Table 3.2 shows the complete list of methods and properties for the Scripting.Dictionary object.

**TABLE 3.2:** Scripting.Dictionary Object Methods and Properties

| Name | Type | Description |
|---|---|---|
| `Add` *key, value* | Method | Adds a new string key to the Dictionary associated with the specified value. If the key already exists, an error occurs. |
| `CompareMode` (`CompareMethod`) | Property Get, Let | Controls the way the Dictionary object compares keys. Sets or returns one of the CompareMethod enumeration constants.<br><br>`vbBinaryCompare (0)` (case-sensitive)<br><br>`vbTextCompare (1)` (case-insensitive)<br><br>`vbDatabaseCompare (2)` (N/A) |
| `Count` | Property Get (read-only) | Returns the count of the number of associations in the Dictionary object. |
| `Exists` *key* | Property Get (read-only) | Returns a Boolean value that shows whether the specified key exists. |
| `Item` *key* or *index* | Property, Get, Let, Set | Returns or sets a value associated with the specified string key or integer index. |
| `Items` | Method | Returns a variant array of all of the values currently stored in the Dictionary. |
| `Key` *key* | Property Let (write-only) | Changes a string key from one string to another. |
| `Keys` | Method | Returns a variant array of all of the keys currently stored in the Dictionary. |
| `Remove` *key* | Method | Removes the specified key, if it exists. |
| `RemoveAll` | Method | Removes all keys. |

> **NOTE** The Microsoft VBScript documentation doesn't list the `vbDatabaseCompare` as a valid `CompareMode` value for a Dictionary object. Although it doesn't raise an error if you use it, it exhibits some strange behavior, so don't use it.

# A (Very) Brief Introduction to HTML and Forms

OK, I told you this book was not for beginners, but those of you who aren't experienced with HTML and forms will appreciate this (I promise) brief introduction before you move on to the other projects in this chapter.

Developers originally used HTML files for read-only display of information. Very quickly though, they realized that they needed a way for people to interact with the pages—specifically, to enter form data, such as names and e-mail addresses, in a way that they could be collected on the central server. It's important to realize that the *display* portion of a form requires nothing beyond standard HTML; however, to save the information generated by a form requires a program running on the server.

All HTML files begin with an `<html>` tag and end with an `</html>` tag. This tag is a containing or block tag—a tag that contains other tags. Following, or "inside" the HTML tag, you always have `<head></head>` tags. Any tags appearing between the `<head>` and `</head>` tags are in the *head* section. The head section contains browser directives, but most importantly, it contains the document title. The title of the document goes inside `<title>` and `</title>` tags. You should be seeing a pattern here. The `</tag>` form ends a tag begun with the `<tag>` form. Tags are not case sensitive in HTML, but they are in XML, SGML, and other markup languages, so you should work on making yourself write case-sensitive HTML right from the beginning. I'm afraid I'm guilty of mixing case in tags, so don't do as I do, do as I say.

After the head section comes the *body* section, which (you guessed it) is delimited by `<body>` and `</body>` tags. All the information displayed by the browser belongs in the body section except for the title, which is in the head section.

Believe it or not, you now have enough information to write a simple HTML file. Here's an example:

```
<html>
<head>
<title>
    Extremely Simple HTML
</title>
</head>
<body>
    Enter your name, then click the Submit button.
</body>
</html>
```

Figure 3.3 shows how this file looks in a browser. To run it, enter the preceding code listing into Notepad or an HTML editor. Save the file, then navigate to it in the browser. I recommend you create a virtual Web site rather than simply saving the file to disk and browsing to it, because you're going to write server-side code next, which requires the Web server.

**FIGURE 3.3:**

Extremely simple HTML file

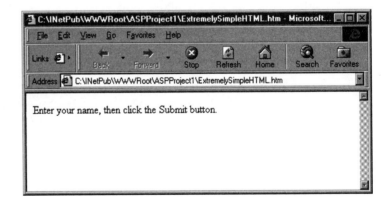

Wait—there's no Submit button! To display a button using standard HTML, you need to create a form. (Sounds like VB, doesn't it?) An HTML form begins with a <form> tag and ends (like most containing HTML tags) with a </form> tag. The form tag can take several parameters; these are the most common:

**Name** The name of the form. Although this parameter isn't required, it's good practice to name your forms so you can refer to them easily in client-side scripts.

**Action**  The URL to which the form will submit data. You may include additional URL-encoded variables in the value portion of the Action parameter (the part after the equals sign), but only if the Method parameter is Post. If you don't specify an action, the form will post itself to the originating filename (in other words, it posts to itself).

**Method**  You can use either the Post or the Get method. If you use the Get method, the browser will create a URL string that consists of the action URL (minus any explicit parameters) with URL-encoded form data appended. You'll see an example of this in a minute.

Here's a very simple form:

```
<form name="frmTest" METHOD="POST"
    action="testform.asp?submitted=true">
    <input type="text" name="Text1" value="">
    <input type="submit" name="Submit" value="Submit">
</form>
```

Copy the form code and insert it after the line that ends with click the Submit button. Save the file as TestForm.asp. Now navigate to the file in your browser. The page should now look similar to Figure 3.4.

**FIGURE 3.4:**

The TestForm.asp file

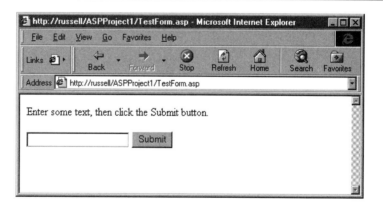

Enter some text in the text field and click the Submit button. Nothing happens. That's because you need to write a program to make something happen. Let's do that. Go back into the TestForm.asp file you just saved and add the following code above the <html> tag. Be sure to enter the <% and %> code delimiters.

```
<%@ Language=VBScript %>
<%
if Request("Submitted") = "true" then
    Response.Write "Request(Text1) = " & _
         Request("Text1") & "<BR>"
    Response.End
end if
%>
```

Refresh the file, enter some text into the text box, and submit the form again. This time, the server should display the text you typed.

You've just written your first ASP program. If you're not familiar with ASP and forms, I encourage you to experiment with this form a little before moving on to the next project. Specifically, you should try these tasks:

- Change the form method from `Post` to `Get`. What happens? (Hint: Look at the address line of your browser.)

- The `Action` parameter is optional. What happens if you delete the `Action` parameter from the `<form>` tag? What if you enter just `action=?submitted=true` as the parameter?

- What values besides the `Text` value does the form submit to the server?

# Creating a Self-Modifying ASP Application

Using interpreted ASP code has many advantages. For instance, because the code lives in text files, it's easy to change. Also, after the ASP engine has been installed, you don't have to install any more DLL installations, registrations, or support files. In this project, you'll see some of the power of ASP files by writing a self-modifying application. Don't worry if you don't completely understand everything in the project at this time—you will by the time you finish this book.

Using Visual InterDev or your favorite HTML editor, start a new text file. This file will consist of a form with a drop-down selection list. When you select a color from the list and submit the form, the file will rewrite itself to reflect your choice, then redisplay itself.

Listing 3.1 shows the entire code.

| LISTING 3.1 | Self-Modifying ASP File (*selfMod.asp*) |
|---|---|

```asp
<%@ Language=VBScript %>
<% option explicit %>
<%Response.Buffer=True%>
<%
dim submitted
dim backcolor
dim fs
dim ts
dim s
dim afilename
dim colors
dim curColor
dim V
dim aPos
dim i
set colors = server.CreateObject("Scripting.Dictionary")
colors.Add "Black", "000000"
colors.Add "Red", "FF0000"
colors.Add "Green", "00FF00"
colors.Add "Blue", "0000FF"
colors.Add "White", "FFFFFF"

submitted=(Request("Submitted") ="True")
if submitted then
    Session("CurColor")=Request("newColor")
    curColor = Session("CurColor")
    afilename=server.MapPath("selfMod.asp")
    Response.Write afilename & "<BR>"
    Response.Write Session("CurColor") & "<BR>"
    set fs = server.CreateObject _
        ("Scripting.FileSystemObject")
    set ts = fs.OpenTextFile(afilename,ForReading,false)
    s = ts.readall
    ts.close
    set ts = nothing
    aPos = 0
    do
        aPos = instr(aPos + 1, s, "bgcolor", _
            vbBinaryCompare)
```

```
            loop while (mid(s, aPos + 7, 1) <> "=")
        aPos = aPos + 9
        if aPos > 0 then
            s = left(s, aPos) & Session("CurColor") & _
                mid(s, aPos + 7)
            set ts = fs.OpenTextFile _
                (afilename,ForWriting,false)
            ts.write s
            ts.close
            set fs = nothing
            Response.Redirect "selfMod.asp"
        else
            set fs = nothing
            Response.Write "Unable to find the position " & _
                "in the file to write the new color value."
            Response.End
        end if
    else
        if isEmpty(Session("Curcolor")) then
            Session("CurColor") = "FF0000"
        end if
        curColor = Session("CurColor")
    end if
%>
<html>
<head>
</head>
<body>
<form name="frmColor" method="post"
    action="selfmod.asp?Submitted=True">
<input type="hidden" value="<%=curcolor%>">
<input type="hidden" value="<%=Session("curcolor")%>" id=hidden1
    name=hidden1>
<table align="center" border="1" width="80%" cols="2">
    <tr>
        <td align="center" colspan="2" bgcolor="#FF0000">
            <% if curColor = "000000" then %>
                <font color="#FFFFFF">
            <% else %>
                <font color="#000000">
            <% end if %>
            Select A Color
                </font>
```

```
            </td>
        </tr>
        <tr>
            <td align="left" colspan="2" bgcolor="#FFFFFF">
                Select a color from the list, then click the
                "Save Color Choice" button.
            </td>
        </tr>
        <tr>
            <td align="right" valign="top" width="20%">
                <b>Color</b>:
            </td>
            <td align="left" valign="top" width="80%">
                <select name="newColor">
                    <%
                    for each V in colors
                        Response.Write "<option "
                        if colors(V)=curColor then
                            Response.Write "selected "
                        end if
                        Response.Write "value='" & _
                            colors(V) & "'>" & V
                        for i = 1 to 12
                            Response.Write " "
                        next
                        Response.Write "</option>"
                    next
                    %>
                </select>
            </td>
        </tr>
        <tr>
            <td align="center" valign="bottom" colspan="2">
            <input type="submit" value="Save Color Choice"
                id=submit1 name=submit1>
            </td>
        </tr>
</table>
</form>
</body>
</html>
<%set colors = nothing%>
```

Web development environments such as Visual Basic and Visual InterDev create Web applications for you automatically, but if you're not using one of these tools, you'll need to create one manually.

If you're still using IIS 3, ignore this procedure. If you're using IIS 4, though, you must create a Web application before IIS will run the global.asa file. If you ever notice that an application isn't running any of the code in global.asa, you should check to make sure that the virtual directory containing your global.asa file is marked as a Web application. To mark the virtual directory for your project as an application, open the Internet Service Manager, select or create your application's virtual directory, then right-click the virtual directory name in the left-hand pane.

Look at the button to the right of the Name field in the Application Settings portion of the Virtual Directory properties dialog. If the button's caption is Create, click the button to create a new Web application, then enter the name for the application in the Name field. If the button is called Remove, then the directory is already marked as a Web application, and you don't need to do anything (see Figure 3.6).

**FIGURE 3.6:**

Internet Service Manager Virtual Directory properties

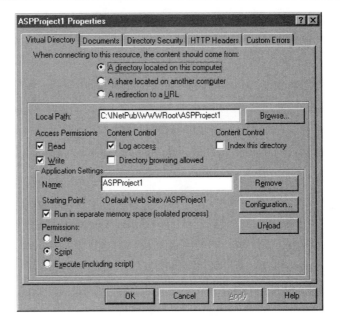

## Setting Up the Project in Visual InterDev

To set up the project outlined in this section in Visual InterDev, you should reference the Microsoft Scripting Runtime Library. You'll also need to allow write access to the virtual directory through the Internet Service Manager program before the project will work. To specify write access, open the Internet Service Manager program, find your virtual directory in the Default Web Site, and right-click it. Select Properties. In the dialog box, make sure the Write check box is checked. For IIS 4, the dialog box looks like Figure 3.6.

In the rest of this chapter, I'll explain the code in the selfMod.asp file.

```
<%@ Language=VBScript %>
```

This line is required in every ASP file (but of course, the language doesn't have to be VBScript—remember, ASP files can host multiple languages).

```
<% Option Explicit %>
```

Just as in VB, the Option Explicit command forces you to declare variables before you use them. Although the command is not required, you should always use this in both ASP and VB.

```
<%Response.Buffer=True%>
```

The server normally writes the HTTP headers immediately, then begins sending output as the ASP engine generates it. If you want to redirect within your code (which requires a change to the HTTP headers), you have to include this line. When you set the Response.Buffer property to True, the server buffers the entire response until page processing is complete. For long requests, this can slow down the perceived response time, because the user has to wait until the entire request has finished processing before the browser can begin to display the result. You should usually use this command in a page only if you plan to redirect, write cookies, or alter the HTTP headers.

```
set colors = Server.CreateObject("Scripting.Dictionary")
```

There are several things to explain in this line. First, the Server.CreateObject method is equivalent to the following VB code:

```
Dim colors as Dictionary
Set Colors = New Dictionary
```

In an ASP file, you need to enter both the project name (`Scripting`) and the class name (`Dictionary`) to obtain a reference to an object.

At any rate, the next five lines simply add the colors to the Dictionary object with the color name as the key and the HTML color string (which is a text representation of a long, or RGB, value) as the value. Each of the six-character strings represents three hexadecimal byte values. Colors are a combination of red, green, and blue. Each color may take a value from 0 to 255 (00 to FF in hex) and requires two characters. You read the value in pairs. The pairs of characters represent the red, green, or blue values, respectively.

```
colors.Add "Black", "000000"
colors.Add "Red", "FF0000"
colors.Add "Green", "00FF00"
colors.Add "Blue", "0000FF"
colors.Add "White", "FFFFFF"
```

This form submits to itself by posting the values entered by the user back to the same page that the form came from—unheard of for straight HTML forms, but common as dirt with ASP files. Submitting a form to itself puts all the code that deals with the form in one file, where you can test it easily, and makes one less file to maintain. If the user has submitted the form, you want to process the submitted request; otherwise, you just want to display the form. The following line determines whether the form is being shown for the first time or whether the user has submitted the form. The Request object will contain a string value of "`Submitted=True`" if the form has been submitted. The following code assigns a local variable called `submitted` a Boolean value of `True` if the form was submitted by the user:

```
submitted=(Request("Submitted") ="True")
if submitted then
    Session("CurColor")=Request("newColor")
    curColor = Session("CurColor")
```

**NOTE**  In the preceding code, note that you do not have to dimension Session variables before using them—even if `Option Explicit` is in effect.

Another way to test whether a user has posted a form is to check the value of `Request.ServerVariables("REQUEST_METHOD")`. The value will be `POST` when the user has posted content, and `GET` when you should display the form. I've used both and prefer using the local variable method. I find that using a local variable is more intuitive and works regardless of whether you use the `Post` or `Get` method.

You can think of the Session object as a Dictionary object (although it's not) because it exhibits almost identical behavior:

```
afilename=Server.MapPath("selfMod.asp")
```

The `Server.MapPath` method translates a virtual directory or filename into a physical directory or filename. In this case, when you pass it the name of the current file, it will return the full physical `drive:\pathname\filename` for the file. On my system, it returns

```
"c:\inetpub\wwwroot\ASPProject1\selfMod.asp"
```

The next few lines create two of the other objects in the Microsoft Scripting Runtime Library—a FileSystemObject and a TextStream object. The FileSystemObject provides methods and properties to work with the native file system. One of those methods is the `OpenTextFile` method, which returns a TextStream object. The TextStream object lets you read from and write to text files. In this case, open the file in read-only mode, then read the entire file at one time by using the `ReadAll` method. Finally, close the TextStream.

```
set fs = server.CreateObject("Scripting.FileSystemObject")
set ts = fs.OpenTextFile(afilename,ForReading,false)
s = ts.readall
ts.close
set ts = nothing
```

At this point, the content of the string `"s"` is the same as the file that's running! You can do this because the ASP engine doesn't lock the file while it's executing—it reads the whole file into memory. You're going to search the string for the first occurrence of the word `bgcolor` that's followed by an equals sign.

```
aPos = 0
do
    aPos = instr(aPos + 1, s, "bgcolor", vbBinaryCompare)
loop while (mid(s, aPos + 7, 1) <> "=")
aPos = aPos + 9
```

The code loops to find the last occurrence of the word `bgcolor` because the first occurrence is inside the loop itself! The final line sets the value of the `aPos` variable to point to the color string value in the first row of the table—the position after the first pound (#) sign in the file, right before the color value you're going to update.

After it finds the position of the color string for the first row of the table, the code simply substitutes the selected color value and saves the file. It then redirects so that the browser will request the just-altered file.

```
if aPos > 0 then
    s = left(s, aPos) & Session("CurColor") & _
        mid(s, aPos + 7)
    set ts = fs.OpenTextFile(afilename, ForWriting, _
        false)
    ts.write s
    ts.close
    set fs = nothing
    Response.Redirect "selfMod.asp"
else
    set fs = nothing
    Response.Write "Unable to find the position " & _
        "in the file to write the new color value."
    Response.End
end if
```

If the form was not submitted, the file provides a default color value of red—FF0000—and assigns it to both a Session variable and a local variable called cur-Color. In general, you should assign Session variable values to local variables if you're going to use them more than once in a file, because looking up the Session variable value based on the key you provide takes several times longer than simply retrieving the value of a local variable. This follows the same principle you use in VB; always assign objects to local variables if you're going to use them more than once in a routine. Similarly, it's the principle behind the introduction of the With...End With block in VB. Local references are much faster than COM references.

```
if isEmpty(Session("Curcolor")) then
    Session("CurColor") = "FF0000"
end if
curColor = Session("CurColor")
```

That's almost all the VBScript code in the file. The remainder of the file displays the table, the drop-down list, and the button inside a <form> tag.

```
<form name="frmColor" method="post"
    action="selfmod.asp?Submitted=True">
```

There are several types of input controls. The available input types correspond roughly to text fields, buttons, combo boxes, and list boxes, although they act slightly differently than the equivalent Windows common controls.

You saw the text field and submit button types in the previous project. The drop-down list is slightly different. It's not an `<input>` tag at all, it's a `<select></select>` tag. The `<select>` tag contains a list of `<option>` tags that contain the list data. Each option tag can take a `value` parameter that specifies the value returned to the server. By default, the browser returns the option value for the item that's visible in the drop-down list. This is similar to a VB list box, which contains both visible items and `itemdata`. The ItemData array contains a list of long values, one for each item in the list. In contrast, the `<option>` tag can take any type of value, although it returns them all as text. You can also preselect a specific option by adding a `selected` parameter to that option tag. The `selected` parameter does not require a value.

One special type of input control is hidden. A hidden input doesn't display, so you can use it to pass values from one file to another. In this case, I'm using hidden inputs just so you can view the value by selecting View Source from the browser.

```
<input type="hidden" value="<%=curcolor%>">
<input type="hidden" value="<%=Session("curcolor")%>">
```

This is a trivial example that you would never use in practice because you would have problems if more than one person accessed the file. However, it does illustrate two important points about ASP files:

- *Because ASP files are text files, you can change them easily*. To update an ASP-based application, you simply update the text files that contain the application code. No registration entries to worry about, no need to stop the server, no DLLs or large executables, and no installation programs to write. That's powerful stuff.

- *ASP files can rewrite themselves*. You can't do that in VB (although you can write VB code that writes ASP pages). You can do this because the code contained in the ASP file is loaded into memory for compilation from the ASP file. After the file is loaded, the ASP engine releases the file lock. Depending on your server settings, the ASP engine can cache the file—but it does check to see if the file has changed for each request. Therefore, when you change the file, the ASP engine will display the contents of the changed file for the next request.

In the next section, you'll learn how to cache data in HTML or simple ASP files, rewriting them as needed when the data changes.

# Tying It All Together—Caching Table Data

Imagine that, instead of changing a color value, you wanted to display the contents of a table. Sure, you can query a database for each request, but if the table data didn't change often, wouldn't it be nice if you could "cache" the table in an HTML file? Whenever the table data changed, you could re-create the HTML file.

I'm going to present the project here despite the data access requirements. Those of you who are not familiar with ActiveX Data Objects (ADO) may want to return to this example after reading Chapter 8, "Maintaining State in IIS Applications." You can also read up on ADO by taking a look at the *VB Developer's Guide to ADO* by Mike Gunderloy (Sybex, 1999).

This project consists of one ASP file. Each time you run the file, it lets you select a table from the pubs database. When you submit your selection, the program checks to see whether it already has the table data cached in an HTML file. If the table cache file exists, the ASP file simply returns the contents of the HTML file. If the table cache file does not exist, the program reads the table from the database, writes a cache file, then displays the contents of the file. The program also refreshes cached data if you pass a Refresh=True parameter in the URL. Administrators could use this feature to force the cached data to refresh.

**NOTE**  The pubs database comes with SQL Server. If you don't have SQL Server, you can download a Microsoft Access database containing the tables of the pubs database from the Sybex Web site.

**NOTE**  To download code (including the Access database), navigate to http://www.sybex.com. Click Catalog and search for this book's title. Click the Downloads button and accept the licensing agreement. Accepting the agreement grants you access to the downloads page for the book.

The complete code for the program is in Listing 3.2 at the end of this chapter. Just like the code in the previous project in this chapter, the selectTable.asp file is a form that submits to itself. The first part of this file contains the logic needed to differentiate between a request containing form data (Submitted=True) and an unsubmitted request, before the user has selected a table to display. Unlike the previous project, though, this one gets all its information from a database by using ADO. To read database information, you need to open a connection to the database:

```
Set conn = Server.CreateObject("ADODB.Connection")
conn.ConnectionString="pubs"
conn.CursorLocation= adUseClient
conn.Mode= adModeRead
conn.Open
```

In this case, you create the Connection object and set its `ConnectionString` property to a valid Data Source Name (DSN), pubs. Next, you set the Connection object's `CursorLocation` property to `adUseClient`, which tells the Connection object that you're going to use open database connectivity (ODBC) client cursors rather than SQL Server server-side cursors for any recordsets you retrieve using the connection. Because you're only going to be reading data, not updating, you set the `Mode` property to `adModeRead`. Finally, you open the connection using the `Open` method of the Connection object.

Next, you want to retrieve information about the tables in the database so you can populate the drop-down list. To do that, you need to get a recordset from the connection.

```
set R = Server.CreateObject("ADODB.Recordset")
R.CursorLocation=aduseclient
call R.Open("SELECT Name FROM SysObjects WHERE " & _
    Type='U' ORDER BY Name ASC",conn, _
    adOpenForwardOnly, adLockReadOnly,adCmdText)
end if
```

This code creates a Recordset object, tells it to use a client-side cursor, and to get a list of all tables in the pubs database. The rest of the code in the file displays the data from the recordset. It's fairly straightforward and similar to the code in the previous project, so I won't spend any time on it.

When the user selects a table from the drop-down list, the code redirects to the relative URL `showTable.asp`. You'll use redirection extensively in Web applications to provide messages and feedback, and to process requests based on user selections or input. The `Response.Redirect` method sends a header to the client browser. The header essentially means that the browser can find the information requested at a new address. The browser immediately makes a new request to the server for the specified page. So, (right now) redirection requires a round-trip to the client.

> **NOTE**
>
> Microsoft will soon provide server-side redirection, which won't require the round-trip to the client and therefore will be much more efficient.

The `showTable.asp` file contains almost no static HTML—just the bare minimum markup and two placeholders for the table data.

```
<html>
<head>
</head>
<body>
<!--Start--><!--End-->
</body>
</html>
```

The first thing the `showTable.asp` file does is check the `TableName` parameter. If the parameter is empty, the program redirects the user "back" to the `selectTable.asp` file:

```
if Request.QueryString("TableName") = "" then
    Response.Redirect "selectTable.asp"
end if
```

This code exists because, as I stated earlier, you don't know and can't control the order in which a user might request files from your application. If users simply type the URL to `showTable.asp` into their browsers, the program wouldn't know which file to display. Simply displaying whichever table the file may currently contain might be confusing; therefore, the code forces the user to make a choice before displaying any table.

Next, it caches the `TableName` parameter in a local variable:

```
requestedTablename= Request.QueryString("TableName")
```

If the requested table name is same as the previous request, the file simply shows the data already cached in the file; otherwise, it reads and formats the table data. It also refreshes the table data if you pass a `"Refresh=True"` parameter in the URL. You'll need some way to refresh the file if the table data changes. An "optional" parameter such as this gives you the opportunity to refresh the file if, for example, an administrator changes the data. Another way of doing this is to keep track of the data by looking at the highest Identity value (AutoNumber in Access), the date/time at which the table was last changed, or via a trigger that updates a row in a separate table whenever data in the main table is changed.

In this project, you "change" the table data by selecting a different table or by passing a `"Refresh=True"` parameter to the ASP page:

```
if requestedTablename <> tablename or _
    Request.QueryString("Refresh") = "True" then
    ' open the file, change the contents to that
    ' of the new table, then save the file.
End if
```

The process of opening a file is similar each time. You query the Server object by using the `MapPath` function to obtain the physical path for the file.

```
set fs = server.CreateObject("Scripting.FileSystemObject")
aFilename = server.MapPath("showTable.asp")
set ts = fs.OpenTextFile(afilename,ForReading,false)
s = ts.readall
ts.close
set ts = nothing
```

> **TIP**  Microsoft's documentation states that one way to speed up sites is to limit or eliminate the use of the `MapPath` function. For greatest efficiency, you should cache path information in Application or Session variables when appropriate. Don't ever hard-code file paths in a Web application unless you're absolutely sure that the path will never change.

Next, you want to replace the old table name with the selected table name. Find the old table name parameter and value in the file string. Use VB's new `replace` function to perform string replacements.

```
s = replace(s, "tablename=" & chr(34) & tablename & _
    chr(34), "tablename=" & chr(34) & requestedTablename _
    & chr(34), 1, 1, vbBinaryCompare)
```

Now replace the table data. Because browsers ignore comments, you can conveniently use them as markers inside HTML files. I've used the two comment tags `<!-Start-->` and `<!-End-->` to mark the beginning and end positions for the table data. To make the replacement, you need to find the markers.

```
do
    startPos = instr(startPos+1, s, _
        "<!--Start",vbBinaryCompare)
loop while mid(s, startPos + 9 ,1) <> "-"
startPos=startPos + len("<!--Start") + 3
```

```
do
     endPos = instr(endPos + 1, s, _
     "<!--End", vbBinaryCompare)
loop while mid(s, endPos + 7, 1) <> "-"
```

To get the data, you create a database connection and read the data from the selected table.

```
set conn = server.CreateObject("ADODB.Connection")
conn.ConnectionString="pubs"
conn.CursorLocation=aduseclient
conn.Mode= adModeRead
conn.Open
set R = Server.CreateObject("ADODB.Recordset")
R.CursorLocation=aduseclient
set R = conn.Execute("SELECT * FROM " & _
     requestedtablename,,adCmdText)
```

Whenever you retrieve data, you should check to make sure that the data you think is there is actually there. The `Execute` method returns a recordset regardless of whether it retrieves any data. Always check the recordset's `End-of-File` (EOF) property. The property will return `True` if the recordset is empty—that is, if no rows were retrieved. If the recordset contains data, then you can format the column headers by using the `Field.Name` property to get the name of each column.

```
if not R.EOF then
     tableData="<table align='center' border='1' _
     width='95%' COLS='" & R.Fields.Count & "'>"
     sTmp="<TR>"
     for each F in R.Fields
          sTmp = sTmp & "<TD><B>" & F.Name & "</B></TD>"
     next
     sTmp = sTmp & "</TR>"
     tableData = tableData & sTmp
end if
```

At the end of this loop, the recordset is still on the first row. You loop until the EOF property becomes true, placing each field value in a table cell. Note that this is a nested loop; the outer loop creates the rows while the inner loop fills the columns with data.

```
while not R.EOF
     sTmp = "<TR>"
     for each F in R.Fields
```

```
            if (F.Attributes and adFldLong) = adFldLong then
                if F.Type=adLongVarBinary then
                    sTmp = sTmp & _
                    "<TD valign='top'>(binary)</TD>"
                elseif F.ActualSize=0 then
                    sTmp = sTmp & _
                    "<TD valign='top'> </TD>"
                else
                    sTmp = sTmp & "<TD valign='top'>" & _
                    F.GetChunk(F.ActualSize) & "</TD>"
                end if
            else
                if isNull(F.Value) then
                    sTmp = sTmp & _
                    "<TD valign='top'> </TD>"
                else
                    sTmp = sTmp & _
                    "<TD valign='top'>" & F.Value _
                    & " </TD>"
                end if
            end if
        next
        sTmp = sTmp & "</TR>"
        tableData = tableData & sTmp
        R.MoveNext
Wend
```

You need to decide what to do if the recordset does not contain any rows. In this case, the program returns a message in the first table row.

```
tableData= "There is no data in the table: " & _
    requestedTablename & ".<BR>"
```

Finally, don't forget to close the recordset and the connection and set them to Nothing. Setting them to Nothing frees up the memory. Strictly speaking, you don't have to do this at the end of a page because the ASP engine destroys the objects and frees the memory for variables created during page processing when the page ends. However, it's good practice for you to clean up explicitly. It also frees the memory somewhat sooner than the ASP engine can.

```
R.Close
set R = nothing
conn.Close
set conn= nothing
```

Finally, concatenate the table data into the file string between the start and end position markers in the file, then write the file string to disk.

```
s = left(s, startPos) & tableData & _
    mid(s, endPos)
set ts = fs.OpenTextFile(afilename,ForWriting,false)
ts.write s
ts.close
set ts = nothing
set fs = nothing
```

Now the file is ready to display, so you can redirect to the file you just wrote.

```
Response.Redirect "showTable.asp?TableName=" & _
    requestedTablename
```

**LISTING 3.2**  Code for Providing Fast Access to Table Data ASP Project (*selectTable.asp* and *showTable.asp*)

```
'*****************************************************
' The selectTable.asp file
'*****************************************************
<%@ Language=VBScript %>
<% option explicit %>
<%Response.Buffer=True%>
<%
dim submitted
dim tablename
dim R
dim conn
submitted=(Request("Submitted") ="True")
if submitted then
    Response.Redirect "showTable.asp?TableName=" & _
        Request("TableName")
Else
    set conn = server.CreateObject("ADODB.Connection")
    conn.ConnectionString="DSN=pubs;UID=sa;PWD="
    conn.CursorLocation=aduseclient
    conn.Mode= adModeRead
    conn.Open
    set R = Server.CreateObject("ADODB.Recordset")
    R.CursorLocation=aduseclient
    call R.Open("SELECT Name FROM SysObjects WHERE Type='U' _
ORDER BY Name ASC",conn,adOpenForwardOnly,adLockReadOnly,adCmdText)
end if
```

```
%>
<html>
<head>
<meta name="generator" Content="Microsoft Visual Studio 6.0">
</head>
<body>
<form name="frmTable" method="post"
    action="selectTable.asp?Submitted=True">
<table align="center" border="1" width="80%" cols="2">
    <tr>
        <td align="center" colspan="2" bgcolor="#FF0000">
            Select Table
                </font>
        </td>
    </tr>
    <tr>
        <td align="left" colspan="2" bgcolor="#FFFFFF">
            Select a table name from the list, then click
            the "Display Table" button.
        </td>
    </tr>
    <tr>
        <td align="right" valign="top" width="20%">
            <b>Table</b>:
        </td>
        <td align="left" valign="top" width="80%">
            <select name="TableName">
                <%
                do while not R.EOF
                    Response.Write "<option "
                    if R("Name").value = tableName then
                        Response.Write "selected "
                    end if
                    Response.Write "value='" & R("Name") &
                        "'>" & R("Name") & "</option>"
                    R.movenext
                loop
                R.close
                set R = nothing
                conn.Close
                set conn=nothing
                %>
            </select>
```

```
                </td>
            </tr>
            <tr>
                <td align="center" valign="bottom" colspan="2">
                    <input type="submit" value="Display Table">
                </td>
            </tr>
        </table>
    </form>
</body>
</html>

'*****************************************************
' The showTable.asp file
'*****************************************************
<%@ Language=VBScript %>
<% option explicit %>
<%Response.Buffer=true%>
<%
dim submitted
dim tablename
dim tabledata
dim sTmp
dim requestedTablename
dim afilename
dim fs
dim ts
dim s
dim startPos
dim endPos
dim conn
dim R
dim F
tablename="authors"
if Request.QueryString("TableName") = "" then
    Response.Redirect "selectTable.asp"
end if
requestedTablename= Request.QueryString("TableName")
if requestedTablename <> tablename or _
    Request.QueryString("Refresh") = "True" then _
    set fs = server.CreateObject _
        ("Scripting.FileSystemObject")
```

```
aFilename = server.MapPath("showTable.asp")
set ts = fs.OpenTextFile(afilename,ForReading,false)
s = ts.readall
ts.close
set ts = nothing
s = replace(s, "tablename=" & chr(34) & _
    tablename & chr(34), "tablename=" & chr(34) & _
    requestedTablename & chr(34),1,1,vbBinaryCompare)
do
    startPos = instr(startPos+1, s, _
    "<!--Start",vbBinaryCompare)
loop while mid(s, startPos + 9 ,1) <> "-"
startPos=startPos + len("<!--Start") + 3
do
    endPos = instr(endPos + 1, s, _
        "<!--End", vbBinaryCompare)
loop while mid(s, endPos + 7, 1) <> "-"
set conn = server.CreateObject("ADODB.Connection")
conn.ConnectionString="pubs"
conn.CursorLocation=aduseclient
conn.Mode= adModeRead
conn.Open
set R = Server.CreateObject("ADODB.Recordset")
R.CursorLocation=aduseclient
set R = conn.Execute("SELECT * FROM " & _
    requestedtablename,,adCmdText)
if not R.EOF then
    tableData="<table align='center' border='1' " & _
        "width='95%' COLS='" & R.Fields.Count & "'>"
    sTmp="<TR>"
    for each F in R.Fields
        sTmp = sTmp & "<TD><B>" & F.Name & _
            "</B></TD>"
    next
    sTmp = sTmp & "</TR>"
    tableData = tableData & sTmp
    while not R.EOF
        sTmp = "<TR>"
        for each F in R.Fields
            if (F.Attributes and adFldLong) = _
                adFldLong then
                if F.Type=adLongVarBinary then
```

```
                                    sTmp = sTmp & _
                                        "<TD valign='top'>" & _
                                        "(binary)</TD>"
                                elseif F.ActualSize=0 then
                                    sTmp = sTmp & _
                                    "<TD valign='top'>" & _
                                    " </TD>"
                                else
                                    sTmp = sTmp & _
                                    "<TD valign='top'>" & _
                                    F.GetChunk(F.ActualSize) & _
                                    "</TD>"
                                end if
                            else
                                if isNull(F.Value) then
                                    sTmp = sTmp & _
                                    "<TD valign='top'>" & _
                                    " </TD>"
                                else
                                    sTmp = sTmp & _
                                    "<TD valign='top'>" & _
                                    F.Value & " </TD>"
                                end if
                            end if
                        next
                        sTmp = sTmp & "</TR>"
                        tableData = tableData & sTmp
                        R.MoveNext
                    wend
                else
                    tableData= "There is no data in the table: " _
                        & requestedTablename & ".<BR>"
                end if
                R.Close
                set R = nothing
                conn.Close
                set conn= nothing
                s = left(s, startPos) & tableData & mid(s, endPos)
                set ts = fs.OpenTextFile(afilename,ForWriting,false)
                ts.write s
                ts.close
                set ts = nothing
                set fs = nothing
```

```
        Response.Redirect "showTable.asp?TableName=" & _
            requestedTablename
end if
%>
<html>
<head>
</head>
<body>
<!--Start-->
<!--End-->
</body>
</html>
```

# CHAPTER FOUR

# Introduction to WebClasses

- Understanding How WebClasses Work
- Understanding HTML Templates
- Writing HTML without Templates
- Exploring the WebClass Event Sequence
- Optimize, Optimize, Optimize
- Comparing the Advantages and Disadvantages of VB/WebClasses vs. ASP

The way you interact with Internet Information Server from a Visual Basic application is with a special type of class called a *WebClass*. WebClasses are new in Visual Basic 6. They work hand in hand with Active Server Pages to provide server-based request processing.

Let me interject here that there's nothing that WebClasses can do that you can't do yourself! If that's so, then what's the point? Why not just write ActiveX DLLs that work with ASP pages and forget the WebClass? Better yet, why not just use ASP so you don't have to compile, install, and register binary code?

The point is that WebClasses handle a great deal of the grunt work of connecting your VB class to the Web server, parsing the variables sent by the browser, and sending new content to the browser. More important, WebClass code, like a DLL, is compiled code; therefore, in certain situations, it's considerably faster than the interpreted ASP code. Still more important, WebClasses encourage separation between the interface code and the application logic. A WebClass acts as the connection point between the user interface (HTML) and back-end databases or middle-tier business objects. Finally, WebClasses let you work in a robust environment that you are familiar with and that has evolved over many years.

In this chapter, you'll see how WebClasses work hand in hand with IIS and the ASP objects to make it easy to provide dynamic information to the browser. You'll also see the importance of optimizing your code to ensure that your application responds quickly and scales well. Finally, you'll see the relative advantages and disadvantages of using WebClasses as opposed to using ASP pages, so you can decide which technology is appropriate for your applications.

# Understanding How WebClasses Work

In their first implementation, WebClasses don't talk directly to the server. When you create an ActiveX DLL in Visual Basic, you typically also create another project that instantiates the objects that your DLL exposes, so that you can test them. Similarly, a WebClass is a DLL that needs to be loaded; the objects it exposes need to be instantiated from another program.

At this time, Microsoft has chosen to let WebClasses work through an intermediary ASP page. The browser requests the ASP page from the server, which starts the

ASP engine. The ASP engine parses the ASP page and executes the code, which instantiates the WebClass. The WebClass typically gets HTML from an HTML template and retrieves data from a database. It inserts the data into the HTML template and returns the resulting HTML page, possibly with embedded client-side script, to the browser. You can see this process in Figure 4.1.

**FIGURE 4.1:**

A typical WebClass request cycle

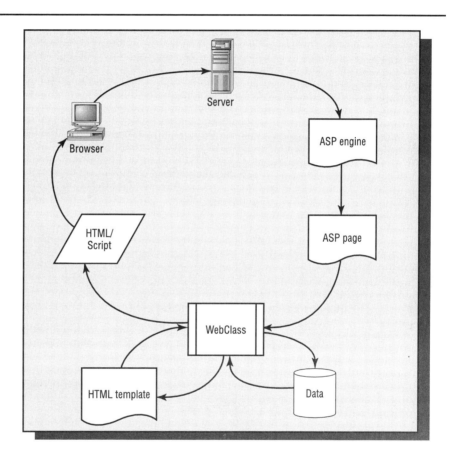

Here's a closer look at what happens in the WebClass request cycle: The user types the URL of an ASP page into the browser. For this example, assume the ASP page's URL is http://myserver/WebClass1.asp. The ASP page does nothing but instantiate a WebClass object. Listing 4.1 shows the code from a VB-generated ASP page that creates a WebClass.

### LISTING 4.1 VB-generated ASP Page to Display a WebClass

```
<%
Response.Buffer=True
Response.Expires=0
If (VarType(Application("~WC~WebClassManager")) = 0) Then
    Application.Lock
    If (VarType(Application("~WC~WebClassManager")) = 0) Then
        Set Application("~WC~WebClassManager") = _
    Server.CreateObject("WebClassRuntime.WebClassManager")
    End If
    Application.UnLock
End If
Application("~WC~WebClassManager").ProcessRetainInstanceWebClass _
    "Project1.WebClassTest", _
        "~WC~Project1.WebClassTest", _
        Server, _
        Application, _
        Session, _
        Request, _
        Response
%>
```

You've already seen information about the `Response.Buffer` call. The line `Response.Expires=0` tells the browser that the page expires immediately—the next time the user requests this page, the browser should request it again from the server, not from the browser's cache.

The If...End If block checks the Application object variable called ~WC~WebClassManager to see whether it's empty (a `VarType` function return of 0 indicates an empty variable). If so, it locks the Application object. The code then immediately checks again to see whether the variable is empty. Why? Because you're now working in a multiuser environment. It's possible that another thread set the application variable object reference sometime after the first check returned zero but before the `Application.Lock` command executed.

> **NOTE** You cannot assume that your session is the only one running. You must either know or perform the appropriate checks. In the preceding example, if a reference already exists and you suddenly overwrite the variable with a new reference, some other user will have problems.

If the variable is still empty, the code tells the Server object to create a new instance of an object called a WebClassManager. You don't need to know anything about this object other than that it manages multiple instances of Web-Classes for you, so that many people can use your WebClass simultaneously in an application.

Finally, the code calls either the `ProcessRetainInstanceWebClass` or `ProcessNoStateInstance` method of the WebClassManager object (you'll see more about these two methods later). It passes two string references—the project and name identifier of your WebClass as found in the Registry, and a `WebClassSessionName` string. It also passes references to most of the ASP objects, so that your WebClass can use the properties and methods of those objects to communicate with the server and return content to the browser.

Now you've seen the first difference between a standard class and a WebClass. VB ensures that a WebClass automatically gets a reference to the ASP objects on start-up. In contrast, here's how you would instantiate a VB5 ActiveX DLL from an ASP page:

```
Dim myObj
Set myObj = Server.CreateObject("MyProject.MyObject")
```

At this point, you could either explicitly pass references to the ASP objects or you could write `OnStartPage` and `OnEndPage` methods in your DLL, which the server automatically calls immediately after creating the object. When the server calls the `OnStartPage` method, it also passes a reference to the ASP ScriptingContext object as a parameter. The ScriptingContext object exposes methods that let your DLL obtain references to the ASP objects.

At any rate, when the ASP engine first creates the WebClass, it will fire the `WebClass_Initialize` event. The `WebClass_Initialize` event lets you perform initialization for that WebClass.

Next, the WebClass will fire one of two events. If the user made the request without asking for a specific WebItem—for example, the user typed only `http://myserver/WebClass1.asp` into the browser—the WebClass will fire the `WebClass_Start` event. If the user requested a specific item, the WebClass will fire the `Respond` event for the requested item. Figure 4.2 shows the complete sequence of events.

**FIGURE 4.2:**

WebClass event sequence

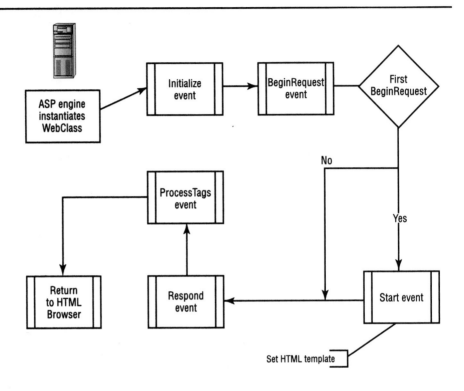

The `WebClass_Start` event lets you select which WebItem will be processed first as well as perform any other initialization for this specific instance of the WebClass.

The `Respond` event fires for the *requested item.* This is important. The requested item is typically an HTML template or a custom WebItem, so the event code has a different name for each item, for example, `Template1_Respond`.

Finally, the `ProcessTag` event—again, an item-specific event—provides you the opportunity to replace WebClass-specific tags with whatever you wish: HTML markup, content, script, input controls, etc.

> **WARNING** The `mswcrun.dll` file that comes with Visual Studio Service Pack 3 (sp3) has some serious problems with tag replacement. When running in design mode, the WebClass truncates the HTML returned to the browser. This behavior does not occur at runtime. To solve this problem, you need to replace the sp3 version of the DLL with an earlier version. For more information, see the Microsoft Knowledge Base article Q234317.

# Understanding HTML Templates

WebClasses work closely with HTML *templates*. An HTML template is a standard HTML page with (optionally) some delimited fields that your WebClass can replace with custom information at runtime. You can call these special tags *WebClass tags* or *custom tags*. This is easier to see than to explain. Suppose you want to put a person's name in the title of an HTML page. You don't want to have separate pages for each person, you only want to change the title. The rest of the page should be the same regardless of who's viewing it. In a standard HTML page, the title goes into the `<head>` section between `<title>` and `</title>` tags:

```
<title>This is a title</title>
```

To display a different title for each user, you would create an HTML template with a single replaceable parameter:

```
<title>Hello <wcName>Name</wcName></title>
```

When the WebClass processes the HTML template at runtime, it will find the `<wcName>` tag and raise a `ProcessTag` event. Inside the event procedure, you use a `Case` statement to determine which tag you're replacing.

```
Private Sub Template1_ProcessTag(ByVal TagName As String, _
    TagContents As String, SendTags As Boolean)
    Select Case TagName
    Case "wcName"
        TagContents = "Bob"
    End Select
End Sub
```

When this page displays in the browser, the title bar will contain `Hello Bob`.

This simple text replacement is a much more powerful concept than it appears at first glance. For example, suppose you have lists of customers, one list per salesperson. Whenever a salesperson signs on, you want to show only that person's customer list. You could write the HTML template so that it contained a WebClass tag, `<wcCustomerList>`, for the list. At runtime, you would replace the WebClass tag with the list for that salesperson. The page will display a customized list for every salesperson, based on their sign-on and that one replacement tag.

The reasoning behind HTML templates is that many programmers don't write HTML and don't want to write HTML. In theory, HTML templates make it easier to split development between graphic artists, Web designers, and programmers by separating the display code from the programming code. In practice, there's often a tight integration between the two. For many projects, there's also a point at which it becomes awkward, inconvenient, and often counterproductive to keep moving back and forth between a layout artist and a programming team. Usually, the programmer takes over the main responsibility at that point. Finally, in instances where the program code requires knowledge of the positions of objects on the screen, the layout/programming split becomes nonexistent.

Personally, I feel that programmers working in the Web medium need to learn the layout language. Part of the appeal of Visual Basic has always been the power it gave programmers to quickly lay out graphical interfaces. If you don't understand the layout language in the Web medium, you have abdicated that power. Some people will argue that the VB forms engine also writes "code" (in .frm files) that you don't need to understand; similarly, HTML editors provide drag-and-drop formatting capability for HTML code. That's a valid argument. So what's the difference? Maybe when the HTML editors get so good at writing code that they always do exactly what you expect, there won't be any difference. Meanwhile, this entire area is changing so rapidly that you should learn the layout language, if only to take maximum advantage of the medium.

# Writing HTML without Templates

Despite their availability, you don't have to use an HTML template to create an IIS project. HTML templates are typically more convenient for complex pages and for pages where the "look" may change often. Sometimes, it's simpler to write the HTML from inside the WebClass.

Here's a simple example. Suppose you want to display a table from a database. Start a new IIS project in VB. Right-click the project and select Properties. Rename the project **showTable**. Right-click the WebClass and rename it **tableViewer**. Save the project.

> **NOTE** When you first run an IIS project, VB will create a virtual Web for you. If you don't save the project, VB creates a source folder for the virtual Web in your **Temp** directory. If you save the project, it creates the source folder for the virtual Web as a subdirectory of the project folder.

Double-click the WebClass Designer. You'll see an Explorer-type view with two folders: one titled HTML Template WebItems and the other titled Custom WebItems. Right-click the Custom WebItems folder and select Add Custom WebItem. Title the new WebItem **showTable**. Your designer window should now look like Figure 4.3.

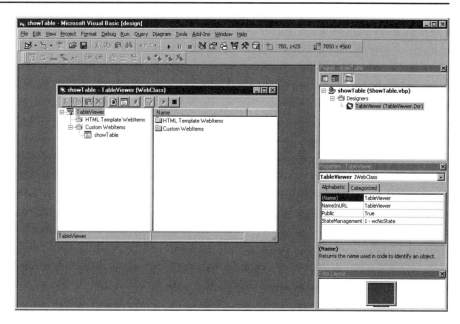

**FIGURE 4.3:**

WebClass Designer window

Double-click the showTable custom WebItem and place the code in Listing 4.2 into the Respond event. Note that this project uses the Microsoft pubs database that comes with SQL Server. If you do not have SQL Server, you can download a Microsoft Access database containing the tables of the pubs database from the Sybex Web site.

> **NOTE** To download code, navigate to http://www.sybex.com. Click Catalog and search for this book's title. Click the Downloads button and accept the licensing agreement. Accepting the agreement grants you access to the downloads page for the book.

### LISTING 4.2 ShowTable_Respond Event

```vb
Private Sub showTable_Respond()
    Dim conn As connection
    Dim R As Recordset
    Dim F As Field
    Dim s As String
    Set conn = New connection
    conn.ConnectionString = "pubs"
    conn.Mode = adModeRead
    conn.Open
    Set R = conn.Execute("authors", , adCmdTable)
    s = "<html><head><title>Pubs Database-" & _
        "Authors Table</title></head>"
    s = s & "<BODY>"
    s = s & "<table align=""center"" width=""95%" & _
        "border=""1"">"
    s = s & "<tr>"
    For Each F In R.Fields
        s = s & "<td align=""center""><b>" & F.Name _
            & "</b></td>"
    Next
    s = s & "</tr>"
    While Not R.EOF
        s = s & "<tr>"
        For Each F In R.Fields
            If IsNull(F.Value) Then
                s = s & "<td> </td>"
            Else
                s = s & "<td>" & F.Value & "</td>"
            End If
        Next
        s = s & "</tr>"
        R.MoveNext
    Wend
    R.Close
    Set R = Nothing
    conn.Close
    Set conn = Nothing
    s = s & "</table></body></html>"
    Response.Write s
End Sub
```

You're almost done. You need to tell the WebClass which item to show first. Find the Start event for the WebClass and place this code into the event, replacing the code that the IIS Application Wizard automatically puts there:

```
Private Sub WebClass_Start()
    Set NextItem = showTable
End Sub
```

Now run the project. VB displays a dialog box stating that it is going to create a virtual Web for your project. Accept the default. The browser appears and should look similar to Figure 4.4.

**FIGURE 4.4:**

WebClass tableViewer display of pubs Authors table

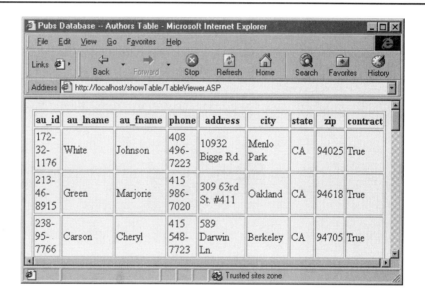

## Exploring the WebClass Event Sequence

Despite the simplicity of this project, it contains all the events in the WebClass event sequence. Use the debugger to step through the code. This is what you should see:

When the WebClass starts, the code in the Start event sets the NextItem property of the WebClass to the showTable WebItem.

Before displaying the WebItem, the WebClass fires the `showTable_Respond` event, which opens the database, retrieves the contents of the Authors table, and formats the HTML return string.

Here's a closer look at the `Respond` event code. After retrieving the contents of the Authors table, the code loops through the field names to create the first row. It creates the row (`<tr></tr>` tags) and a column (`<td></td>`) for each field, places each field name in the center of the column (`align="center"`), and displays the field name in bold text (`<b></b>` or `<strong></strong>`). Finally, it closes the row.

```
s = s & "<tr>"
For Each F In R.Fields
    s = s & "<td align=""center""><b>" & F.Name & "</b></td>"
Next
s = s & "</tr>"
```

Next, the code loops through the recordset. For each row, it tests the value of each column. If the value is `Null`, it adds a non-breaking space (` `). If you don't do this, the browser creates the null table cell with no border.

```
s = s & "<tr>"
While Not R.EOF
    s = s & "<tr>"
    For Each F In R.Fields
        If IsNull(F.Value) Then
            s = s & "<td> </td>"
        Else
            s = s & "<td>" & F.Value & "</td>"
        End If
    Next
    s = s & "</tr>"
    R.MoveNext
Wend
```

Finally, the code closes the recordset and the connection. Although VB destroys local variables when the method completes, you should get into the habit of destroying object variables (setting them to nothing) yourself. When you're working with databases particularly, you want to close any connections or free the table locks as quickly as possible. Remember, the Web is a multiuser medium. You should get in the habit of writing code as if a million people might be using your application. (Maybe they will be!)

# Optimize, Optimize, Optimize

This routine that creates the HTML table at the end of the preceding section concatenates the entire HTML string into the string variable s, then writes the contents of that variable to the browser by using the `Response.Write` method. You could make the routine write the contents directly, by substituting `Response.Write` wherever the code has s = s &. If you do that in a WebClass, you'll slow down the code considerably. In fact, for long tables, you'll get a significant increase in speed by creating a temporary string for each row, then concatenating them once at the end of the display. There are two reasons.

First, you should avoid making unnecessary object references whenever possible. A good rule of thumb is that if you're going to use an object more than once in a routine, create a local variable reference. Similarly, if you need to access a property of an object more than once in a routine, create a local variable and copy the property into it. Calling the `Response.Write` method multiple times forces VB to make unnecessary object reference calls. This routine could be optimized even more by using the `With...End With` structure to avoid referencing the recordset variable R as often as it does.

Second, the routine is slow because VB must allocate memory and create a new string every time you concatenate two strings. The longer the two strings are, the more memory (and time) it takes to concatenate them. By using shorter strings or byte arrays, you can often dramatically speed up a routine with little work.

If you want to see how much you can speed up a routine, create a new standard .exe and paste the routines in Listing 4.3 into the form; then run the project. You can find the code in the `StringConcatenation` project on the Sybex Web site.

> **NOTE** To download code, navigate to `http://www.sybex.com`. Click Catalog and search for this book's title. Click the Downloads button and accept the licensing agreement. Accepting the agreement grants you access to the downloads page for the book.

**LISTING 4.3**     **Optimizing Responses (frmConcatenate.frm)**

```
Private Sub Form_Load()
    Dim s1 As String
```

```vb
Dim s2 As String
Dim s3 As String
Dim s4 As String
Dim startTimer
Dim diff
Text1.Text = ""
Me.Caption = "String Concatenation Comparison"
Me.Show
DoEvents

Text1.Text = Text1.Text & "Start longConcat: "
Text1.Refresh
startTimer = Timer
s1 = longConCat
diff = Timer - startTimer
Text1.Text = Text1.Text & diff & vbCrLf & vbCrLf
Text1.Refresh

Text1.Text = Text1.Text & "Start shortConcat: "
Text1.Refresh
startTimer = Timer
s2 = shortConCat
diff = Timer - startTimer
Text1.Text = Text1.Text & diff & vbCrLf & vbCrLf
Text1.Refresh

Text1.Text = Text1.Text & "Start reallyShortConcat: "
Text1.Refresh
startTimer = Timer
s3 = reallyShortConCat
diff = Timer - startTimer
Text1.Text = Text1.Text & diff & vbCrLf & vbCrLf
Text1.Refresh

Text1.Text = Text1.Text & "Start VariantConcat: "
Text1.Refresh
startTimer = Timer
s1 = variantConcat()
diff = Timer - startTimer
Text1.Text = Text1.Text & diff & vbCrLf & vbCrLf
Text1.Refresh
```

```
        Text1.Text = Text1.Text & "Start byteConcat: "
        Text1.Refresh
        startTimer = Timer
        s4 = byteConcat
        diff = Timer - startTimer
        Text1.Text = Text1.Text & diff & vbCrLf & vbCrLf
        Text1.Refresh
End Sub
Function longConCat() As String
    Dim s As String
    Dim i As Long
    For i = 1 To 10000
        s = s & "abcdefghijklmnopqrstuvwxyz"
    Next
    longConCat = s
End Function
Function shortConCat() As String
    Dim s As String
    Dim tmp As String
    Dim j As Long
    Dim i As Long
    For i = 1 To 1000
        tmp = ""
        For j = 1 To 10
            tmp = tmp & "abcdefghijklmnopqrstuvwxyz"
        Next
        s = s & tmp
    Next
    shortConCat = s
End Function
Function reallyShortConCat() As String
    Dim s As String
    Dim tmp As String
    Dim j As Long
    Dim i As Long
    For i = 1 To 100
        tmp = ""
        For j = 1 To 100
            tmp = tmp & "abcdefghijklmnopqrstuvwxyz"
        Next
        s = s & tmp
```

```
        Next
        reallyShortConCat = s
    End Function
    Function variantConcat() As String
        Dim s As String
        Dim V As Variant
        Dim tmp As Variant
        Dim j As Long
        Dim i As Long
        For i = 1 To 100
            tmp = ""
            For j = 1 To 100
                tmp = tmp & "abcdefghijklmnopqrstuvwxyz"
            Next
            V = V & tmp
        Next
        s = V
        variantConcat = s
    End Function
    Function byteConcat() As String
        Dim s As String
        Dim b() As Byte
        Dim i As Long
        Dim j As Long
        Dim ptr As Long
        Dim letters() As Byte
        letters = StrConv("abcdefghijklmnopqrstuvwxyz", vbFromUnicode)
        ReDim b(259999) As Byte
        ptr = 0
        For i = 1 To 10000
            For j = 0 To 25
                b(ptr) = letters(j)
                ptr = ptr + 1
            Next
        Next
        s = b()
        s = StrConv(s, vbUnicode)
        byteConcat = s
    End Function
```

Each function in the project creates a string that contains the letters of the alphabet repeated 10,000 times. The longConCat function appends the alphabet string to a single string variable 10,000 times in a loop. On my computer, an NT-based 400Mhz Pentium II running this program in the development environment, the longConCat function takes about 17 seconds. The shortConCat function appends 10 alphabet strings together, then appends the resulting string to another string 1,000 times. Breaking the string into 1,000 shorter strings decreases the time dramatically—the shortConCat function takes less than 3 seconds. The reallyShortConCat function takes only about .3 seconds. It appends 100 alphabet strings together, then appends the result to another string 100 times. The result shows that fewer, larger concatenations are more efficient than many smaller ones. The byteConcat function is even more efficient—it takes only .15 seconds. That's a speed improvement of 11,333% (no, that's not a misprint) without any special API calls. When you compile the project with all compiler optimizations turned on, the difference is even more dramatic. Sometimes small changes make a big difference.

Imagine the difference in load on your server when you're serving large tables to many users! Although routine efficiency isn't the main theme of this book, you should carefully consider what effect your routines will have on the complete application—especially under a heavy multiuser load. This whole discussion of efficiency points out nicely why Microsoft has added WebClasses to VB. The increase in efficiency of a compiled application over similar code in interpreted mode isn't as high as you might expect, but the increase in efficiency of strongly typed code is considerable and can be well worth the increased complexity of installing and updating a VB application compared to a set of text-file ASP pages.

# Comparing the Advantages and Disadvantages of VB/WebClasses vs. ASP

Now that you've built both an ASP and a WebClass project, it's useful to compare the relative strengths and weaknesses of each for building Web applications.

Because VB uses the full Visual Basic language, whereas ASP uses VBScript, VB is much more powerful.

First, VBScript uses only the Variant data type. If you assume that the speed of an ASP application is similar to the speed of the variant routine (and you can), then you just saw an example of how using VB and WebClasses can speed up your code. Variants, due to their size and the need to check variable subtypes, usually run slightly slower and in some cases much more slowly than "primitive" data types.

Second, you can compile VB code—the ASP engine always interprets code. Because the VB interpreter is highly efficient already, compiling an inefficient application won't usually provide a large increase in speed. Using the previous example, however, compiled with all optimizations selected, the `byteConcat` function executes five times as fast—in .03 seconds rather than .15 seconds. In contrast, the other functions execute in almost exactly the same amount of time whether you compile the application or run it in interpreted mode. I used this example because a great deal of Web application programming consists of merging data with HTML for presentation. Therefore, in certain situations, a compiled application can provide both better response and greater scalability.

Finally, compiled code has one more advantage—nobody can see your application code. If you have security issues, are selling applications commercially, or just don't want anyone to copy your code, you will want to avoid ASP, in which the code is available to anyone who has access to the server.

ASP does have some advantages. For instance, it needs only one standard installation because the IIS setup program installs and registers the ASP DLLs with the Web server. After that, to install a new application you need only create a virtual directory and copy the ASP files. In contrast, *you* have to install the VB runtime files. You must individually install and register VB WebClasses—but after you've accomplished that, you can run them on remote or multiple servers. ASP code runs only on the Web server. Therefore, the trade-off here is ease of delivery vs. scalability.

In addition, ASP code (without the Windows Scripting Host) is relatively safe for Internet Service Providers (ISPs) to run on their servers. Even if you write an endless loop, an ASP page will eventually time out (in 90 seconds by default). ASP programs can't write binary files. In contrast, VB WebClasses present security and reliability risks. Because they're regular Windows DLLs, they're free to do whatever they like (including crash the server), within the permissions assigned to the account under which they run. Many ISPs and business clients won't install them on their servers.

Finally, ASP can run on other platforms besides Windows (currently some Unix platforms), whereas VB runs only on Windows.

Having used both, I recommend that you choose VB when the application requires a lot of server-side processing, when you have the ability to install ActiveX code on the server, or when security needs dictate the use of compiled code.

Choose ASP when the application doesn't need the power of a compiled language, when delivering to a location where you are not allowed to install ActiveX code, or when delivering to non-Windows-based servers.

Taking the long view, ASP was never intended to be both a formatting engine and a code engine; it was meant to be a "glue" environment that lets you connect browsers and Web servers to back-end business and database components. Because VB has been honed and optimized over the years, it's an ideal system for building those components. With the advent of ActiveDirectory services and COM+, you'll be able to build your business components in VB, connect them to multiple back-end databases, and deploy them on multiple servers using MTS (or COM+) to control transactions and cache objects. These capabilities lead to an "ideal" Web application, where rather than trying to increase your server speed, you can simply offload most of the processing to other servers as your application's user base grows.

This ideal Web application looks something like Figure 4.5. There's a set of clients, one or more Web servers and one or more Name servers, a Business Services layer, and a Data Services layer. The clients make requests to the Web servers. The Web servers call the Name servers to find business objects on the network and pass requests on to these business objects. The business objects retrieve and store data in multiple back-end databases and return formatted HTML combined with data to the Web servers, which return the pages to the client.

Remember that this is an ideal application. Certainly, you do not need to develop every Web application using this model, but if you need scalability, you should be working toward a model similar to this one.

**FIGURE 4.5:**

An ideal Web application

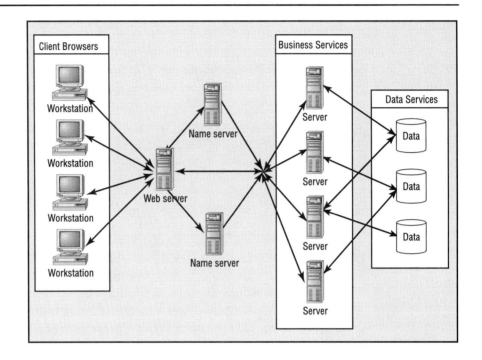

# CHAPTER FIVE

# Securing an IIS Application

- Understand How Security Works
- Create the Project
- Create an HTML Template
- Add a Custom Event
- Add a Custom WebItem
- Test the Security
- Compile the Project
- Improve Site Security
- Take Advantage of NT Security

In this chapter, you're going to build a complete IIS application, not just a single page. This is an interactive chapter. To get the most out of this chapter, you should start Visual Basic and follow along step by step. This interactive process will let me explain procedures while you do them, which will help both of us. You'll see how to add HTML templates and use WebClass replacement tags.

The application you're going to build is a template for a site secured by a sign-on and password. To secure a site, you need to make sure that every person entering the site has successfully signed on. You need to keep valid sign-ons somewhere—a database is the best place, but for small sites like this one, a file works just as well.

# Understand How Security Works

In a stand-alone Windows program, you would simply show the sign-on page first—users would have to sign on before they could see any other screens in the application. In a Web site, any user can request any page for which they know the URL. They can (and often do) bookmark pages to which they want to return later. The Web application must intercept page requests from users who have not signed on and reroute them through the sign-on screen. Figure 5.1 shows a generic logic flow for handling sign-on/password security. You should note that the figure does not show any exception handling.

The application requires only one HTML screen—the sign-on screen. All input and messages will occur on this screen. For illustration purposes, though, you'll add a second screen that will be "secured" behind the sign-on page. When the application is complete, you will not be able to get to the second screen unless you have successfully logged on.

# Create the Project

First, start VB. You will see the New Project dialog. If VB is already running, select New Project from the File menu. Select the IIS Application project type as shown in Figure 5.2.

**FIGURE 5.1:**

Program flow for sign-on/password validation

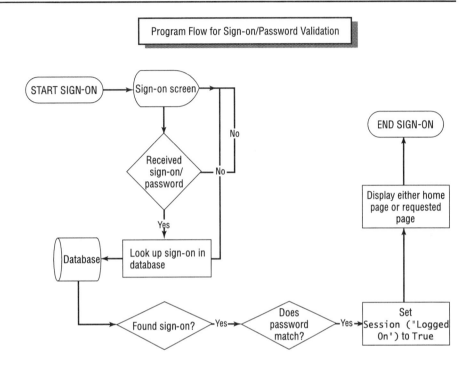

**FIGURE 5.2:**

Visual Basic New Project dialog

Visual Basic will automatically create a new project containing a single Web-Class Designer named `WebClass1`. As usual, the first thing to do is to rename the project and the default items so that you'll be able to differentiate between them later. Right-click the project name, select Properties, and rename the project **SecuredSite**. Double-click `WebClass1` and rename it **Signon**. Select the `NameInURL` property and rename it **Signon** as well. Your screen should now look similar to Figure 5.3.

**FIGURE 5.3:**

SecuredSite project window

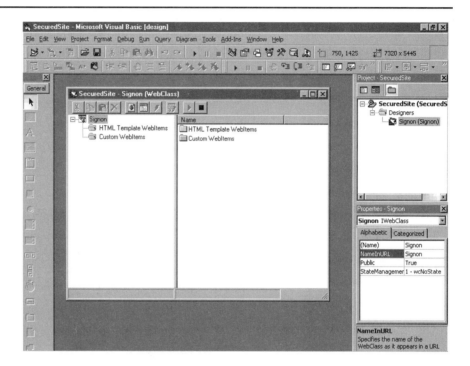

Table 5.1 shows the list of design-time properties available in the Property Editor.

**TABLE 5.1:** WebClass Design-Time Properties

| Property | Description |
| --- | --- |
| Name | The class name of this WebClass object. Use this name to refer to the object within the project. The name you select is also the class name that appears in the Registry. |
| NameInURL | Controls the name given to the ASP page to start the WebClass. For example, if you assign the name `Signon` to the `NameInURL` property, VB will name the ASP page `Signon.asp`. |

*Continued on next page*

**TABLE 5.1 (CONTINUED):** WebClass Design-Time Properties

| Property | Description |
|---|---|
| Public | Determines whether other programs can use methods and properties of this WebClass. |
| StateManagement | There are two options:<br><br>**wcNoState** This is the default value, and the one you should usually use. With no state management, the server will create a new instance of your WebClass for each page request and destroy it when the request has finished processing.<br><br>**wcRetainInstance** You should not use this except on sites with small numbers of users. With **wcRetainInstance** set to **True**, the server will create a new instance of your WebClass for the *first* page request by a user, then store a reference to the WebClass object in a Session variable. |

> **WARNING** The wcRetainInstance setting is so convenient that it is tempting to set it to True for every WebClass. Unfortunately, it also means that the server must then use the same thread on which it created the WebClass object for all subsequent requests by that user. This setting reduces the problems associated with maintaining state but severely reduces the scalability of your site. Don't use it unless you're sure the site will never have many visitors. That said, at times it's perfectly acceptable to keep a WebClass instance alive. If you're creating a site that will run on a stand-alone computer—for example, an application for mobile sales users who may not always be connected—then you don't have to worry about scalability. In such cases, you can take advantage of the persistent WebClass object to improve your development time and improve the application's response time. Without the overhead involved in creating the WebClass object and retrieving state information for the user's page request, the application's response time will improve.

Save the project in a directory called **SecuredSite**. Using Windows Explorer, create two subdirectories of the project directory, one called **images** and one called **HTMLTemplates**. Figure 5.4 shows the project directory on my computer at this stage.

**FIGURE 5.4:**

Directory structure for SecuredSite project

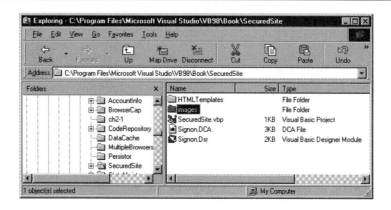

## Create an HTML Template

Now you're going to add an HTML template. The process of editing HTML templates or files is not part of VB (yet), so you'll need to create a new template with another program.

Listing 5.1 shows the HTML for the sign-on screen. To create a new HTML template file, open an HTML or text editor—Notepad works fine—and enter the code in Listing 5.1. Alternately, you can download the code and graphics for this project from the Sybex Web site.

> **NOTE** When you copy HTML from this book, ignore the line breaks; the HTML parser ignores them as well. It's perfectly acceptable (and somewhat faster) to format the entire HTML screen as a single unbroken string of text. Of course, if you do this, the source code in the browser becomes difficult to read.

> **NOTE** To download code, navigate to http://www.sybex.com. Click the Catalog button and search for this book's title. Click the Downloads button and accept the licensing agreement. Accepting the agreement grants you access to the downloads page for the book.

### LISTING 5.1   HTML for Sign-On Screen (*Signon.htm*)

```html
<html>
<head>
<title>Signon</title>
</head>
<body background="CAJBKGRN.GIF" bgcolor="#ffffff" leftmargin="100">
<center>
<P><font size="5">Please Sign In</font></P>
Enter your sign-on and password, then click the Signon button<BR>
<font color="#ff0000"><WCMessage></WCMessage></font>
<form action="" method="post" name="frmSignon">
<table width="50%" border="1">
<tr>
   <td valign="top" align="right">
   <b>Signon:</b>
   </td>
   <td align="left" valign = top>
      <WCSignon></WCSignon>
   </td>
</tr>
<tr>
<td valign="top" align="right">
   <b>Password:</b>
   </td>
   <td align="left" valign="top">
   <WCPassword></WCPassword>
   </td>
</tr>
<tr>
<td align="middle" colspan="2">
   <input type="submit" value="Sign On">
   </td>
</tr>
</table>
</form>
</center>
</body>
</html>
```

Save the completed HTML template file as **Signon.htm** in the `SecuredSite\HTMLTemplates` directory.

> **TIP**
> 
> VB always makes a copy of HTML templates that you add to the WebClass. It never uses an HTML template directly. If you don't create a separate directory for the templates, VB will rename them for you. For example, when you add an HTML template file named `Template1.htm`, VB will copy the file to `Template11.htm`. It quickly becomes difficult to keep track of the names. You can avoid this problem altogether by storing the original copy of your templates in a directory other than your project directory.

Now add the template to the WebClass. Right-click the HTML Template Web-Items entry in the WebClass Designer and select Add HTML Template. Select the `Signon.htm` file you just saved from the `HTMLTemplates` directory. Behind the scenes, VB will copy the file, parse the HTML in it, and create a new item called `Template1`. Right-click the `Template1` item, select Rename from the pop-up menu, and rename the item **Signon**. Your screen should now look like Figure 5.5.

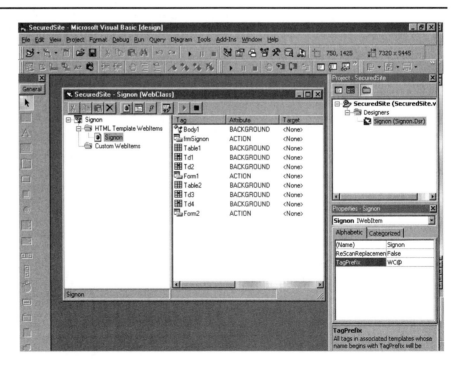

**FIGURE 5.5:**

SecuredSite project WebClass Designer window

The right-hand pane of the designer lists the programmable items that the HTML Template parser found in the HTML file. In DHTML, all these objects expose events, methods, or properties that you can alter at runtime. You'll connect some of these events later.

For now, click the Signon item and look at the Properties window. HTML Templates have three properties at design time, as shown in Table 5.2.

**TABLE 5.2:** HTML Template Design-Time Properties

| Property | Description |
|---|---|
| Name | The class name of this HTMLTemplate object. Use this name to refer to the object within the project. |
| ReScanReplacements | This Boolean property controls whether the tag replacement engine scans once for replacement tags or whether it scans continuously until it has replaced all the tags. This concept is confusing until you realize that you can replace tags with content containing other tags. If you need to do this, set ReScanReplacements = True; otherwise, leave it set to False. |
| TagPrefix | The default setting WC@ is a bug. Although it works most of the time, Microsoft recommends that you change it to WC: without the ampersand. I've found the colon to be unnecessary. (See the Microsoft Knowledge Base Article Q189539 for more information.) |

Leave the ReScanReplacements setting set to False. Change the TagPrefix setting to **WC**, without the default ampersand, then save the project.

The HTML file contains three WebClass replacement tags: WCMessage, WCSignon, and WCPassword.

> **NOTE** The HTML Template parser often changes the case of WebClass replacement tags. If you edit the Signon template after adding it to the WebClass, you will probably see that the tags have changed to WCMESSAGE, WCSIGNON, and WCPASSWORD. The change to uppercase is inconsistent. For example, if you enter the tags in the template in all lowercase, the HTML Template parser changes only the second tag to uppercase, which will cause a runtime error.

In the file, these replacement tags appear as block elements, with a starting and ending tag, for example, `<WCMessage></WCMessage>`. Both tags must be present and, except for the slash, the contents must match for the replacement to work properly. Case is relevant. Let me restate that a little louder: CASE MATTERS! Mismatched tags cause a runtime error, not a design-time error, probably because the WebClass HTML parser, like other HTML parsers, is not case sensitive. If you have mismatched tags in a template, the WebClass will generate an error similar to this in the Application event log:

```
WebClass Runtime error '800a2332'
Corresponding close tag, </WCSignon>, not found in <file>
```

> **TIP** Always check the Application event log for errors if your WebClass application behaves in an unexpected manner.

Unfortunately, this first version of WebClasses doesn't have a very "smart" HTML parser. It often alters your HTML code in irritating ways, such as removing or adding white space, changing the case of WebClass tags, or rewriting angle brackets as HTML encoded text (for example, < becomes &lt; and > becomes &gt;). The parser is also unable to correctly parse embedded WebClass tags (tags contained within tags). For this reason, Microsoft recommends that you insert WebClass tags only as markers for complete replacement of tags, not as markers for single parameters. For example, the following WebClass tag will be replaced at runtime with an `<input>` tag.

```
<WCTextInput1>Insert input tag</WCTextInput1>
```

In contrast, the parser will not correctly parse the following HTML tag because it contains an embedded WebClass tag:

```
<input type="text" value="<WCTextInput1></WCTextInput1>">
```

If you look at Listing 5.1, you'll see that it follows Microsoft's recommendation.

Because the HTML parser sometimes changes the case of your WebClass tags, you should always force the tag names to either uppercase or lowercase in comparison tests. Alternately, you can always write your WebClass tags in uppercase to begin with. Remember, though, humans are fallible; your programs will work better if you write the tags however you like, then force the case conversion before any tag comparison.

You need to tell the WebClass which item to display first. Right-click the Signon HTML Template and select View Code from the pop-up menu. Find the

WebClass_Start event. VB automatically inserts some default response code in the Start event:

```
'Write a reply to the user
With Response
.Write "<html>"
    .Write "<body>"
    .Write "<h1><font face=""Arial"">" & _
    "WebClass1's Starting Page</font></h1>"
    .Write "<p>This response was created " & _
    "in the Start event of WebClass1.</p>"
    .Write "</body>"
.Write "</html>"
End With
```

You'll want to delete that default response code in almost every case and substitute your own Start code. In this case, the first thing you want to do is display the Signon screen. You use the NextItem property to control which item the WebClass will process next.

```
Private Sub WebClass_Start()
    Set NextItem = Signon
End Sub
```

> **TIP**
> To eliminate the default Start event code altogether, use Notepad or another text editor to open the file WebClass.dsr from the Template\Projects directory where you installed VB. Scroll to the bottom of the file and delete the contents of the WebClass_Start event. Save the file. The next time you create an IIS project, the default Start event code will not appear.

Unlike standard VB classes, you can't refer to the WebClass itself with the keyword Me. You can refer to any WebClass generically using the syntax WebClass.propertyName or WebClass_methodName. Note that *WebClass* in the preceding sentence does *not* stand for the name of your WebClass; use the word *WebClass* itself.

When the WebClass executes the NextItem command, it calls the Respond method for the specified item. In the Respond event for the Signon item, tell the item to display itself:

```
Private Sub Signon_Respond()
    On Error Goto ErrSignon_Respond
    Signon.WriteTemplate
```

```
ExitSignon_Respond:
    Exit Sub
ErrSignon_Respond:
    Response.Write "Error: " & Err.Number & "<br>" & Err.Source & _
    "<br>" & Err.Description
    Resume ExitSignon_Respond
End Sub
```

> **WARNING** You should always trap for errors that may occur during the `WriteTemplate` method. When an error occurs at runtime during HTML template processing, the WebClass fires the `FatalErrorEvent` event. Unfortunately, the WebClass clears the Error object *before* the `FatalErrorEvent` occurs, so the only way to find the error is to look in the Application event log.

The `WriteTemplate` method loads the HTML template file, then scans for replacements. Each time the scanner finds a replacement tag, it calls the `ProcessTag` event for the item. Although WebClasses automate the process of making the replacement, you need to write code to tell VB which tags to replace, and what content to replace each tag with. In this program, you'll replace all three tags. Enter this code into the `Signon_ProcessTag` event:

```
Private Sub Signon_ProcessTag(ByVal TagName As String, _
TagContents As String, SendTags As Boolean)
Select Case lcase(TagName) ' note forced case conversion
    Case "wcmessage"
        TagContents = Session("msg")
        Session("msg") = ""
    Case "wcsignon"
        TagContents = "<input type=""text""" & _
            "name=""Signon"" value=""" & _
            Session("LastSignon") & """>"
    Case "wcpassword"
        TagContents = "<input type=""password""" & _
            "name=""Password"" value=""" & _
            Session("LastPassword")& """>"
    End Select
End Sub
```

The `ProcessTag` event occurs before a WebClass sends HTML to the browser. The WebClass looks for replacement tags in a WebItem *only* if it's based on an

HTML template, and it *always* looks for the replacement tags unless you set the `TagPrefix` property of the WebItem to a null string. The WebClass never fires the `ProcessTag` event for a custom WebItem.

The following list shows the three arguments passed to the `ProcessTag` event and their purposes.

> **TagName** Contains the name of the replacement tag—the text inside the brackets.
>
> **TagContents** Contains the text between the start and end replacement tag, for example, for the tag `<WCSignon>Signon</WCSignon>`, the Tag-Contents would contain `Signon`, whereas the `TagName` would contain `WCSignon`.
>
> **SendTags** This flag controls whether the WebClass sends the replacement tags along with the replacement value or *replaces* the tags with the replacement value—in other words, does *not* send the tags. Here's the difference:
>
> If your WebClass Tag = `<WCSignon></WCSignon>`, then the `TagName=` `"WCSignon"`. Assume you set the `TagValue` to `Bill`.
>
> When `SendTags=True`, the string sent to the browser contains `<WCSignon> Bill </WCSignon>`.
>
> When `SendTags=False`, the string sent to the browser contains only `Bill`.
>
> The default is `False`.

The `ProcessTag` event code replaces the three WebClass tags, (`WCMessage`, `WCSignon`, and `WCPassword`) with temporary values stored in Session variables called `msg`, `lastSignon`, and `lastPassword`, respectively. During the first replacement, the Session variables have no value—or rather, they have a variant subtype of `Empty`, so they're interpreted as null strings.

> **TIP** Using the same variable names in all the various layers of code is good practice when possible; you'll find that Web applications typically pass values from databases to business objects, to WebClasses, to the browser, to client-side script or input tags, and often back again. Your applications will be much easier to debug and maintain if you name the variables consistently in all these locations.

# Add a Custom Event

You need to write the code to process the sign-on and password when the user submits the form. Form submission is an *event*. Because VB doesn't know which events you'll want to process, you need to connect an item with an event. Right-click the frmSignon entry in the right-hand pane of the WebClass Designer window and select Connect to Custom Event. A new event, called frmSignon, appears under the Signon item (see Figure 5.6).

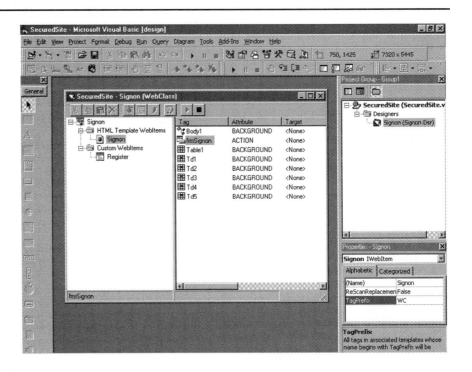

**FIGURE 5.6:**

Adding a custom event

For now, because you'll want to check for errors before continuing, you'll just write a stub to check the values entered by the user. When the user has entered both values, the event code displays the entered values in the browser. If the user did not enter a valid value for either the sign-on or password, the event code places a message into the Session("msg") variable and redisplays the form.

To add the code, double-click the frmSignon event in the Designer window. The code window opens and your cursor is inside the new event. Enter the following code into the event stub:

```
Private Sub Signon_frmSignon()
    Dim aSignon As String
    Dim aPassword As String
    Dim action As String
    Dim tmpSignon As String
    Dim tmpPassword As String
    Dim arrSignonInfo As Variant
    Dim V As Variant
    action = Request.Form("Submit")
    Session("LastSignon") = ""
    Session("LastPassword") = ""
    aSignon = Request.Form("Signon")
    aPassword = Request.Form("Password")
    If Trim(aSignon) = vbNullString Then
        Session("msg") = "You must enter a signon."
        Set NextItem = Signon
        Exit Sub
    End If
    Session("LastSignon") = aSignon
    If aPassword = vbNullString Then
        Session("msg") = "You must enter a password."
        Set NextItem = Signon
        Exit Sub
    End If
    Session("LastPassword") = aPassword
End Sub
```

Make sure you have no more than one browser open. Otherwise, the debugger can get confused. Save the project, then press F8 to step through the project. The Signon screen should look like Figure 5.7.

> **TIP** When debugging, you need to switch to the browser manually whenever the WebClass completes a response. After running a WebClass many times, stepping may cease to work. In that case, set a breakpoint. The WebClass code window appears when execution reaches the breakpoint. You still need to switch back to the browser manually.

**FIGURE 5.7:**

The SecuredSite Signon screen

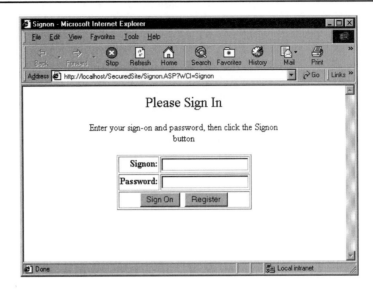

After you enter a sign-on and a password, the application displays the sign-on and password you entered. If you experiment, you'll see that both the sign-on and password are required. The server returns error messages to the browser if either value is missing.

You have the first part of the application running. Now, you're ready to add some more features. You'll need a registration screen into which people will enter information (a sign-on and password) and a database in which to store the registration information they enter. For a large site, you would want to use a real database, but for this practice application, you'll use a file on the server. Each line in the file will contain two string items, the sign-on and password.

Adding the registration screen changes the flow of the program slightly. Figure 5.8 shows the flowchart after adding the registration screen.

**FIGURE 5.8:**

Sign-on/password with registration

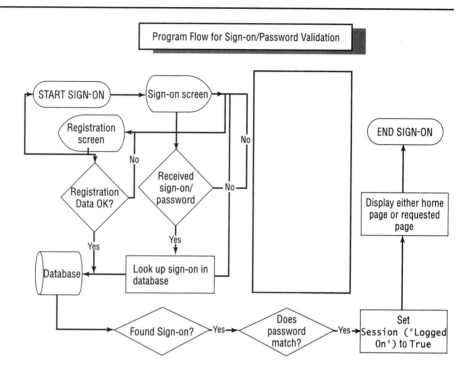

## Add a Custom WebItem

This time, instead of creating an HTML template, you'll create a custom WebItem, so you'll become familiar with the difference between the two. Right-click the Custom WebItems entry in the WebClass Designer window and select Add Custom WebItem from the pop-up menu. Rename the new item **Register**, then right-click it again and select View Code.

The WebClass will create a new subroutine stub called `Register_Respond`. The WebClass calls the respond event on a WebItem when you set the WebClass `NextItem` property to that item.

You'll need to add a Registration button to the Signon template so users can reach your registration screen. To modify the Signon template, right-click the

Signon WebItem and select Edit HTML Template. VB will launch your default HTML editor.

> **TIP** To modify the editor that VB uses for editing HTML, click Tools ➢ Options, then click the Advanced tab. Enter the path to the editor you want to use in the External HTML Editor field, then click OK.

Change the last row in the table so it contains two buttons instead of one:

```
' Before
<tr>
    <td align="middle" colspan="2">
            <input type="submit" value="Sign On">
    </td>
</tr>

' After
<tr>
    <td align="middle" colspan="2">
        <input type="submit" name="submit" value="Sign On"> 
        <input type="submit" name="submit" value="Register">
    </td>
</tr>
```

Notice that the name of both buttons is Submit. That way, you can easily add a check in the `Signon_frmSignon` event code to determine which button the user clicked. If the user is trying to register, you can reroute them to the Registration screen. Add the following code immediately after the line `action = Request.Form("Submit")` in the `Signon_frmSignon` event code.

```
If action = "Register" Then
    Set NextItem = Register
    Exit Sub
End if
```

When the code executes, setting the `NextItem` property to `Register` fires the `Register_Respond` event for the Register custom WebItem. In the `Register_Respond` event, you'll return the HTML to show the Registration screen. Listing 5.2 shows the HTML for the Registration screen. Place this code in the `Register_Respond` event stub.

### LISTING 5.2 HTML for Registration Screen (in Signon.dsr)

```
Private Sub Register_Respond()
Dim s As String
Dim sBody As String
    s = getHTMLTemplate()
    s = Replace(s, "<!-Title->", "SecuredSite Registration")
  sBody = "<form name=""frmRegister"" action=""" & _
    URLFor("Register", "register") & """ method=""post"">"
  sBody = sBody & "<table align=""center"" width=""60%""" & _
    "cols=""2"" border=""1"">"
  sBody = sBody & "<tr><td align=""left"" colspan=""2"">" & _
    "Enter a signon and password. Your signon and " & _
    "password may be up to 20 characters (numbers, " & _
    "letters and symbols), and may not contain spaces. " _
    & "You must enter both a signon and password to " & _
    "register.</td></tr>"
  If Session("msg") <> "" Then
      sBody = sBody & "<tr><td align=""left""" & _
      "colspan=""2""><font color=""#FF0000"">" & _
      Session("msg") & "</font></td></tr>" & _
      Session("msg") = ""
  End If
  sBody = sBody & "<tr><td align=""right""><b>Signon" & _
    "</b>:</td><td align=""left""><input " & _
    "type=""text"" name=""Signon""" & _
    "maxLength=""20""></td></tr>"
  sBody = sBody & "<tr><td align=""right""><b>Password" & _
    "</b>:</td><td align=""left""><input " & _
    "type=""password""" & _
    "name=""Password"" maxLength=""20""></td></tr>"
  sBody = sBody & "<tr><td align=""center""" & _
    "colspan=""2""><input type=""submit""" & _
    "value=""Register""></td></tr>"
  s = Replace(s, "<!-Body->", sBody)
  Response.Write s
End Sub
```

> **NOTE** You cannot run the WebClass successfully until you add the `getHTMLTemplate` function. You'll see that within a few paragraphs.

Because we're not asking for much information in this application, there's little difference between the HTML for the Signon and the Registration screens. Normally, you would also ask for other information during registration, such as e-mail addresses, telephone numbers, street addresses, titles, etc. In any event, the important thing to notice here is that you can use WebClasses to *manage* the presentation layer or to *generate* it. Which one is best for you depends on your work situation and the needs of the program.

The `Register_Respond` event does contain some useful code. First, you'll eventually get tired of writing the standard HTML tags. That's why HTML editors invariably provide a template. The line `s=getHTMLTemplate()` shows you how easy this is to do in code. The `getHTMLTemplate` function returns an HTML string containing some replaceable markers for the title and body of the document. The markers are formatted as HTML comments, so (except for the title) they won't be visible in the browser if you don't replace them with valid HTML.

```
Private Function getHTMLTemplate() As String
    getHTMLTemplate = "<html><head><title>" & _
        "<!-Title-></title></head><body>" & _
        "<!-Body-></body></html>"
End Function
```

The rest of the `Register_Respond` routine sets up the HTML to display the screen. Finally, the routine uses the `replace` function to insert the title and body of the document in place of the markers.

In the Signon HTML Template, you hard-coded the URL for the form submission. In this routine, you let the WebClass dynamically create the URL by using the `URLFor` function. The `URLFor` function takes one or two parameters—a WebItem object (or a string containing the name of a WebItem) and, optionally, the name of a method for the WebItem. The function returns a URL referencing the specified WebItem or method.

The advantage of using `URLFor` is that you can change the URL based on factors unknown at design time. For example, suppose you have administrative users and non-administrative users, who have different privilege levels. If you use hard-coded URLs in HTML templates, you need to have more than one template. If you use dynamic URLs, you make a decision at runtime to display the appropriate URL based on the user's privilege level. If you want to see what the WebClass inserts into the HTML string, right-click the Registration page at runtime and select View Source from the pop-up menu.

When the user clicks the Submit button, you need to validate the registration information and store it in the registration file. You need to create another custom event. Right-click the Register WebItem in the WebClass Designer window and select Add Custom Event. Name the event **Register** so it will match the name in the URLFor function call.

Listing 5.3 contains the `Register_Register` event code.

**LISTING 5.3  SecuredSite Registration Event Code (in Signon.dsr)**

```
Private Sub Register_Register()
    Dim i As Long
    Dim s As String
    Dim aSignon As String
    Dim aPassword As String
    Dim success As Boolean
    On Error GoTo Err_Register
    Session("msg") = ""
    aSignon = Request("Signon")
    ' check for valid values
    If Len(Trim(aSignon)) = 0 Then
        Session("msg") = "You must enter a sign-on."
        Set NextItem = Register
        Exit Sub
    End If
    aPassword = Request("Password")
    If Len(Trim(aPassword)) = 0 Then
        Session("msg") = "You must enter a password."
        Set NextItem = Register
        Exit Sub
    End If
    If InStr(aSignon, " ") > 0 Or _
  InStr(aPassword, " ") > 0 Then
        Session("msg") = "You may not enter " & _
            "spaces in your signon or password."
        Set NextItem = Register
        Exit Sub
    End If
```

```
        If findSignon(aSignon) Then
            ' signon already used
            Session("msg") = "That sign-on is not " & _
                "available. Try again."
            Set NextItem = Register
        Else
            Call appendToTextFile(App.Path _
                & "\registration.txt", aSignon _
                & "," & aPassword)
            Set NextItem = Congratulations
        End If
Exit_Register:
        Exit Sub
Err_Register:
        Session("msg") = "Error: " & Err.Number & _
            "<BR>Source: " & Err.Source & "<BR>Description: " & _
            Err.Description
        Set NextItem = Register
        Resume Exit_Register
End Sub
```

> **NOTE** The code in the `Register_Register` event will not execute successfully until you add the code from the remainder of this section.

The first part of this routine only validates the information entered. After you're sure that you have valid information, the routine tries to find the sign-on. For this program, finding the sign-on is a two-part process. First, the `findSignon` function calls a function called `readTextFile`:

```
s = readTextFile(App.Path & "\registration.txt")
```

You'll see the code for the `readTextFile` function shortly, but I want to introduce two new objects first. The `readTextFile` function uses the Scripting.FileSystemObject to open and read the text file. It returns a string containing the textfile contents. The FileSystemObject is part of the Microsoft Scripting Runtime Library installed with both ASP and Visual Basic 6. It can check for the existence of files and can copy or move files. The FileSystemObject by itself cannot read files, but it provides an `OpenTextFile` method, which returns a TextStream object that can read and write text files. The VB documentation explains how to use the

FileSystemObject and the TextStream object in detail, but basically, you provide a filename, a constant describing the action you want to take (ForReading, ForWriting, or ForAppending), and optionally, a Format constant that sets the TextStream object to use either ASCII or Unicode. The Format constants are TriStateTrue, TriStateFalse, TriStateMixed, and TriStateUseDefault. Of course, you don't have to use the FileSystemObject—you could use standard VB file access methods instead.

Add the readTextFile function to the Signon WebClass.

```
Private Function readTextFile(aFilename As String) As String
    Dim fs As FileSystemObject
    Dim ts As TextStream
    Dim s As String
    On Error GoTo Err_readTextFile
    Set fs = New FileSystemObject
    Set ts = fs.OpenTextFile(aFilename, ForReading, _
True, TristateUseDefault)
    If Not ts.AtEndOfStream Then
        s = ts.ReadAll
    End If
    ts.Close
    Set ts = Nothing
    Set fs = Nothing
    readTextFile = s
Exit_readTextFile:
    Exit Function
Err_readTextFile:
    Err.Raise Err.Number, "readTextFile", Err.Description
    Resume Exit_readTextFile
End Function
```

Remember, we decided to store the sign-ons and passwords as comma-delimited items, one per line. The findSignon routine splits the string returned from the readTextFile function into an array, then iterates through the array, splitting each line item into a two-item array at the comma.

Add the findSignon function to the Signon WebClass.

```
Private Function findSignon(aSignon, Optional retInfo _
As Variant) As Boolean
    Dim vArr As Variant
    Dim lRegCount As Long
```

```
            Dim i As Integer
            Dim arrSignonInfo As Variant
            Dim s As String
            On Error GoTo Err_FindSignon
            s = readTextFile(App.Path & "\registration.txt")
            If Len(s) > 0 Then
                s = Left$(s, Len(s) - 2)
                vArr = Split(s, vbCrLf)
                lRegCount = UBound(vArr)
                For i = 0 To lRegCount
                    arrSignonInfo = Split(vArr(i), ",")
                    If StrComp(aSignon, arrSignonInfo(0), _
                        vbTextCompare) = 0 Then
                        findSignon = True
                        If Not IsMissing(retInfo) Then
                            retInfo = vArr(i)
                        End If
                        Exit Function
                    End If
                Next
            End If
Exit_FindSignon:
    Exit Function
Err_FindSignon:
    Err.Raise Err.Number, Err.Source, Err.Description
    Resume Exit_FindSignon
End Function
```

If the routine finds a matching sign-on, it returns True. If you include the optional retInfo parameter, the findSignon routine sets it to the matching item.

The Register_Register routine checks the return value from findSignon to see whether any other user has already selected the requested sign-on. If so, it asks the user to select a different sign-on; if not, it appends the sign-on and password to the registration file and displays a Congratulations message containing a link back to the Signon screen. After registration, the user should be able to sign on successfully.

The Register_Register routine calls an appendToTextFile method to append the new sign-on and password. Again, the code uses the Scripting.FileSystem-Object and TextStream objects to write to the registration.txt file. Add the code for the appendToTextFile method to the Signon WebClass.

```vb
Private Sub appendToTextFile(aFilename As String, _
    value As Variant)
    Dim fs As FileSystemObject
    Dim ts As TextStream
    Dim v As Variant
    Dim i As Long
    Dim itemCount As Long
    On Error GoTo Err_appendToTextFile
    ' open the text file in Append mode
    Set fs = New FileSystemObject
    Set ts = fs.OpenTextFile(aFilename, ForAppending, _
        True, TristateUseDefault)
    If (VarType(value) And vbArray) = vbArray Then
        itemCount = UBound(value)
        For Each v In value
            ts.WriteLine v
        Next
    Else
        ts.WriteLine value
    End If
    ts.Close
    Set ts = Nothing
    Set fs = Nothing
Exit_appendToTextFile:
    Exit Sub
Err_appendToTextFile:
    App.LogEvent "Unable to append to the file: " & _
    aFilename & " in the appendtoTextFile routine."
    Err.Raise Err.Number, "appendToTextFile", _
        Err.Description
    Resume Exit_appendToTextFile
End Sub
```

You need to add another Custom WebItem to display the Congratulations message. Right-click the Custom WebItems entry in the WebClass Designer and select Add Custom WebItem. Rename the new WebItem **Congratulations**. Double-click the Congratulations WebItem and replace the empty Congratulations_Respond event code with the following code:

```vb
Private Sub Congratulations_Respond()
    Dim s As String
    Dim sBody As String
    s = getHTMLTemplate()
    s = Replace(s, "<!-Title->", "Congratulations")
```

```
        sBody = "You have successfully registered. Click <a href=""" _
        & URLFor(Signon) & """ target=""_top"">here</a> to continue."
        s = Replace(s, "<!-Body->", sBody)
        Response.Write s
    End Sub
```

You're almost done. You have all the routines needed for the sign-on; now you just need to call them from the Signon_frmSignon method. Here's the completed code for the Signon_frmSignon method:

```
Private Sub Signon_frmSignon()
    Dim aSignon As String
    Dim aPassword As String
    Dim action As String
    Dim tmpSignon As String
    Dim tmpPassword As String
    Dim arrSignonInfo As Variant
    Dim v As Variant
    action = Request.Form("Submit")
    If action = "Register" Then
        Set NextItem = Register
        Exit Sub
    End If
    Session("LastSignon") = ""
    Session("LastPassword") = ""
    aSignon = Request.Form("Signon")
    aPassword = Request.Form("Password")
    If Trim(aSignon) = vbNullString Then
        Session("msg") = "You must enter a signon."
        Set NextItem = Signon
        Exit Sub
    End If
    Session("LastSignon") = aSignon
    If aPassword = vbNullString Then
        Session("msg") = "You must enter a password."
        Set NextItem = Signon
        Exit Sub
    End If
    Session("LastPassword") = aPassword
    If findSignon(aSignon, arrSignonInfo) Then
        arrSignonInfo = Split(arrSignonInfo, ",")
        If StrComp(aPassword, arrSignonInfo(1), _
            vbTextCompare) = 0 Then
```

```
            Session("Signon") = aSignon
            Session("Password") = aPassword
            With Response
                .Write "Finished checking password" _
                    & "/signon." & "<BR>"
                .Write "Signon=" & aSignon & "<BR>"
                .Write "Password=" & aPassword & "<BR>"
            End With
        Else
            Session("msg") = "Invalid Password"
            Set NextItem = Signon
        End If
    Else
        Session("msg") = "Unrecognized Signon. " _
            & "Try again or click the Register button " _
            & "to register."
        Set NextItem = Signon
    End If
End Sub
```

You should now be able to run the project. When you register successfully, you should see the Congratulations message in your browser. In the next section, you'll see how to use the sign-on and password WebClass to force users to sign on before viewing any content pages in your application.

## Test the Security

Take one more look at the `Signon_frmSignon` code. Notice that when the user has successfully signed on, it sets two Session variables—`Signon` and `Password`. These variables will always have a value of `Empty` until the user has successfully signed on. By implementing a check at the beginning of each page request, you can route the user to the Signon screen when `Session("Signon")` is empty.

In an ASP site, you'd typically do this with an include file. In WebClasses, you can use the `BeginRequest` event to do the same thing.

```
Private Sub WebClass_BeginRequest()
    If IsEmpty(Session("Signon")) Then
        Select Case Request("WCI")
            Case "Signon", "Register"
```

```
        ' OK, let users see pages in these WebItems
        Case Else
            Session("msg") = "This is a secured " & _
            "site. You must sign in before you may " & _
            "view any of the pages."
            Response.Redirect URLFor(Signon)
        End Select
    End If
End Sub
```

The `BeginRequest` routine lets people see pages associated with the `Signon` and `Register` WebItems, but restricts all other pages by redirecting to the Signon page if the user has not successfully signed on. Using this method, you may add WebItems to this WebClass without worrying about whether the user is signed on.

To test the security, you'll need to create another WebItem. The item doesn't need to do anything but write a message to the screen. If you request it, though, you'll need to sign on before you can see it. Right-click the Custom WebItems in the WebClass Designer window and select Add Custom WebItem from the pop-up menu. Name the new item **TestSecurity**. Double-click the `TestSecurity` item and add this code to the `Respond` event:

```
Private Sub TestSecurity_Respond()
    With Response
        .Write "<center><h2>This page is " & _
            "secured.</h2></center><BR>"
        .Write "To test the security, add a bookmark " & _
            "to your Favorites list or make a note of " & _
            "the URL in the address field. "
        .Write "Close your browser, open a new instance "
        .Write "of the browser, and try to navigate to " & _
"this URL."
    End With
End Sub
```

Save and then run your project. After you have registered and signed on, you should be able to see the TestSecurity page by typing the URL into your browser. Although your server name and path may be different, the last part of the URL should be the same as the following example:

```
http://localhost/SecuredSite/Signon.ASP?WCI=TestSecurity
```

Follow the instructions on the TestSecurity page to see how the security works. You've completed the project, but your site may not be as secure as you think.

# Compile the Project

Unlike in standard types of Visual Basic projects, running a WebClass in design mode and running it as a compiled DLL are different kinds of operations.

Create a new directory on your C drive called **SecuredSite** and move the `registration.txt` file into that directory. Make sure to change the path reference in the `Signon_frmSignon` and `Register_Register` routines. Now run the site again. You shouldn't see any difference in the site.

Make sure you set the project options like those shown in Figure 5.9, and then compile the program.

**FIGURE 5.9:**

SecuredSite project options

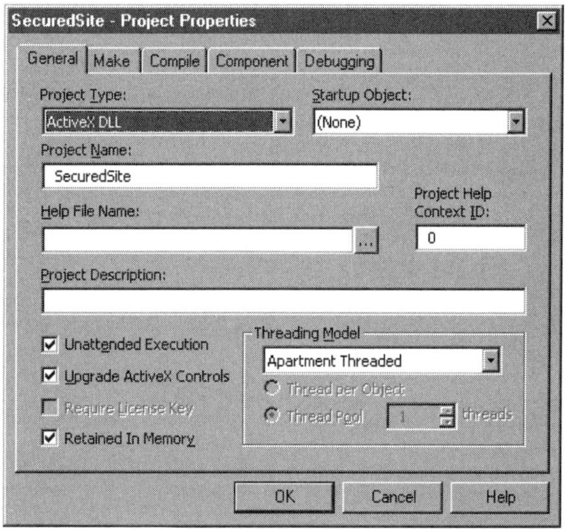

You must check the Unattended Execution option, because WebClasses run on the server. Unhandled errors in a VB program display a modal dialog box—and no one's likely to see it. When you check this option, the VB runtime translates all `MessageBox` calls into Application log events.

You also need to check the Retained in Memory option for WebClasses. This flag tells IIS to keep the Visual Basic runtime DLL loaded even when the last instance of a WebClass has been destroyed. If you don't check this option, the entire runtime DLL will be unloaded after each request, then loaded again for the next request, which will slow down the response time considerably.

> **NOTE**
> 
> If you're developing on Windows 95 or 98, which don't have event logs, VB writes the information into a file. You specify the name of the file with the `App.Logpath` property. If you haven't specified a filename, VB writes the information into a file called `VBEvents.log` in the `Windows` directory.

After you've compiled the project, run it by opening a new instance of the browser and typing the URL for the `Signon.asp` page. Make sure your WebClass project is *not* running when you do this; otherwise, you'll still be in the development environment.

> **TIP**
> 
> If you don't know the URL, run the program once more in development mode and copy the URL from your browser's address field.

You will likely get an error when the program tries to open the registration file. If you don't get an error, either your security is lax or IIS may have its security settings set to NT Challenge/Response mode. Even if you don't get an error, you may want to read through this section anyway and possibly change some settings.

Why do you get an error while running with a compiled DLL but not while running in development mode? Because when you run the program in compiled mode, *you aren't you*! That's confusing, isn't it. Instead, you're running the program with the permissions assigned to the default IIS Web user—usually called `IUSR_MachineName`, where `MachineName` is the name of the server on which IIS is running. Worse, sometimes you're running with the permissions assigned to the default ISAPI extension user, usually called `IWAM_MachineName`. (IUSR stands for Internet User, and IWAM stands for Internet Web Application Manager.) The permission level you have in these various modes is called your *security context*. The reasons it can be different at different times lie in how you set up IIS and your Web application.

When IIS is set up to allow anonymous access (the default setting), it doesn't try to authenticate the user requesting a file; instead, it impersonates another account—by default, the `IUSR_MachineName` account—to gain access to files and other resources.

I'll go into more detail about this later; for now, follow these rules and you should be able to run your projects without security problems:

- When you run a WebClass in development mode, you have all the security permissions assigned to your account. You should be able to read and write files and access databases through your IIS application in exactly the same way as you can by changing files in Explorer or any other application.

- If you have security problems when running a WebClass in compiled mode (and you will), adjust the permissions assigned to the IIS anonymous user account (IUSR_MachineName). If the application runs in an isolated process, change the rights for the IWAM_MachineName account instead.

- Your security context can change during the course of a request, from the LocalSystem account to IUSR_MachineName, to IWAM_MachineName. You should ensure that all three of these accounts have appropriate access rights to files and COM objects.

- If your application runs in an isolated process, you may also need to change the MTS package permissions in order to instantiate other COM objects from your WebClass. For the present, you won't have to worry about that. I'll take it up in more detail in Chapter 12, "IIS Applications and Microsoft Transaction Server."

To solve the security problem associated with the registration file, open Windows Explorer, navigate to the registration.txt file or the SecuredSite directory, and right-click it. Select the Security tab. Add the IUSR_MachineName account and the IWAM_MachineName account to the access control list (ACL) for that file or to the directory. Make sure you give these accounts Change (Read, Write, eXecute and Delete—usually abbreviated as RWXD) permissions, or at least read/write (RW) permissions for the file, depending upon your needs. Run the project again. This time, you should not get an error.

Unfortunately, security problems are the most common problems you'll run into when you deploy your application. If you're building an in-house application and are lucky enough to have an all-Windows intranet-only client base, you might want to consider changing the default to NT Challenge/Response mode and removing the Anonymous browse option. Figure 5.10 shows the properties dialog for the SecuredSite virtual directory. These are the default security settings.

**FIGURE 5.10:**

Internet Service Manager properties

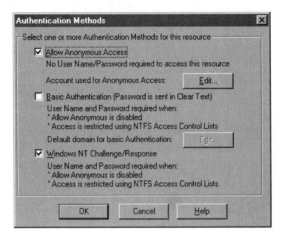

To get to the screen shown in Figure 5.10, open the Internet Service Manager, expand the Default Web Site item, then right-click the SecuredSite entry. Select Properties from the pop-up menu. Click the Directory Security tab, then click the Edit button. If you don't want to run IIS under the default `IUSR_MachineName` account, click the Edit button next to Allow Anonymous Access and change the account to a different network account. Alternately, you can disable anonymous access altogether by clearing the check box, but you should do that only if all users of the application can authenticate on your network

Try to keep this security model in mind as you design your Web applications. It becomes especially important if you'll be using COM objects from other servers, connecting to a separate SQL server, or accessing remote files. If you need anything more than read-only resource access to files inside your Web site, you'll need to make sure that the account permissions for IIS are properly set. It's a good idea to write down the application's security settings somewhere where you or the server administrator will be able to find them later. Servers aren't static—they change all the time. If an administrator rebuilds the server, if resources are moved or renamed, or if an administrator accidentally changes permissions for your directories or accounts, you'll need to restore the permissions before your application will execute properly.

# Improve Site Security

You've implemented the rudiments of sign-on/password security, but there are some serious security holes in the site. First, the way the project is set up, you have to provide write access to the application so it can write the registration file. That's a bad security practice because it's relatively easy to fool a server into writing files. Someone might manage to upload malevolent code onto your server. Worse yet, try typing this URL into your browser (you will need to substitute your own server name and virtual directory name):

```
http://myServer/SecuredSite/registration.txt
```

Bad isn't it? Any person who knows the name of the registration file could obtain all the sign-ons and passwords.

Second, anybody can register—and there's little point in providing security if you then let anyone in who can invent a sign-on and password, unless you're just trying to capture personal information, such as contact information for visitors to your site. It would be much better to have a site administrator assign sign-ons to individuals. If you're really looking for good security, you should assign passwords as well, because people tend to select easy-to-guess passwords or to reuse them in many places.

Here are several ways you could improve the security for the site:

- Move the registration file to a directory outside of your Web root and outside of your File Transfer Protocol (FTP) root. That way, people won't be able to find it easily.

- Change the method for storing registration information from a file-based system to a secured database.

- Add administrative options to assign sign-ons and passwords.

- Add automatic password changes after a specific period of time has elapsed. For example, you might force people to change passwords each month, with a one-week grace period. People with expired passwords would need to contact an administrator to obtain a new one.

- Use NT user- or group-level security to restrict access to the directory. You'll see more about this in the next section. If you do this, you may not need sign-on and password security in your application; you can use the NT security instead.

# Take Advantage of NT Security

Have you ever browsed to a site and seen a modal sign-on/password dialog box appear? The dialog appears when a server returns a status of 401, which means "access denied." Figure 5.11 shows the dialog box that appears in IE.

**FIGURE 5.11:**

Built-in sign-on/password dialog

You can control the status returned to the browser through the `Status` property of the `Response` object.

```
Response.Status = "401 Unauthorized"
```

By default, the dialog box displays the name of the server that sent the access denied message. You can replace that with a custom message by returning an HTTP header value along with the status. The custom message must be in quotes, inside the quotes surrounding the header value, so make sure you enter it exactly as shown here:

```
Response.AddHeader "WWW-Authenticate", _
    "BASIC REALM=""Your custom message here"""
```

When the browser receives the 401 status, what happens depends on the Authentication settings for IIS. There are three authentication methods (see Figure 5.10):

**Anonymous**  This is the default. Using this method, all IIS permissions depend on the settings for the `IUSR_MachineName` account.

**Basic Authentication**  Use this method when you need to provide network authentication but not all your clients are running IE.

**NT Challenge/Response**  Use this method to provide transparent (no sign-on required) authentication for IE browsers.

If all your clients use IE browsers, you can avoid having them log in at all by setting the security to NT Challenge/Response. IE sends the logged-on user's sign-on and password hash value (an encrypted form of the sign-on and password) for each request. IIS can use the hash value to authenticate the user and fulfill the request without the user having to manually enter a sign-on and password.

Unfortunately, IE is the only browser that contains the built-in mechanism to make this work. For other browsers, you need to allow both Basic Authentication and NT Challenge/Response. IE browsers will attempt to authenticate transparently by using Challenge/Response, whereas other browsers such as Netscape will display the sign-on/password dialog.

For either of these methods to work, the user must have a sign-on and password that provides access to your network. From then on, IIS impersonates the user by providing that sign-on/password and does *not* use the `IUSR_Machine-Name` sign-on discussed earlier in this chapter.

You can easily see this in action. Change the authentication method for the `SecuredSite` virtual directory to Basic Authentication. Ignore the warning. Clear the other two check boxes. Close your browser. Change the `Signon_Response` event code so it checks the value of `Request.ServerVariables("LOGON_USER")`. If the value is empty, return the 401 status code and the HTTP header; otherwise, continue.

```
If Request("LOGON_USER") = vbNullString Then
    Response.Status = 401
    Response.AddHeader "WWW-Authenticate", _
        "BASIC REALM=""Your custom message here"""
    Exit Sub
End If
```

When you run the program, you won't be able to bypass the dialog box until you have entered a valid NT sign-on and password.

If you're using IE, go back to the IIS administration program and check the NT Challenge/Response check box. Stop the `SecuredSite` program, close your browser, then run the program again. This time you won't see the dialog box. When the server returns the 401 status, IE immediately sends the hashed sign-on/password value for the logged-on user to IIS, which then authenticates by using Challenge/Response.

Obviously, this method applies primarily to intranet applications and to situations in which you want to offer remote users access to an internal application.

Remember the warning you got when you checked the Basic Authentication check box? You should be aware that the browser sends the user's sign-on and password encoded using Base64 (a common Internet encoding scheme). Although any encryption/encoding scheme is sufficient to deter most users, any decent hacker can decrypt Base64 encoded values with little effort. You should avoid forcing users to send unencrypted sign-ons and passwords over the Internet. It's much easier to do this if the clients are using IE. If they're not, you should consider authenticating via a secure channel, such as HTTPS.

You've seen how to create a WebClass application and how to implement either your own sign-on/password security or NT-based security. In the next chapter, you'll use the debugger to explore WebClasses in more detail.

# CHAPTER SIX

# WebClass Debugging and Error Handling

- Exploring the WebClass Event Sequence
- Debugging Client-Side Script
- Logging and Displaying Errors
- Trapping Errors

One of the main advantages of using VB over ASP is the strength of the Visual Basic debugging environment. Microsoft's latest version of Visual Interdev includes some debugging capabilities and is a huge improvement over the first version, in which debugging was limited to printing debug messages in the browser. Still, VB's debugger is the best in the business.

My rule of thumb is that VB developers should spend about 60 percent of their time in the debugger. Nevertheless, I've run across numerous programmers over the years who seem to think that debuggers are for wimps and that real programmers just think their way through the problems. Such people always remind me of those who insist that great composers created masterworks out of whole cloth, with no rewriting. Historians have long since disproved that theory; I doubt that inspired programming is any different.

Because I think the debugging capabilities of VB are so important, I'm going to walk you through a debugging session. Of course, all of you experienced VB programmers already know how to use the debugger, so before you decide to ignore this section, let me assure you that you may learn a few things about WebClasses from it—I know I did.

# Exploring the WebClass Event Sequence

Create a new IIS project. Rename the project **WebClassDebug**. Change the name of `WebClass1` to **debugTest**. In each event stub available to the WebClass, write a response to the browser as follows:

```
Private Sub WebClass_BeginRequest()
    Response.Write "Entered BeginRequest<br>"
End Sub

Private Sub WebClass_EndRequest()
    Response.Write "Entered EndRequest<br>"
End Sub

Private Sub WebClass_FatalErrorResponse(SendDefault _
    As Boolean)
SendDefault=False
    Response.Write "A fatal error occurred.<br>"
    Response.Write "Error# " & Err.Number & ", " & _
      "Source: " & Err.Source & ", " & "Description: " & _
```

```
        Err.Description
    Response.Write "WebClass Error# " & _
        WebClass.Error.Number & _
        ", Source: " & WebClass.Error.Source & _
", Description: " & WebClass.Error.Description
End Sub

Private Sub WebClass_Start()
    Response.Write "Entered Start<br>"
End Sub

Private Sub WebClass_Initialize()
    Response.Write "Entered Initialize"
End Sub

Private Sub WebClass_Terminate()
    Debug.Print "Entered Terminate"
End Sub
```

Now press F5 to run the project. You should immediately get an error in VB. If you continue (as if you had compiled the project), you will see an error message in the browser window. (By the way, you can compile this application with no compile errors and get the same error—it's a runtime error.)

> **WARNING** The `mswcrun.dll` file that comes with Visual Studio Service Pack 3 (sp3) has some serious problems with tag replacement. When running in design mode, the WebClass truncates the HTML returned to the browser. This behavior does not occur at runtime. To solve this problem, you need to replace the sp3 version of the DLL with an earlier version. For more information, see the Microsoft Knowledge Base article Q234317.

```
WebClassDebug error '800a005b'
Object variable or With block variable not set
/debugTest/debugTest.ASP, line 14
```

The first thing experienced ASP programmers will notice is that this is a typical ASP error message, and properly so, as the error occurred because an external object (your WebClass) encountered a fatal error. The second thing you'll notice is that the error message is not very helpful—it includes little useful information. Some object couldn't be instantiated. If a user calls you up and says, "I'm getting an error when I try to reach your site," this is all the information you'll have to go on unless you add some extra error trapping to your application.

Look at the `debugTest.asp` file. Line 14 contains the call that instantiates your WebClass object:

```
Application("~WC~WebClassManager").ProcessNoStateWebClass _
    "WebClassDebug.debugTest", _
        Server, _
        Application, _
        Session, _
        Request, _
        Response
```

Some other object must have failed. You know it isn't the WebClassManager object, or the failure message would refer to the previous line in the ASP file, where the WebClassManager object is instantiated. Your application doesn't create any objects—it doesn't use `New` anywhere, so the program must not be able to start an instance of the WebClass, right? Actually, that's not correct. The WebClass object was created properly.

Try again. This time, press F8 to start the application. You will reach the `Initialize` event code, but the program fails on the only code line in the routine:

```
Private Sub WebClass_Initialize()
    Response.Write "Entered Initialize"
End Sub
```

Why? Because the Response object—a global object—doesn't yet exist when the `WebClass_Initialize` event occurs. So you can't use `Response.Write` to print messages from the `Initialize` event. Before you try again, change the `Response.Write` statement to `Debug.Print`.

```
Private Sub WebClass_Initialize()
    Debug.Print "Entered Initialize"
End Sub
```

While you're at it, note that the code in the `WebClass_Terminate` event contains `Debug.Print` also, because the `Response` object has been destroyed when this event executes, and you will get an error if you try to use the Response object.

This time, you should be able to step through all the code. The browser should list three events:

- Entered BeginRequest
- Entered Start
- Entered EndRequest

**NOTE** Sometimes, the debugger refuses to step through WebClass code (although the code runs fine) after errors occur, or after you have repeatedly run the project. Stopping and starting the Web server will usually solve this problem. You can start and stop the Web server from within the WebClass Designer by clicking the black, square Stop icon on the Designer toolbar (see Figure 6.1).

**FIGURE 6.1:**

WebClass Designer toolbar

Stop icon

At any time, you can press F5 to continue program execution. When the debugger reaches a breakpoint in your code, it will bring up the VB development environment, and you can step through your code. To reach the browser to view the output, you must press Alt+Tab to get back to the browser window—VB will not automatically switch back to the browser even if you press F5.

At present, you should always start your WebClass with only one browser window open. If more than one browser is open, the debugging environment has trouble determining which one to use for output. If you start the program with no browser open, VB will launch an instance of the browser and use that for output. There's a project option to tell the VB environment to use an already open browser instance for output. You can select that option by checking the Use Existing Browser option at the bottom of the Debugging tab in the Project Properties dialog box (see Figure 6.2).

It can be useful to spend a short time experimenting in the debugger with new VB features such as WebClasses. Although most features are documented, it's often unclear exactly how they fit together, or when events occur relative to each other.

For example, the WebClass has a `NextItem` property. When you set this property, the WebClass calls the `Respond` event for the specified WebItem. Let's watch that happen in the debugger. First, you'll need to modify the project slightly. Add two custom WebItems, called **TestItem1** and **TestItem2**. If you don't remember how to do that, review Chapter 5, "Securing an IIS Application." From now on, I'll assume that you know how to work with the environment to add HTML templates and custom WebItems, and to modify code.

**FIGURE 6.2:**

Debugging tab in the Project Properties dialog box

Add the following code to the Respond event for the two WebItems:

```
Private Sub TestItem1_Respond()
    Set NextItem = TestItem2
    Response.Write "Got to TestItem1<br>"
End Sub

Private Sub TestItem2_Respond()
    Response.Write "Got to TestItem2<br>"
End Sub
```

You also need to tell the WebClass to use the two new items, so change the Start event so it sets the WebClass NextItem property to TestItem1:

```
Private Sub WebClass_Start()
    Set NextItem = TestItem1
    Response.Write "Entered Start<br>"
End Sub
```

In the Start event, you set the NextItem property to TestItem1. In the Respond event for TestItem1, the code directs the WebClass to immediately set the NextItem property to TestItem2. In each routine, the code commands the Response object to write a message. By following the messages, you should get a good idea of the order in which the WebClass executes the commands. Because you set the

`NextItem` property *before* issuing the `Response.Write`, you should get this output if the code works as expected:

```
Entered BeginRequest
Got to TestItem2
Entered EndRequest
```

Instead, you get output from all five of the event routines:

```
Entered BeginRequest
Entered Start
Got to TestItem1
Got to TestItem2
Entered EndRequest
```

What happened? It turns out that the `NextItem` command doesn't take effect until *after* the routine in which it is set has completed. In other words, the program doesn't execute the commands in the order in which they appear in the code; instead, it executes as follows:

```
Initialize event
BeginRequest event
Start event
    Set NextItem
    Write Response
    Fire Respond event for TestItem1
TestItem1_Respond
Set NextItem
Write Response
    Fire Respond event for TestItem2
TestItem2_Respond
    Write Response
EndRequest event
Terminate event
```

So, to call another WebItem or method in a WebItem after a response has begun, you need to use VB's standard `Call` syntax. Change the code in `TestItem1_Respond` to call `TestItem2_Respond` explicitly, then run the program again.

```
Private Sub TestItem1_Respond()
    Call TestItem2_Respond
    Response.Write "Got to TestItem1<br>"
End Sub
```

Now you'll see the output you expected:

```
Entered BeginRequest
Entered Start
Got to TestItem2
Got to TestItem1
Entered EndRequest
```

So, unlike standard VB calls, setting the `NextItem` property causes an indirect and possibly out-of-sequence or *deferred* execution (depending on where you put the code). It turns out that other events also execute in ways you might not expect. For example, you can set the `ReScanReplacements` property of a WebItem at either design time or at runtime. In Chapter 5, Table 5.2 shows that the `ReScanReplacements` property controls whether the tag replacement engine scans once for replacement tags or whether it scans continuously until it has replaced all the tags. Regardless of when you set it, it doesn't work exactly as you would expect. The documentation states that "The `ReScanReplacements` property causes the WebClass to make an additional pass through the replacement tags during the `ProcessTag` event."

Let's explore it with the debugger. Tag replacement begins when the WebClass fires the `ProcessTag` event. The event never fires for custom WebItems, so you'll need to change one of the custom WebItems into an HTML template. Delete `TestItem1` and replace it with an HTML template containing this HTML content:

```
<html>
<head><WCHead></WCHead></head>
<body><WCBody></WCBody></body>
</html>
```

> **TIP** Remember to place the original copy of the HTML template in a directory *other* than your project directory; otherwise, VB will make a copy of the file and call it `TestItem11.htm` rather than `TestItem1.htm`.

Be sure to change the `TagPrefix` property to `WC` instead of `WC@`.

Leave the `ReScanReplacements` property set to the default `False` value. You'll also need to change the `TestItem1_Respond` event to display the template:

```
Private Sub TestItem1_Respond()
    TestItem1.WriteTemplate
End Sub
```

Finally, you need to add code to the ProcessTag event to designate the replacement text:

```
Private Sub TestItem1_ProcessTag(ByVal TagName As String, _
TagContents As String, SendTags As Boolean)
    Select Case lcase(TagName)
    Case "wchead"
        TagContents = "<title><WCTitle></WCTitle></title>"
    Case "wcbody"
        TagContents = "This is the body of the document"
    Case "wctitle"
        TagContents = "Test RescanReplacements"
    End Select
End Sub
```

Now step through the project. Figure 6.3 shows the output you should get.

**FIGURE 6.3:**

TestItem1 output when ReScanReplacements = False

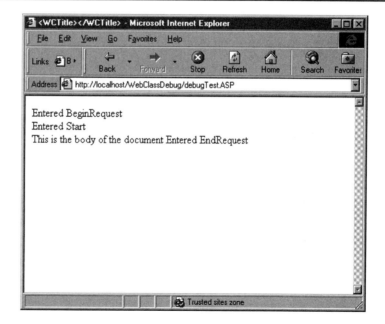

> **WARNING**
>
> The HTML parser often changes the case of replacement tags. It does this inconsistently and always (so far) changes them to uppercase. There are three workarounds: Make sure to write your replacement tags in uppercase; force the `TagName` parameter in the `ProcessTag` event to a known state, either uppercase or lowercase; or use the `TagContents` property to differentiate between tags. Notice that the title bar contains an HTML tag. That's because the `ProcessTag` event returned a `TagContents` value containing another replacement tag. The browser interprets the tag as title text and places it in the title bar of the browser.

Set `ReScanReplacements` to `True` and run the project again; you don't need to step through it this time. Now, the title bar should show `Test ReScanReplacements`. Setting the `ReScanReplacments` property works as advertised. Stop the project, set a breakpoint on the line `Select Case Lcase(TagName)` in the `ProcessTag` event, and run the project again. This time, pay close attention to the order in which the tags get replaced. From the description in the documentation (an "additional pass"), I would have expected the program to replace the tags in this sequence: `WCHead`, `WCBody`, and `WCTitle`. Instead, the WebClass finds and replaces the tags in this sequence: `WCHead`, `WCTitle`, and `WCBody`. Apparently, the WebClass reads the contents of the HTML template into a string, then always searches from the beginning of the string each time for replacement tags. So, after the first replacement, the string looks like this:

```
<html>
<head><title><WCTitle></WCTitle></title></head>
<body><WCBody></WCBody></body>
</html>
```

Therefore, during the second pass, the WebClass finds the `WCTitle` tag before it finds the `WCBody` tag. This sequence affects the way you think about recursive tag replacement. Remember, you can set the `ReScanReplacements` property at runtime. Let's try setting the property to `True` *after* the WebClass has replaced the `WCBody` tag. Change the `ReScanReplacements` design-time setting back to `False` and add this line to the `Case` statement in the `ProcessTag` event:

```
Case "wcbody"
    TagContents = "This is the body of the document"
    TestItem1.ReScanReplacements=True
```

Doesn't work, does it? Apparently, the WebClass also keeps track of whether the current item being replaced is the last one. You might be able to force the

WebClass to replace the title tag if you also add one last replacement tag to the WCBody replacement text:

```
Case "wcbody"
    TagContents = "This is the " & _
        "<WCIgnore></WCIgnore>body of the document"
    TestItem1.ReScanReplacements=True
```

Still doesn't work. You can make it work only by setting the `ReScanReplacements` property to `True` either at design time or immediately after replacing the WCHead tag. Try that if you like. You've learned one more thing about the way tag replacements work: The WebClass will rescan for replacement tags only in the portion of the response that occurs *after* the `ReScanReplacements` property has been set to `True`.

I wouldn't go so far as to call this behavior a bug, but I first ran across this "feature" at my company when adding some processing in the `ProcessTag` event to select a graphic based on a user's input. I wanted to write an `<img>` tag to the browser that contained one image or another. There was a `<WCImg></WCImg>` tag at the top of the template that I would replace with the `<img>` tag.

The problem was, I didn't know which image to use until after my code reached a `<WCTotal>` replacement tag further down in the template file. During processing, that replacement calculated and displayed a total. The totaled values were themselves embedded in still other replacement tags. If the total was greater than a certain value, I'd use one image, if less, a different image. I decided the order of the tags wouldn't matter; I'd replace the `<WCImg>` tag with another replacement tag, then replace that secondary tag by setting `ReScanReplacements` to `True` after performing the replacement on the `<WCTotal>` tag. As you've seen, that didn't work. Fortunately, I was dealing with only version 4.*x* browsers. For that particular template, because I was under time pressure to deliver the application, I used cascading style sheet (CSS) absolute positioning to move the HTML reference to the graphic further down in the file. That way, the WebClass tag scanner found the tags in the sequence I needed—the `<WCTotal>` tag first, then the `<WCImg>` tag.

Before we leave this topic, note that you don't have to place the replacement tags right next to each other; you can put default text between the tags. In fact, you don't even have to use unique names for the replacement tags. Instead, you can differentiate the tags based on the `TagContents` property. As an example, edit the `TestItem1` template and replace its contents with this HTML:

```
<html>
<head><WC>Head</WC></head>
```

```
<body><WC>Body</WC></body>
</html>
```

Also, add another `Case` statement to the `ProcessTag` event:

```
Case "WC"
    Select Case TagContents
    Case "Head"
        TagContents = "<title><WCTitle></WCTitle>" & _
            "</title>"
        TestItem1.ReScanReplacements = True
    Case "Body"
        TagContents = "This is the " & _
            "<WCIgnore></WCIgnore> body of the document"
    End Select
End Select
```

Run the project again. It should run identically. So which value should you use to differentiate tags, the `TagName` or the `TagContents`? I don't think there's a tremendous difference. All of Microsoft's documentation references the `TagName` property, but it might be easier and less subject to error to decide on a standard `TagPrefix`, then use that for all replacement tags in conjunction with a unique `TagContents` value. For absolute safety, you can create the initial `TagContents` as an HTML comment, much like the `getHTMLTemplate` function in Chapter 5. As a side benefit, the HTML parser doesn't seem to change the case of the text between tags, only that of the tags themselves. In either case, as is true with all Web processing, you'll need to match up the names between the HTML and the WebClass.

# Debugging Client-Side Script

Stepping through code with the debugger can teach you a tremendous amount about the way VB and WebClasses work. In the Web environment, though, code isn't limited to the server. You're perfectly free to write code that runs on the client as well. Because this book isn't about scripting code for browsers, I'm not going to discuss the code in any depth. Nonetheless, I can't leave the topic of the debugger without pointing out that if you have the right combination of hardware and software (and I realize that's a big if in the Web world), you can extend your debugging session into the browser itself.

To debug client-side script, you must first use the IIS administration program to create an IIS application, then configure the application for client-side debugging.

To do that, open the IIS administration program, find the virtual Web for the WebClassDebug site, right-click it, and select Properties. You'll see the dialog box in Figure 6.4.

> **NOTE**
>
> Client-side debugging works only with Internet Explorer 4 and higher, so if you're running Netscape or another browser, go out and get a real...(just kidding)...you can skip the rest of this section. It also works only if you have Internet Information Server or Personal Web Server version 4 or higher.

**FIGURE 6.4:**

IIS Virtual Directory Properties dialog

Click the Create button in the Application Settings section of the dialog. The Name field will become active. Type **WebClassDebug** in the Name field and then click the Apply button at the bottom of the dialog box.

Next, click the Configuration button in the Application Settings section. You will then see the Application Configuration dialog. Click the App Debugging tab, then check the check box labeled Enable ASP Client-Side Script Debugging (see Figure 6.5). Click the Apply button and then click OK until you've closed all the dialogs.

Now you need to write some client-side script so you can debug it. One of the hardest things for people first programming in the ASP/WebClass/browser environment to understand is that on the server, client-side script is text. It's sent to the browser just like any other text. After it reaches the browser, though, it's code. The two environments are completely separate—the server code knows nothing about the browser code and the browser code knows nothing about the server code. There's no automatic method to share variable values between client-side script and server-side programs. You can't set a server variable directly from client-side script. At any rate, you write client-side scripts with the `Response` `.Write` method just as you do with all other text and HTML.

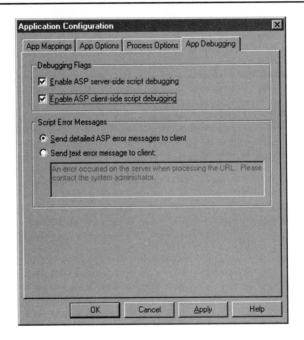

**FIGURE 6.5:**

IIS Application Configuration dialog

In the `WebClass_BeginRequest` event, enter the code to write the client-side script.

```
With Response
    .Write "Entered BeginRequest<br>"
    .Write "<script language=""vbscript"">"
    .Write "   sub onButtonClick()"
    .Write "      msgbox " & Chr(34) & _
      "Your session ID is:" & Session.SessionID & _
      Chr(34) & ", vbInformation + vbExclamation, " _
```

```
    & """How Did The Browser Know?"""
        .Write "    end sub"
        .Write "</script>"
        .Write "<input type=""button"" value=""Click Me""" & _
          "onClick=""onButtonclick()""><p>"
End With
```

Save and run the project. When you click the Click Me button, the browser displays a message box containing your current SessionID. Note that you *can* set client-side variables explicitly with server-side code, but not the reverse.

With Visual Interdev, you can set breakpoints in client-side script, but from within VB, you'll need to introduce an error to view the debugger.

Switch back to the project, press Ctrl+Break to enter break mode, and change the word `msgbox` in the script to **msgBx**. Press F5 to switch back into run mode, press Alt+Tab to move back to the browser, and press F5 to refresh the page. This time when you click the button, you'll get an error, and IE will ask whether you want to debug. Click the Yes option.

If IE does not ask whether you want to debug, make sure you haven't disabled debugging within the browser. To check, click the View menu ➣ Internet Options ➣ Advanced tab (see Figure 6.6).

**FIGURE 6.6:**

Internet Explorer 4.*x* Advanced Internet Options

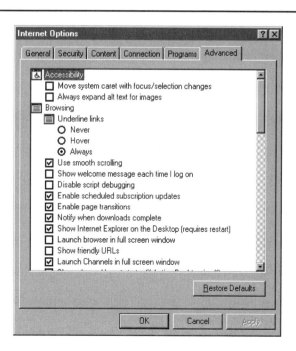

If IE *does* ask whether you want to debug, but the debugger doesn't appear, make sure you have the latest version of VBScript and JScript. You can download the latest versions free from Microsoft at http://msdn.microsoft.com/scripting/default.htm.

# Logging and Displaying Errors

All this has been interesting but doesn't solve the matter of the unhelpful error message displayed by the ASP page when a problem occurs. Unfortunately, although I have a solution, it's not elegant. In most cases, you can improve the error message by using the FatalErrorResponse event to return an intelligible error message if an internal untrapped error occurs. This event functions much like VB's default failure MessageBox, except that you can override the default message and provide your own. WebClasses also provide a WebClass.Error property. This property returns an Error object with only three properties rather than the usual five—Number, Source, and Description. The easiest way I know of to see this in action is to change the case of the first two <WC></WC> tags in TestItem1 HTML template to lowercase.

```
<html>
<head><wc>Head</wc></head>
<body><WC>Body</WC></body>
</html>
```

Why this causes an error I can't explain, but it does. Figure 6.7 shows the error output of the FatalErrorResponse event after changing the tags.

Why doesn't the FatalErrorResponse event fire if you do something like you did at the beginning of this chapter—use the Response object in the Initialize event? OK, I can rationalize that: The Response object hasn't been created yet, and that causes an error that can't be returned to the browser by the FatalErrorResponse event, because (circular logic) the Response object hasn't been created yet.

That logic also explains the behavior of the WebClass if you place a Response.Write statement in the WebClass_Terminate event. Stepping through the program with the debugger, VB will raise Error 91, Object variable or With block variable not set, when it reaches the Terminate event. If you compile the project and run it, the FatalErrorResponse event never fires. But you don't get the ASP error, either. VB does document the error for you, though—in the Application log. Figure 6.8 shows the error from the Application log. Interestingly,

VB itself apparently uses the MessageBox command internally, which the runtime engine then translates into an Application log message.

**FIGURE 6.7:**

Output from the FatalErrorResponse event

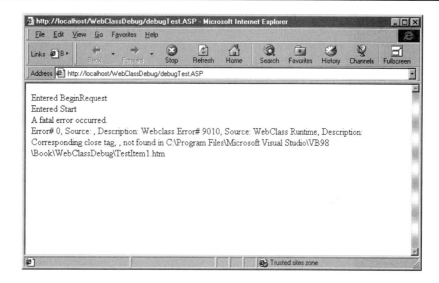

**FIGURE 6.8:**

Application log error message

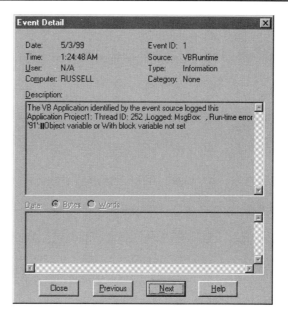

Here's the inelegant solution I promised you. This solution works only *after* you've compiled your WebClass into a DLL (unless you fiddle around with the ASP file that VB uses to instantiate your WebClass). Although Microsoft's documentation says that you can't add code to the ASP file, you can. If you set `On Error Resume Next` in the ASP file before the WebClassManager creates your WebClass, you can trap errors that occur within the WebClass, which it would normally send to the Application log.

One more time, change the code in the `WebClass_Initialize` event to:

```
Private Sub WebClass_Initialize()
    On Error GoTo Err_Init
    Response.Write "Entered Initialize"
Err_Init:
    Err.Raise Err.Number, "WebClass_Initialize", _
        Err.Description & "<br>Error during " & _
        "WebClass initialization."
    Exit Sub
End Sub
```

Stop the Web server, compile the project, and then restart the Web server. If you leave your browser open between iterations of the program, it will still contain the correct URL in the address field. Don't run it yet, though. First, wrap the line in the ASP file that creates the WebClass with error-trapping code so that the last part of it looks like the following:

```
On Error Resume next
Application("~WC~WebClassManager").ProcessNoStateWebClass _
    "WebClassDebug.debugTest", _
      Server, _
      Application, _
      Session, _
      Request, _
      Response
If Err.Number <> 0 then
    Response.Write "Error #" & Err.Number & ", Source: " & Err.Source & _
        _", Description: " & Err.Description
End if
```

Save the file and navigate to the URL for the project. This time, you should get the output shown in Figure 6.9.

**FIGURE 6.9:**

Result of modifying the WebClass ASP file

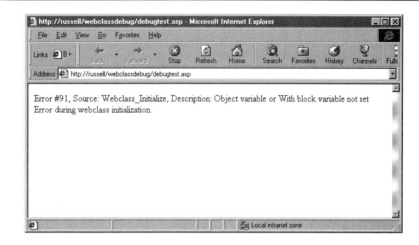

If you combine this method with some internal error trapping, you can get reasonably good error messages for debugging. I'm not advocating this as a primary method of debugging your application, but you have to admit that it's better than

```
WebClassDebug error '800a005b'
Object variable or With block variable not set
/debugTest/debugTest.ASP, line 14
```

It's not an elegant solution because the VB development environment *overwrites* the ASP file each time you run the project in design mode. So during development, the usefulness of this solution is limited to helping you discover what's going on inside the WebClass when you compile the application. After you compile the project, though, the ASP file is static (until the next compile) so this solution can work long-term to help you find problems.

For those of you developing on servers that you can't control, it's a useful way to get most error messages back to the browser. Even more useful, you can cause the program to "switch modes" by passing a parameter in the URL. You can check for the presence of the parameter to enable debugging code that traps the error inside the ASP file. In the following example, when you pass a QueryString parameter called DebugMode with a value of True, the error handler returns messages to the browser; otherwise, they go to the Application log by default.

```
If Request("DebugMode") = True then
On Error Resume Next
Application("~WC~WebClassManager").ProcessNoStateWebClass _
```

```
            "WebClassDebug.debugTest", _
        Server, _
        Application, _
        Session, _
        Request, _
        Response
            If Err.Number <> 0 then
            Response.write "Error #" & Err.Number & _
                & ", Source: " & Err.Source & ", Description: " _
                & Err.Description
    End if
Else
Application("~WC~WebClassManager").ProcessNoStateWebClass _
        "WebClassDebug.debugTest", _
        Server, _
        Application, _
        Session, _
        Request, _
        Response
End If
```

You can extend this as needed to help you debug your applications at runtime, but just remember that you must re-create your special error-handling code to the ASP file each time you recompile. Also remember that the development environment will overwrite the file each time you run the application in design mode.

WebClasses do log fatal errors to the Application event log on NT. But even if you have access to the Application event log, this solution can still help, because without the extra error code, you get only the default error message.

# Trapping Errors

If your job involves developing COM (ActiveX) objects or controls for use by other programmers in varying environments, then you'll probably be well aware of the error-handling requirements. Basically, you're creating a "black box" component that must be able to communicate with other people's code, must adhere to the requirements of its environment (in this case, the Web server), and must degrade gracefully if its own requirements are not met.

For example, in a personal application, the fatal error message box is often enough error handling. If you wrote the app, and you're running it on your own machine, you can probably re-create the situation and fix the problem. When you're running in client-server mode and your client-side app fails, it at least affects only one person—the person working on the client computer. But if your WebClass fails, you could conceivably affect hundreds of people simultaneously. In the worst of situations, you could potentially also affect all other applications running on the Web server, by taking up bandwidth or even crashing the server.

That's why many ISPs won't install WebClass-based applications on their servers. In contrast, ASP applications run in the scripting environment. You can certainly slow down the server by writing endless loops inside an ASP file, but it's difficult to crash the server altogether. Although you may not be able to run your WebClass applications on an ISP's server, you have the same problems on your own servers.

The answer is error trapping. You're trying to trap several types of problems, and it's good to keep them in mind right up front:

- Parameter/input errors
- Logic errors
- Errors in external code
- Resource errors

Your goals in trapping these types of errors should be, in order of importance, to:

1. Keep your application from crashing
2. Provide as much information as possible about the error
3. Propagate all errors back to a critical decision point
4. Degrade gracefully

If your application crashes, you've lost the game. You won't be able to accomplish any of the other three goals. The more information you provide about the error, the easier it will be for you to find and fix it. You don't want your application to stop—even with good error messages—if you can work around the error, so you'll want to categorize errors based on how they affect your application. For example, input errors should never be fatal—you should trap them all and provide reasonable error messages so that the user or programmer providing the information can solve the problem. During development, you should focus primarily on the first two goals. In some cases, you won't have enough information to do more than approach the third goal during initial development. Later in the development cycle, after several users have tested your application, you should be able to improve your error handling to solve common problems. Spending lots of time degrading gracefully does no good if that causes you to miss fatal errors that crash the application.

Your first line of defense in a WebClass application, as in any application, is to decide which type of error handling is appropriate inside each routine. VB provides two error-handling methods: `On Error GoTo` and `On Error Resume Next`. Which one is best depends on what you're doing at the time. The overriding rule is that using either is better than using none. I routinely use `On Error GoTo` at the start of each routine, then change to `On Error Resume Next` for code that accesses external objects—those that aren't under my control.

Your biggest problems will arise when you don't have any error handling in a routine. Code that works every time in development will fail in production, sometimes due to outside factors.

## Error-Handling Scenario

Consider this scenario: You have a recordset populated with data from a database query that you use to fill an HTML select list on the browser. You want to display a list of names associated with UserIDs. The user submits a form containing the UserID associated with the selection back to your application. What are the possibilities for failure?

- You could fail to obtain a recordset.
- The recordset could be empty.
- Critical data may be missing.
- Some of the fields could contain a null value.
- The user could submit the form without selecting an item.
- The item selected might not match an item in the database.

Generic error handlers will catch all these errors but may not provide enough information to solve the problem. Let's take some of these errors in turn and analyze them from the standpoint of each error type and your goals in trapping them.

## You Could Fail to Obtain a Recordset

This is a call to external code. You can't control whether the connection to the database will be valid, whether the database server is running, or whether the network is running; therefore, you should trap the call with On Error Resume Next. You always test for errors after the call. If the call fails, you can raise an error in your routine. If you follow the guidelines in this section, your application will either decide what to do at that point, or it will propagate the error back to a critical decision point.

The following code illustrates one way to handle external errors:

```
Sub showSelectList
    Dim R as Recordset
    Dim methodName as string
    methodName = "showSelectList"
    On Error Resume Next
    Set R = conn.execute(someSQLStatement, ,adCmdText)
    If Err.Number <> 0 then
        Err.Raise Err.Number, Err.Source & ", " & _
        methodName, Err.Description & _
        "Error obtaining data " & _
        "for selection list."
    End If
    ' continue processing
End Sub
```

**NOTE**  The methodName variable is necessary because VB doesn't provide runtime access to the call stack. This is an irritating oversight that should have been remedied several versions ago. By appending the methodName to the source, you can log the call stack state without too much effort. You can also maintain a global array or stack object to store the state of the call stack, thus allowing you to log it when errors occur.

For external errors, use On Error Resume Next and test for errors when the call returns. If the external code raises an error, you'll catch it in the trap If Err.Number <> 0. You have two choices whenever you catch an error: You can decide how to handle the error at that point (create a critical error handler) or you can defer the decision to the calling code. Of course, you can also choose to ignore the error, but that's only advisable under certain circumstances, when you're expecting the error to occur and know exactly what you'll do if the error does occur. One such example is testing the upper bound of an array:

```
Function getUboundIntArray(anArray() as Integer) as long
    On Error Resume Next
    getUboundIntArray= Ubound(anArray)
End Function
```

## The Recordset Could Be Empty

Treat this as a parameter or input error. If the external code returned a Recordset object, then it has performed successfully. It's your responsibility to check if the data returned is valid. Normally, your critical error handler for parameter or input errors is internal to the routine. You don't always want to raise an error for parameter/input validation failure—sometimes, you want to return a message. The deciding factor here is usually the type of person using your application. If the person calling your code is an end user, return an error code and an informative status message. The purpose is to enable the end user to communicate coherently with technical support so they can help solve the problem. Remember, in many cases *you'll* be the one supporting the application. If the user is another programmer using your DLL as a data source or functional component, return a detailed error message.

```
Sub showSelectList
    Dim R as Recordset
    Dim methodName as string
    methodName = "showSelectList"
    On Error Resume Next
    Set R = conn.execute(someSQLStatement, , adCmdText)
    If Err.Number <> 0 then
        Err.Raise Err.Number, Err.Source & methodName, _
        Err.Description & "Error obtaining data " & _
        "for selection list."
    End If
    If (R.EOF and R.BOF) then
        ' no data, do something
    End If
End Sub
```

## Critical Data May Be Missing

At this point, you're reasonably sure that no error occurred while retrieving the recordset and that the recordset contains at least one row of data. Now you need to make sure that the recordset contains the fields that you need. I call errors like these *resource* errors because they stem from missing, unreachable, or invalid resources, which include file and database data, network connections, database connections, etc.

If you are a careful person, you will have requested only those fields in your SQL statement, so you can skip this step. If you're the kind of person who typically opens tables or uses SQL statements such as SELECT * FROM MyTable rather then executing specific SQL statements or stored procedures, then you can't be sure that the database hasn't changed. If the database administrator deleted a column, changed a data type, or renamed a column, the changes will affect your application. You'll either have to ensure that the anticipated columns exist or trap for the errors that will occur when you try to reference the fields. When you think about it this way, requesting exactly the fields you need from the database is a lot less work than trapping all the potential errors.

```
    Sub showSelectList
        Dim R as Recordset
        Dim methodName as string
        Dim F as Field
        Dim requiredFields as integer
        methodName = "showSelectList"
        ' code to retrieve recordset
        ' …
        For Each F in R.Fields
            If F.Name = "UserID" or F.Name="LastName" _
                or F.Name="FirstName" then
                requiredFields = requiredFields + 1
            End If
        Next
        On Error Goto Err_showSelectList
        If requiredFields <> 3 then
            Err.Raise 50001, methodName, "A required field " _
                & "is missing in the list of user names."
        End If
        ' continue processing

Exit_showSelectList:
    Exit Sub
Err_showSelectList:
    Err.Raise Err.Number, methodName, Err.Description
End Sub
```

You're now sure that the required fields are present, but unless you wrote a specific SQL query, you don't know the order in which they appear in the recordset. If you use field index numbers to reference the fields, you may not get an error, but you won't get the desired result either. In other words, suppose the SELECT * query returns LastName, FirstName, and UserID. If your code is expecting UserID, FirstName, LastName, the code will fail. If you use explicit field names instead, the code will run as expected.

```
' This code will fail if the field order changes
Response.write "<select name='UserID'>
Do While Not R.EOF
    Response.write "<option value='" & R(0) & "'>" _
    & R(1) & " " & R(2) & "</option>"
    R.MoveNext
Loop
Response.Write "</select>"

' This code will run even if the field order changes
Response.write "<select name='lstUsers'>
Do While Not R.EOF
    Response.write "<option value='" & R("UserID") & _
        "'>" & R("FirstName") & " " & R("LastName") & _
        "</option>"
    R.MoveNext
Loop
Response.Write "</select>"
```

You have only one more check to make to avoid errors. Both of the loops to fill the select list will break if any data field contains a null value. Here's the fixed code:

```
Response.write "<select name='lstUsers'>"
With Response
    Do While Not R.EOF
        .write "<option value='"
        If Not isNull(R("UserID") then
            .Write R("UserID") & "'>"
        Else
            .Write "0" & "'>"
        End If
        If Not isNull(R("FirstName")) then
            .Write R("FirstName") & " "
        End If
        If Not isNull(R("LastName")) then
            .Write & R("LastName")
```

```
            Else
                .Write "N/A"
            End If
            .Write "</option>"
          R.MoveNext
      Loop
   End With
   Response.Write "</select>"
```

You have to be sure to activate a generic error handler for all code not explicitly wrapped in On Error Resume Next followed by an error test; otherwise, your code can fail.

```
        ' Activate internal code error handler
        On Error Goto Err_showSelectList
        ' process data here
    Exit_showSelectList:
        Exit Sub
    Err_showSelectList:
        Err.Raise Err.Number, methodName, Err.Description
    End Sub
```

When the user submits the form, you need to ensure that the data you're expecting is present:

```
If isEmpty(Request.Form("UserID")) then
    ' return message to user
End If
```

One type of error specific to Web applications is caused by people being able to bookmark a place in your application. They can also create their own forms and submit them to your application—even in the wrong place. Although this may not be common for form data, it's extremely common with QueryString data. You need to perform a data-type check, just to be sure. Data stored in the Request object is always Variant data—and it's always string data. One way to ensure that you have the correct data type is to attempt to cast the variable to the correct type, and—you guessed it—trap the resulting error.

```
Dim vUserID as Variant
Dim lUserID as Long
vUserID = Request.Form("UserID")
If isEmpty(vUserID) then
    ' return message to user
End If
```

```
On Error Resume Next
LUserID = CLng(vUserID)
If Err.Number <> 0 then
    ' raise error
End If
```

Finally, after all that code, you're ready to do something with the data returned by the form.

The code you've just written is strong error-trapping. It meets the requirements for the first two goals of error trapping nicely. It will keep your application from crashing and provide reasonably good error messages, but it doesn't fulfill all the goals. Recall that goals 3 and 4 are to propagate all errors back to a critical decision point and to degrade gracefully.

Error propagation is the process of raising errors back up the call stack via installed error-handlers until you reach a point where you can logically decide, based on the error source and number, what you should do next. Propagation requires that you activate error handling in every routine in the call stack. A critical error-handler is a routine that can make a decision about what to do. The reason they're critical is that if you don't make the decision, VB will make it for you—every unhandled error is fatal, and your application quits. That's not a good response in most situations, and it's unacceptable for a server-based application.

Where should you create critical error-handlers? I believe that they properly belong at the beginning points of each state operation. You can think of your application as entering one state after another: "Now I'm initializing; now I'm displaying a form; now I'm retrieving data; now I'm validating input, etc." At the beginning of each state, you should be able to decide what to do if the operation fails. To continue the example, if you're retrieving a list of users and you can't make a database connection, you can simply write a message to the screen saying the data is unavailable. The point is, you *have* to make the decision somewhere. For me, the placement of these critical error-handlers is usually an iterative process. I start with critical error-handlers at the beginning of large operations and add more as the starting points of sub-states within the operations becomes clear. Experience will show you the best places to create them, but it's most important to realize that you have to have at least one at the beginning of each operation to keep your application from crashing.

The final goal is to degrade gracefully. Although any unhandled error can crash your application, you will want to respond to different trapped errors in different ways. In many cases, you can provide default values when data is missing. This is relatively easy to do for parameter/input errors but more difficult to do for resource errors. For example, if the database server is unavailable, it's usually impossible to substitute default values: "I don't know why last quarter's sales total is $0.00, sir." Often, you can defer the decision to the end user, for example, "Unable to communicate with the database. Do you want to try again?"

Logic errors are generally fatal, because you don't know why they occurred. The best thing you can do is to log as much information as possible so that you can find and fix the error. External code errors are the most dangerous. In the age of modular programming and million-line operating systems, you have to trust a lot of code just to get your application to run. If the API call to `getSystemTime` returns an incorrect time, you may not even know that an error occurred, possibly leading to many other problems.

How can you know that all your routines have active error traps, or that your critical error handlers are working properly? You can (almost) solve the problem with code reviews and testing. No one is immune from writing sloppy code sometimes. It's all too easy to write a few lines that you *know* are going to work (until they don't). For small applications, you can check the code, but you should always get someone else to test the application. A good rule of thumb is that five users will find 95 percent of the errors in your program. Unfortunately, it takes many more users to find the last 5 percent. Most programmers are aware that many bugs are never found—but that's not to say that they never cause problems.

You don't have to handle every error in each method. Although VB doesn't have an `On Error Call` *<subroutine>* name, you can solve part of the problem by writing generic error-handling, display, and/or logging routines. Here's a simple example that logs an error:

```
Sub testError()
    On Error Goto Err_testError
    Err.Raise 50000, "testError", "This is a test error."
Err_testError:
    Call LogError
    Exit Sub
End Sub
Sub LogError()
    App.LogEvent "Error #" & cstr(Err.Number) & _
        " Source: " & Err.Source & " Description: " _
        & Err.Description
    Err.Raise Err.Number, Err.Source, Err.Description
End Sub
```

Usually VB clears the Err object when it encounters an `Exit Sub`, `Exit Function`, or `Exit Property` line, but when you call a function or subroutine inside an active error-handler, VB does *not* clear the Err object until it encounters a `Resume` statement. You can use this feature to process errors with generic routines and still have access to the error information when the generic routine exits.

I've taken you through this discussion because I want to make sure you realize that server applications are fundamentally different from stand-alone applications. Visual Basic is a powerful programming language that gives you direct access to the operating system kernel calls. You can easily cause serious problems by writing bad code or by failing to anticipate or trap errors. Conditions you may have taken for granted in stand-alone or standard client-server applications—permanent database connections, homogeneous client operating systems, and almost exclusive use of file resources—are no longer available in the server-based application space. Your application may not be the only one on the server. When the server crashes, bringing the company intranet down with it, your WebClass application had better not be the cause of the problem.

# CHAPTER SEVEN

# Controlling Program Flow

- Understanding Program Flow
- Creating the AccountInfo Project
- Repurposing WebClasses
- Using Multiple WebClasses in an Application

In this chapter, you'll see how to create Web applications that let you exert programmatic control over when, where, and in which direction users can navigate within your application. You'll also see how easy it is to reuse and repurpose WebClass code and learn how to use multiple WebClasses to partition tasks cleanly between code modules.

# Understanding Program Flow

Have you ever tried to read a hypertext novel? In a hypertext novel, Chapter 2 doesn't necessarily follow Chapter 1. You are at perfect liberty to read chapters in random order, in linear sequence, or any combination. As you can imagine, the plot of a hypertext novel—and the planning that goes into it—are considerably different from the plot or the plan for a standard, sequential novel.

The Web is a hypertext medium. It is *meant* to be a hypertext medium, and although you can force pages into a linear sequence, you are working against the natural order of things. When you write a Web application, you need to change the way you think about applications because Web applications run in a nonlinear medium. The harder you try to force your application to behave like a Windows application, the harder you will have to work. Sure, you can use a customized Web-browser control or Java to write your applications, but only by hiding the standard browser controls, menus, and functionality. My advice is to take advantage of the browser and the Web; don't fight them—work with them.

The track a person takes through your application is called *program flow*. As a programmer or application designer, there are times when you don't care about program flow—you're perfectly happy to let the user control the path through the application. On the other hand, there are times when you absolutely must control the track a user takes. For example, in a testing program, you may not want a user to be able to back up and change the answer to a previous question. The program flow in this case is forward only. When your application has complete control of the client computer, controlling flow is relatively straightforward. When your client computer is a browser that is connected to your program only through an intermittent Web connection, controlling flow is more difficult.

The basic problem with controlling program flow on the Web is that browsers can move from place to place using Uniform Resource Locators (URLs). At any time, a user can type a URL into the address field, and the browser will attempt to navigate to that page. That's one difference between a typical Windows application and a browser-based application. In a Windows application, users can't move from one screen to another unless you provide them with the control (for example, menu selection, button click, list selection, etc.) to do so.

A standard Windows program spends most of its time looping, waiting for mouse or keyboard activity. You can assume that as long as your program is running, the potential exists for user interaction. Even if the user gets up and goes away for the weekend, leaving your program running, it still sits there spinning, waiting for specific events. One important event that your program will recognize is the user's desire to quit. Typically, you provide a Close or Exit option on the File menu. You also trap other methods through which the user might quit, such as closing the window or shutting down Windows. The important concept here is that the only way the user can exit your program without you knowing is to shut off the power to the computer.

In contrast, a Web application has no concept of waiting for user input because it's running on the server, where there is no user input. The browser interface portion of the program may still be running—but you can't know that. Consequently, you can't know when the user has closed your program, either. Therefore, server applications tend to *time out* after a definable period of inactivity.

In addition, in a typical Windows program, the program always moves "forward." Even if you provide a Back button, as in a Wizard, you know when users are moving backward because you know that they pressed the Back button. In a browser-based application, users always have a Back button. They also have Favorites and a Refresh option. You don't typically know *how* a user got to a page in your application; therefore, when you want to control where they go next, you need to track their progress so you'll first know where they are now. Given that information, you can decide whether the user is trying to move backward, forward, or simply trying to refresh the current page.

This is a difficult concept until you begin to work with a browser as your application host, and it's easier to see than to explain. The best way to understand it is—you guessed it—to create a project and explore it with the debugger. You'll do that in the next section.

# Creating the *AccountInfo* Project

Imagine that you're a Web applications programmer for The Great Bank of America. Your task is to create a home-banking application so that people can use their browsers to view the balance or history of their checking and savings accounts. Your boss gives you a beautiful flowchart created by the mainframe programming group some years ago. The flowchart shows the screens in the application and the steps a customer must go through to view his or her account balance (see Figure 7.1).

**FIGURE 7.1:**

Account information application flowchart

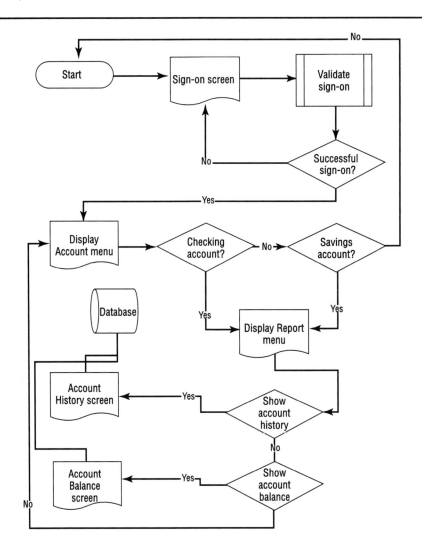

Let's write the application. If you haven't worked with databases and ADO, you may want to skip ahead and read Chapter 10, "Retrieving and Storing Data in Databases." You need a sign-on screen—you can reuse parts of the

SecuredSite project in Chapter 5, "Securing an IIS Application," for that. You'll also need a database. I'll provide the database tables and relational structure. You can use any database to which you can connect with ADO. If you don't want to build the database, you can download the Microsoft Access database (AccountInfo.mdb) used in this project from the Sybex Web site.

> **NOTE** To download code, navigate to http://www.sybex.com. Click Catalog and search for this book's title. Click the Downloads button and accept the licensing agreement. Accepting the agreement grants you access to the downloads page for the book.

Create a new IIS application. Name the project **AccountInfo** and save it in a directory called **AccountInfo**. IIS applications use your project directory as the default Web site; therefore, you should always create a new directory when you save the project. That way, you can reuse filenames without worrying about overwriting your earlier work.

Figure 7.2 shows the tables, field names, and table relationships in the MS Access version of the AccountInfo project database.

**FIGURE 7.2:**

Account information database structure (MS Access)

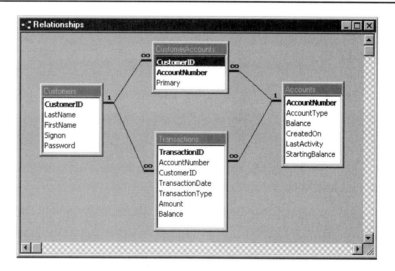

Figure 7.3 shows the field information for each table in the SQL Server version of the database. You can download the AccountInfo.sql file from the Sybex Web site to obtain the DDL commands that will create the database on SQL Server.

**FIGURE 7.3:**

Field information for the AccountInfo database (SQL Server)

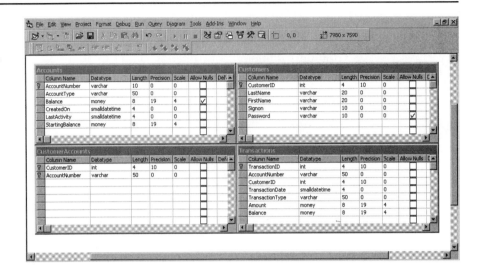

The Accounts table contains account information. The Customers table holds information about the people who own or use the accounts. Each customer and each account has a unique ID. A single customer may have multiple accounts, and each account may have one or more customers who are authorized to use the account. The CustomerAccounts table maps customers to accounts. Any activity in any account is called a *transaction*.

For this project, you can pretend that some other application logs every activity to the Transactions table. Because this is a report application, you're going to read only the information that already exists in the tables; therefore, you're going to have to populate the tables with data before the application will work. The `WebClass_Start` event in the `Reports` WebClass (see Listing 7.1) populates the Accounts, Customers, and CustomerAccounts tables if necessary. The `Start` event is a good place to put the code because it executes only the *first* time the WebClassManager creates a WebClass.

As written, the code creates 50 checking accounts and 50 customers who each own one or two accounts. If you'd prefer to type in your own sample data or change the data provided, feel free—just remember to comment out, delete, or modify the `WebClass_Start` code.

| LISTING 7.1 | Code to Populate the AccountInfo Database Tables (*AccountInfoWebClass.dsr*) |
|---|---|

```
Private Sub WebClass_Start()
  Dim anAccNum As String
  Dim i As Integer
    Dim SQL As String
    Dim cm As Command
    Dim initBalance As Long
    Dim rAccounts As Recordset
    Dim rCustomers As Recordset
  Dim firstname As String
    Dim lastname As String
    Dim accountType As String
    Dim R As Recordset
    Set cm = New Command
    Set cm.ActiveConnection = conn
    Dim aPassword As String
    Dim aSignon As String
    Dim randValue As Integer
    Dim accountOwnerCount As Integer
    ' create some accounts
    SQL = "SELECT count(*) as AccountCount FROM Accounts"
    Set R = conn.Execute(SQL, , adCmdText)
    If R("AccountCount").value < 50 Then
        For i = 1 To 50
            initBalance = Int((5000 * Rnd) + 1)
            anAccNum = getNewAccountNumber()
            randValue = getRandomInt(100, 1)
            If randValue <= 50 Then
                accountType = "Checking"
            Else
                accountType = "Savings"
            End If
            SQL = "INSERT INTO Accounts "
            SQL = SQL & "(AccountNumber, AccountType, "
            SQL = SQL & "Balance, CreatedOn, "
            SQL = SQL & "LastActivity, StartingBalance) "
            SQL = SQL & "VALUES ('" & anAccNum & "', '" _
                & accountType
            SQL = SQL & "', " & CStr(initBalance) & _
```

```
                    ", '" & _
                    Format$(Now(), "general date") & "', '" & _
                    Format$(Now(), "general date") & "', " & _
                    CStr(initBalance) & ")"
            cm.CommandText = SQL
            cm.Execute , , adCmdText
        Next
    End If
    ' create customers if needed
    SQL = "SELECT count(*) AS CustomerCount FROM Customers"
    Set R = conn.Execute(SQL, , adCmdText)
    If R("CustomerCount").value = 0 Then
        Set rAccounts = New Recordset
        SQL = "SELECT AccountNumber FROM Accounts"
        rAccounts.Open SQL, conn, adOpenStatic, _
            adLockReadOnly, adCmdText
        i = 1
        While Not rAccounts.EOF
            aSignon = "Test" & CStr(i)
            aPassword = LCase(aSignon)
            SQL = "INSERT INTO Customers "
            SQL = SQL & "(LastName, FirstName, "
            SQL = SQL & "Signon, Password) "
            SQL = SQL & "VALUES ('" & CStr(i) & "',"
            SQL = SQL & " 'Customer', '" & _
                aSignon & "', '" & aPassword & "')"
            conn.Execute SQL
            i = i + 1
            rAccounts.MoveNext
        Wend
        rAccounts.Close
    End If

    ' create some account owners, if needed
    Set R = conn.Execute("SELECT count(*) AS " & _
        "CustomerAccountsCount FROM CustomerAccounts", _
        , adCmdText)
    If R("CustomerAccountsCount").value < 50 Then
        ' get the account numbers
        Set rAccounts = New Recordset
        SQL = "SELECT AccountNumber "
        SQL = SQL & "FROM Accounts"
        rAccounts.Open, conn, adOpenStatic, _
```

```
            adLockReadOnly, adCmdText
    ' and a list of customers
    Set rCustomers = New Recordset
    SQL = "SELECT CustomerID FROM Customers"
    rCustomers.Open SQL, conn, adOpenStatic, _
        adLockReadOnly, adCmdText
    While (Not rCustomers.EOF And Not rAccounts.EOF)
        ' match a customer to an account
        SQL = "INSERT INTO CustomerAccounts "
        SQL = SQL & "(CustomerID, AccountNumber) "
        SQL =  SQL & "VALUES & "(" & _
            CStr(rCustomers!CustomerID.value) & _
            ", '" & rAccounts!AccountNumber.value _
            & "')"
        conn.Execute SQL
        ' create some transaction records
        ' for each account.
        Call createTransactionRecords _
            (rAccounts!AccountNumber.value, _
            rCustomers!CustomerID.value)
        ' some customers should have
        ' more than one account
        randValue = getRandomInt(100, 1)
        If randValue <= 50 Then
            rCustomers.MoveNext
            accountOwnerCount = 0
        Else
            ' don't move the customers recordset
            accountOwnerCount = accountOwnerCount + 1
        End If
        ' nobody gets more than two accounts
        If accountOwnerCount = 2 Then
            accountOwnerCount = 0
            rCustomers.MoveNext
        End If
        rAccounts.MoveNext
    Wend
    rCustomers.Close
    rAccounts.Close
End If
R.Close
Set R = Nothing
```

```
        Set rAccounts = Nothing
        Set rCustomers = Nothing
        ' delete any customers who don't have accounts
        SQL = "DELETE FROM Customers WHERE "
        SQL = SQL & "Customers.CustomerID NOT IN "
        SQL = SQL & "(SELECT CustomerAccounts.CustomerID "
        SQL = SQL & "FROM CustomerAccounts INNER JOIN "
        SQL = SQL & "Customers ON Customers.CustomerID = "
        SQL = SQL & "CustomerAccounts.CustomerID)"
        conn.Execute SQL
        Response.Redirect "Signon.asp"
    End Sub
```

> **NOTE** When you run this project, you can sign on by typing **test** and a number from 1 to 25. Use the same text as your password, for example, (`Signon=Test25, Password=Test25` or `Signon=test11, Password=test11`). Sign-ons and passwords are not case sensitive in this application. If the sign-on you select is not recognized, sign on with a lower number.

Most of the code to populate the database is fairly straightforward, but you will notice that it contains several subroutine calls, some of which may be useful to you in future programs. When I first wrote the code to populate the database, I created 50 customers and 50 accounts, one per customer. But that didn't seem realistic, so I added the code to loop through the Accounts table and the Customers table, randomly assigning two accounts to some users. I also needed to randomly create either savings or checking accounts. That need led to a function called `getRandomInt`. You provide the maximum and minimum values for the random integer, and the function returns an integer between those bounds. I wrote an almost identical function to get random Long values.

```
    Private Function getRandomInt _
        (upperbound As Integer, _
        lowerbound As Integer) As Integer
        getRandomInt = Int((upperbound - lowerbound + 1) _
            * Rnd + lowerbound)
    End Function
```

I had more problems with initializing a set of transactions. Transactions are deposits, withdrawals, and inquiries by a customer for a specific account. Transactions occur sequentially, by date. I didn't want the transactions to occur on regular intervals, so I needed a way to generate random dates but still have the overall sequence of dates move from the past toward the present. To add the transactions, I created a separate subroutine called `createTransactionRecords`. The `Start` event code calls this subroutine once for each account.

```
Private Sub createTransactionRecords(AccountNumber _
    As String, CustomerID As Long)
    Dim accountBalance
    Dim R As Recordset
    Dim SQL As String
    Dim tranType As String
    Dim tranDate As Date
    Dim tranAmount As Currency
    Dim curBalance As Currency
    Dim i As Integer
    Dim tranCount As Integer
    Dim maxDays As Integer
    Dim dayOffset As Integer
    Dim lastDayOffset As Integer
    Dim tmpBalance As Currency
    maxDays = 365 * 20
    ' get the current balance
    curBalance = getCurrentBalance(AccountNumber)
    ' insert a random number of transaction records
    tranCount = getRandomInt(10, 3)
    For i = 1 To tranCount
        tranType = getRandomTransactionType()
        If i = 1 Then
            dayOffset = getRandomInt(maxDays, 1000)
        Else
            dayOffset = getRandomInt(lastDayOffset - 1, 1)
        End If
        lastDayOffset = dayOffset
        tranDate = getDateOffsetBy(dayOffset)
        If tranType = "Inquiry" Then
            tranAmount = 0
        Else
            tranAmount = Cur(getRandomLong( _
                CLng(curBalance) * 100, 350) \ 100)
        End If
        tmpBalance = curBalance
        If tranType = "WithDrawal" Then
            curBalance = curBalance - tranAmount
```

```
            ElseIf tranType = "Deposit" Then
                curBalance = curBalance + tranAmount
            End If
            ' write the transaction
            SQL = "INSERT INTO Transactions "
            SQL = SQL & "(AccountNumber, CustomerID, "
            SQL = SQL & "TransactionType, TransactionDate, "
            SQL = SQL & "Amount, Balance) "
            SQL = SQL & "VALUES ('" & AccountNumber & "'," _
                & CustomerID & ", '" & tranType & "', '" _
                & tranDate & "', " & tranAmount & ", " _
                & curBalance & ")"
            conn.Execute SQL
        Next
    End Sub
```

The `createTransactionRecords` subroutine creates between 3 and 10 transactions for each account.

```
tranCount = getRandomInt(10, 3)
```

I needed a function not only to get random dates but to force them to be sequential in time. I did this by using two variables, `dayOffset` and `lastDayOffset`, to hold an integer value representing the offset, in days, from the current date. To ensure that the first value would not be too close to the current date, I forced the first date to be at least 1,000 days earlier than the current date. Subsequent dates had to be at least one day later than the first date.

```
If i = 1 Then
    dayOffset = getRandomInt(maxDays, 1000)
Else
    dayOffset = getRandomInt(lastDayOffset - 1, 1)
End If
lastDayOffset = dayOffset
tranDate = getDateOffsetBy(dayOffset)
```

Finally, to get the date itself, the `getDateOffsetBy` function calculates a date offset from today by the value of the semi-random `dateOffset` variable. The `getDateOffsetBy` function returns the formatted date.

```
Private Function getDateOffsetBy(days As Integer) As Date
    getDateOffsetBy = CDate(Format$(DateAdd("d", _
        CDbl(days) * -1, Now), "short date") & " " & _
        getRandomTime())
End Function
```

The `getDateOffsetBy` function calls a function called `getRandomTime` to get the time portion of the random date/time value:

```
Private Function getRandomTime() As String
    Dim hour As Integer
    Dim minute As Integer
    Dim second As Integer
    Dim AmPm As String
    hour = getRandomInt(24, 1)
    minute = getRandomInt(59, 0)
    second = getRandomInt(59, 0)
    If hour > 12 Then
        AmPm = "PM"
        hour = hour - 12
    ElseIf hour < 12 Then
        AmPm = "AM"
    Else
        AmPm = "PM"
    End If
    getRandomTime = Format$(hour, "00") & ":" & _
        Format$(minute, "00") & ":" & Format$ _
        (second, "00") & " " & AmPm
End Function
```

Finally, the `createTransactionRecords` function executes a SQL insert command string to insert the record into the Transactions table. The process inserts transaction records in a loop, then returns so the `WebClass_Start` code can continue matching accounts to customers.

Take another quick look at Listing 7.1. You want the routine to add records to the database only if the database is empty; therefore, each part of the routine checks the count of records in a table before it begins adding records. The account insertion loop counts account records, the customer insertion loop counts customer records, etc. If you step through the code with the debugger, you'll see that the insertion code executes only if the records are missing.

If you want to start over or change the code to populate the database, you'll need to delete the records first, so that the check condition will fail. In Access, I've created a table relationship with cascading deletes so that records in the CustomerAccounts and Transactions tables are deleted whenever you delete an associated "parent" record in either the Accounts or Customers table.

# Repurposing WebClasses

You've already written a WebClass that requires a sign-on and password in the `SecuredSite` project (see Chapter 5). Because the requirements for sign-on/password protected sites are so similar, you can reuse or *repurpose* that WebClass in this project, with minor changes. Repurposing differs from reuse; repurposing implies that you will change the code, whereas reuse implies that you can use the same code, without changes, in multiple situations.

Add the `Signon` WebClass from the `SecuredSite` project to this project. Be sure to save it in the `AccountInfo` directory. You will need to copy the `signon.htm` template manually.

> **WARNING** You should be aware that VB stores file locations in the project (.vbp) file. When you add an *existing* file, VB dutifully writes the location of the file into the project directory. If you then make changes to the file, you are changing the *original* file, not a copy. In some cases—such as a module containing well-tested, generic routines—that may be exactly what you want, but usually, you'll want to modify the code. To avoid overwriting the original file when you add an existing file, you should immediately right-click the filename, then select Save <File> As from the pop-up menu. Save the file in your current project directory.

Think back to the `SecuredSite` application. In that project, you saved sign-on and password information in a file. In this application, sign-on and password information resides in a database. Therefore, to repurpose the WebClass, you'll need to modify the code that reads and writes sign-on information. Open the code window for the `Signon` WebClass. Click the Search icon and search for the `findSignon` function.

The original `findSignon` function opened a text file and looked for a specific sign-on. If it found the sign-on, it optionally created a comma-delimited string containing the sign-on and password. You'll do two things differently with this database version. Instead of reading a file, you'll open a database connection and attempt to retrieve the record containing the sign-on entered by the user. If the record exists, the function returns `True`. Optionally, rather than returning a comma-delimited string, you'll return the record data in a Dictionary object. Replace the original `findSignon` function with this one:

```
Private Function findSignon(aSignon, Optional dRet As _
    Dictionary) As Boolean
```

```
        Dim conn As Connection
        Dim SQL As String
        Dim R As Recordset
        Dim F As Field
        On Error GoTo Err_FindSignon
        Set conn = New Connection
        conn.ConnectionString = Application("ConnectionString")
        conn.Mode = adModeRead
        conn.CursorLocation = adUseClient
        conn.Open
        SQL = "SELECT * FROM Customers WHERE Signon='" & _
            aSignon & "'"
        Set R = conn.Execute(SQL)
        If Not R.EOF Then
            findSignon = True
            If Not IsMissing(dRet) Then
                Set dRet = recordToDictionary(R)
            End If
        End If
        R.Close
        Set R = Nothing
        conn.Close
        Set conn = Nothing
Exit_FindSignon:
    Exit Function
Err_FindSignon:
    Err.Raise Err.Number, Err.Source, Err.Description
    Resume Exit_FindSignon
End Function
```

The new `findSignon` function does three things. First, it creates an ADO Connection object, sets its properties, and opens it. In this case, the connection string has already been created and stored in an `Application` variable. You'll see that code shortly:

```
Set conn = New Connection
conn.ConnectionString = Application("ConnectionString")
conn.Mode = adModeRead
conn.CursorLocation = adUseClient
conn.Open
```

The `ConnectionString` property must be set before you open the connection. I've opened the connection in read-only mode (`adModeRead`). Although you don't have to set this property to open a read-only recordset, the default value is adModeUnknown, which decreases performance. You don't have to set this property explicitly, but it improves readability. I set the CursorLocation property to adUseClient. The default CursorLocation is adUseServer, which tells SQL Server to create a server-side cursor. Server-based cursors are less network-intensive than client-side cursors, but are also less flexible.

Second, the function sets up a query. Queries sent to the database server as strings are called *dynamic SQL*. When you send a query this way, the database engine parses the string, creates an execution plan, compiles the query, and (finally) retrieves the data. It's much more efficient to create stored procedures whenever possible. On the other hand, it's sometimes harder to update stored procedures than to update dynamic SQL. I'll show you how to call a stored procedure in Chapter 10; for now, we'll live with the performance penalty. The SQL query attempts to retrieve an entire row from the Customers table where the sign-on matches the sign-on entered by the user.

```
SQL = "SELECT * FROM Customers WHERE Signon='" & _
      aSignon & "'"
```

Note that the variable aSignon is the parameter passed from the Signon_frmSignon routine. Because it's a string value, you need to surround it with single quotes.

You use the Execute method of the Connection object to execute a dynamic SQL statement. The Execute method returns a Recordset object containing the data retrieved from the database if the sign-on matched a sign-on in the Customers table.

```
Set R = conn.Execute(SQL)
```

The most convenient way to package a database row is in a Dictionary object, because it has key-value pairs—similar to the fields of a recordset. You can use the Recordset itself instead, but Recordset objects carry a great deal of overhead, and (unless you disconnect them from the Connection object) use expensive database connection resources. By transferring the data to a Dictionary, you can get in, get the data, and get out of the database as fast as possible, thus freeing the connection for another request. The new findSignon function calls a general purpose routine called recordToDictionary that moves a row of data from a Recordset to a Dictionary object:

```
Private Function recordToDictionary(R As Recordset) _
    As Dictionary
    Dim d As Dictionary
```

```
            Dim F As Field
            Set d = New Dictionary
            d.CompareMode = TextCompare
            If R.State = adStateOpen And Not R.EOF And _
                Not R.BOF Then
                For Each F In R.Fields
                    If (F.Attributes And adFldLong) = _
                        adFldLong Then
                        If Not IsNull(F.value) Then
                            d.Add F.Name, F.GetChunk(F.ActualSize)
                        Else
                            d.Add F.Name, vbNullString
                        End If
                    Else
                        If Not IsNull(F.value) Then
                            d.Add F.Name, F.value
                        Else
                            d.Add F.Name, vbNullString
                        End If
                    End If
                Next
            End If
            Set recordToDictionary = d
        End Function
```

The function loops through each field in the recordset. It tests explicitly for fields that contain text (Memo in Microsoft Access) or image (OLE Object in Microsoft Access) data, because you retrieve data from those field types using the `GetChunk` method rather than the `Value` method. It also tests for null field values and substitutes null strings instead.

When the `findSignon` function returns, the original `Signon_frmSignon` code expects an array. You'll need to change a few lines. In the original code, replace the lines that dimension the array and retrieve the password from the array with this code:

**ORIGINAL CODE**

```
        Dim arrSignonInfo as variant
        arrSignonInfo = Split(arrSignonInfo, ",")
        If StrComp(aPassword, arrSignonInfo(1), vbTextCompare) _
            = 0 Then
```

**NEW CODE**

```
Dim dSignonInfo as Dictionary
If StrComp(aPassword, dSignonInfo("Password"),
    vbTextCompare) = 0 Then
```

It's convenient and considerably more readable to retrieve the password by name than by position. Code dependent on position makes me nervous because the position of data within resources tends to change over time. For instance, I see a great deal of code in which people use index numbers instead of field names to access field values in recordsets—for example, `rs(0)` rather than `rs("UserID")`. True, using the index numbers is marginally faster, but that should be an optimization of last resort; the loss in readability outweighs the performance gain in all but the most demanding circumstances. If you control both the code and the database, and you're absolutely sure that you'll never add a column to the database and that you'll never change the order in which a SQL statement or stored procedure returns the data, it's probably OK to write code based on the position of a resource. I just feel sorry for the poor programmer who inherits the code.

# Using Multiple WebClasses in an Application

After you have completed the code changes to the `Signon` WebClass, you should be able to sign on. You'll need to change what happens for a successful sign-on. In this case, you want execution to continue, but in a different WebClass. You can't use the `NextItem` property of the `Signon` WebClass, for example, `Set NextItem= Reports`, because the `Signon` WebClass doesn't know anything about the `Reports` WebClass.

Remember, the server instantiates WebClasses via a `Server.CreateObject` request from an ASP page, so to activate any particular WebClass, you need to execute the ASP page associated with that WebClass. Change the code in `Signon_frmSignon` as follows.

## ORIGINAL CODE

```
With Response
    .Write "You are signed on." & "<BR>"
    .Write "Signon=" & aSignon & "<BR>"
    .Write "Password=" & aPassword & "<BR>"
    .Write "Click <a href='" & URLFor(TestSecurity) _
        & "'>Test Security</a> to "
    .Write "go to the secured page."
End With
```

## NEW CODE

```
With Response
    .Redirect "Reports.asp?WCI=SelectAccount"
```

As with any redirection, you lose some efficiency because the browser needs *two* round trips to the server to retrieve a page. The browser sends a request, the server responds with a redirect header, then the browser sends a second request to the new URL. Only then will the server respond with the page. You should keep that process in mind. It's not a problem unless you start redirecting between WebClasses often.

If you haven't tried it already, run the program. Try to sign on. If you can sign on properly, you'll get an error when the `Reports` WebClass receives the `SelectAccount` request, because it doesn't exist yet. When everything seems to be working, create a new HTML template file and name it **SelectAccount.htm**.

> **TIP**
> Remember to create a `Templates` subdirectory of the `AccountInfo` directory. Save the original copies of any HTML template files there to keep VB from renaming them with numeric extensions as you import them into your WebClasses.

Listing 7.2 contains the HTML code for the `SelectAccount` HTML template.

**LISTING 7.2** **Code for the *SelectAccount* HTML Template**

```html
<html><head><title>Select Account</title></head>
<body>
```

```
<center>
<h2>
Accounts List For: <WCACCOUNTHOLDER></WCACCOUNTHOLDER>
</h2>
</center>
<table align="center" width="90%" border="1" cols=2>
   <tr>
      <td colspan="2" align="middle"
      bgColor="lightblue"><b><font
      size=5>Directions</font></b>
      </td>
   </tr>
   <tr>
      <td colspan="2" align="left">
         Click on an account to view the account options
      </td>
   </tr>
</table>
<table align="center" width="90%" border="1">
   <tr>
      <td colspan="2" align="middle"
         background=""><b>Accounts</b>
      </td>
   </tr>
   <WCACCOUNT></WCACCOUNT>
</table>
</body>
</html>
```

The two replaceable markers hold the positions for the customer name and the list of accounts belonging to that customer. You'll replace the <WCACCOUNT></WCACCOUNT> marker with table rows containing anchor tags that display the account type and number. Each anchor is a link to an AccountOptions options page that displays a list of actions a customer can take—in this case, inquire about the account balance or view the account history. The `SelectAccount_ProcessTag` event code handles the replacements:

```
Private Sub SelectAccount_ProcessTag _
    (ByVal TagName As String, TagContents As String, _
    SendTags As Boolean)
    Dim R As Recordset
    Dim i As Integer
```

```
        Select Case LCase(TagName)
        Case "wcaccountholder"
            TagContents = Session("FirstName") & " " _
                & Session("LastName")
        Case "wcaccount"
            ' show the list of accounts for the signed-on user
            ' create a table row for each account
            If getAccountList(R, _
                CLng(Session("CustomerID"))) Then
                While Not R.EOF
                    URLData = R!AccountNumber.value
                    TagContents = TagContents & _
                        "<tr><td><a href=" _
                        & Chr$(34) & _
                        URLFor("AccountOptions") _
                        & Chr$(34) & ">" _
                        & R!accountType & " (" & _
                        R!AccountNumber & ")</a>" _
                        & "</td></tr>"
                    R.MoveNext
                Wend
                R.Close
            End If
        End Select
End Sub
```

You should notice several things in this code. Replacing the <WCACCOUNT­HOLDER> tag is straightforward, but replacing the <WCACCOUNT> tag with the list of accounts is not. Because it seemed likely that I might want to get the list of accounts in other places in the program, and because retrieving the list requires database access, I wrote a separate subroutine. The getAccountList subroutine takes a Recordset parameter and a CustomerID. The subroutine sets the Recordset parameter to a list of accounts by looking in the CustomerAccounts table to find which account numbers are associated with that CustomerID, then selecting those rows from the Accounts table.

```
Private Sub getAccountList(R As Recordset, _
    aCustomerID As Long) As Boolean
    Dim SQL As String
    Dim methodName As String
    methodName = "getAccountList"
    On Error GoTo Err_GetAccountList
    SQL = "SELECT * FROM Accounts "
```

```
        SQL = SQL & "INNER JOIN CustomerAccounts ON "
        SQL = SQL & "Accounts.AccountNumber = "
        SQL = SQL & "CustomerAccounts.AccountNumber "
        SQL = SQL & "WHERE CustomerAccounts.CustomerID = " _
            & aCustomerID
        SQL = SQL & " ORDER BY AccountType"
        Set R = conn.Execute(SQL)
        getAccountList = True
Exit_GetAccountList:
        Exit Function
Err_GetAccountList:
        Err.Raise Err.Number, Err.Source & ", " & _
        methodName, Err.Description & vbCrLf & _
        "Error retrieving account information " _
        & " for CustomerID '" & aCustomerID & "'."
        Resume Exit_GetAccountList
End Sub
```

The most important thing to notice in the `SelectAccount_ProcessTag` event code is that for each account, the program sets a WebClass property called URL-Data. The `URLData` property accepts a string, which the WebClass subsequently appends to all URLs generated by the `URLFor` method. When used in this way, `URLData` is equivalent to QueryString data on an ASP page. When a user clicks on an anchor tag created by `URLFor`, the browser navigates to the URL, and also returns the `URLData` that the WebClass appended to the `href` parameter in the anchor tag.

Here's how it works:

1. You set the `URLData` property to a string, `"XXX"` for example.

2. You use the `URLFor` method to create a URL for an item or method in your WebClass.

3. The WebClass appends the string `"&WCU=XXX"` to the URL.

4. The browser returns XXX to the WebClass when the user clicks the anchor tag containing the URL.

5. You can retrieve the value by checking the `URLData` property.

Although this is by no means the only way to pass data from page to page, it is convenient, partly because it saves you from having to format the URL in code.

You'll see more about passing information from page to page in Chapter 8, "Maintaining State in IIS Applications."

One other convenient side effect of using the `URLData` property rather than hand-formatting QueryString data is that the WebClass will append the `URLData` to every link that it finds in an HTML template when you call the `WriteTemplate` method that contains a `WCU` parameter. In other words, you neither have to know the data that you want to send in advance nor add it in the `ProcessTag` event for that template; the WebClass will do that for you. All you need to do is make sure that each URL for which you want to return the `URLData` ends with either ?WCU= or &WCU= (the equals sign is optional).

In this application, the `URLData` parameter serves to maintain a property page sequence. It ensures that the user must select an account before getting a report, because you can check the `URLData` property in the report pages and redirect to the `AccountOptions` WebItem if the property is blank. Here's the relevant code:

```
' check for out-of-sequence inquiry
If Len(URLData) = 0 Then
    Response.Redirect URLFor(AccountOptions)
End If
```

The report pages are custom WebItems. Both of them check to ensure that the user has selected an account before displaying the information.

An unfortunate side effect of using `URLData` to pass information from page to page is that the value is visible in the browser's address bar. For example, you would see a URL similar to this after selecting an account: http://localhost/AccountInfo/Reports.asp?WCI=AccountOptions&WCU=451-586-67. Therefore, you can't use `URLData` to pass sensitive information unless you encrypt the information. In this case, you're passing an unencrypted bank account number—something you might not want to do in a real application.

To guard against the possibility of a person requesting information about an account that they do not own, the application also performs a database lookup in the `Respond` event for each report. If the user identified by the sign-on and password does not own the requested account, the report code returns a message stating that the user is not authorized to view the account.

Figure 7.4 shows the SelectAccount page for a typical customer.

Each of the links constructed in the `SelectAccount` WebItem points to the `AccountOptions` WebItem. As soon as the user selects an account, the WebClass fires the AccountOptions_Respond event. At that point, you can retrieve the value of the URLData property to find out which account the user selected.

**FIGURE 7.4:**

SelectAccount page

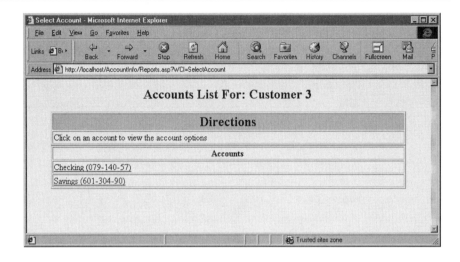

```
Private Sub AccountOptions_Respond()
    On Error GoTo Err_AccountOptions_Respond
    methodName = "AccountOptions_Respond"
    Session("CurrentAccount") = URLData
    Dim R As Recordset
    Set R = conn.Execute("SELECT * FROM Accounts " & _
        "WHERE AccountNumber='" & URLData & _
        "'", , adCmdText)
    Session("AccountNumber") = R!AccountNumber
    Session("AccountType") = R!accountType
    Session("Balance") = Format$(R!Balance, "currency")
    Session("CreatedOn") = R!CreatedOn
    Session("LastActivity") = R!LastActivity
    R.Close
    AccountOptions.WriteTemplate
Exit_AccountOptions_Respond:
    Exit Sub
Err_AccountOptions_Respond:
    Err.Raise Err.Number, Err.Source & methodName, Err.Description
    Resume Exit_AccountOptions_Respond
End Sub
```

The `AccountOptions_Respond` event performs a database lookup on the requested account number and caches the account information in Session variables. You'll use those Session values to display specific information about the selected account on the report pages. After caching the account information, the `AccountOptions.WriteTemplate` command causes the WebClass to process the `AccountOptions` template. Figure 7.5 shows the Account Options page for a typical customer.

**FIGURE 7.5:**
Account Options page

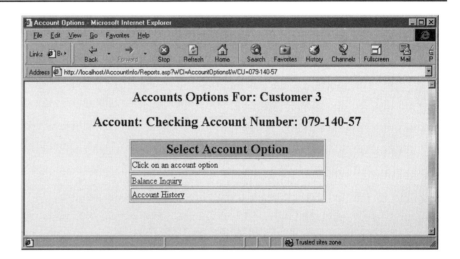

The reports themselves are relatively straightforward. At this point, you've set up a sequence of three conditions that the request must pass before the WebClass will display either the Balance Inquiry or the Account History report:

1. The user must have signed on with a valid sign-on and password.
2. The user must have selected an account.
3. The request must be for one of the accounts owned by the user.

If all the conditions have been met, the browser displays the requested report for the account number contained in the `URLData` property. Looked at another way, in pseudocode, the tests look like this:

```
If (the user is not signed on) Then
   Redirect to the signon page
End If
```

```
If (the user has not selected an account) Then
    Redirect to the account selection page
End If
If (the account requested does not belong to the user) Then
    Display an "unauthorized" message
End If
```

The first check is in the `BeginRequest` event for the WebClass, because users should not be able to reach *any* item in the `Reports` WebClass until they have signed on successfully. The other two checks are within the `Respond` events for the `BalanceInquiry` and `AccountHistory`. I chose to create the reports as custom WebItems, but there's no reason why they couldn't be HTML templates just as easily. Here's the code for the `BalanceInquiry_Respond` event:

```
Private Sub BalanceInquiry_Respond()
    On Error GoTo Err_BalanceInquiry_Respond
    methodName = "BalanceInquiry_Respond"
    Dim V As Variant
    Dim authorized As Boolean
    ' check for out-of-sequence inquiry
    If Len(URLData) = 0 Then
        Response.Redirect URLFor(AccountOptions)
    End If
    ' check for unauthorized inquiry
    For Each V In Session("AccountList")
        If V = URLData Then
            authorized = True
            Exit For
        End If
    Next
    If Not authorized Then
        Response.Write "You are not authorized " & _
            "to view this account."
        Exit Sub
    End If
    With Response
        .Write "<html><head><title>Balance " & _
            "Inquiry Report</title></head><body>"
        .Write "<table align='center' " & _
            "width='70%' border='1'>"
        .Write "<tr><td align='center' "& _
            "bgcolor='#80FFFF'><b>Account Balance " & _
            "</b></td></tr>"
```

```
            .Write "<tr><td align='left'>Current Balance " & _
                "for Account " & URLData & " is " & _
                Session("Balance")
            .Write "</td></tr>"
            .Write "</table></body></html>"
        End With
        ' add an Inquiry record
        Dim SQL
        SQL = "INSERT INTO Transactions (AccountNumber, " & _
            "CustomerID, TransactionDate, " & _
            "TransactionType, Amount, Balance) "
        SQL = SQL & "VALUES('" & _
          Session("AccountNumber") & "', "
        SQL = SQL & Session("CustomerID") & ", '" & _
            CStr(Now) & "','Inquiry', 0, " & _
            CDbl(Session("Balance")) & ")"
    conn.Execute SQL
Exit_BalanceInquiry_Respond:
    Exit Sub
Err_BalanceInquiry_Respond:
    Err.Raise Err.Number, Err.Source & _
        methodName, Err.Description
    Resume Exit_BalanceInquiry_Respond
End Sub
```

Just to keep things realistic, querying the account balance writes a transaction inquiry record. The AccountHistory WebItem doesn't add a transaction record, it just writes all the applicable rows from the Transactions table to the browser, in reverse date order:

```
Private Sub AccountHistory_Respond()
    On Error GoTo Err_AccountHistory_Respond
    methodName = "AccountHistory_Respond"
    Dim R As Recordset
    Dim F As Field
    Dim dAccount As Dictionary
    Dim d As Dictionary
    Dim V As Variant
    Dim s As String
    Dim authorized As Boolean
    ' check for out-of-sequence inquiry
    If Len(URLData) = 0 Then
        Response.Redirect URLFor(AccountOptions)
```

```
        End If
        ' check for unauthorized inquiry
        For Each V In Session("AccountList")
            If V = URLData Then
                authorized = True
                Exit For
            End If
        Next
        If Not authorized Then
            Response.Write "You are not authorized to " & _
                "view this account."
            Exit Sub
        End If
        Set R = conn.Execute("SELECT * FROM Accounts WHERE " _
            & "AccountNumber='" & URLData & "'", , adCmdText)
        If Not isEmptyRecordset(R) Then
            Set dAccount = recordToDictionary(R)
        Else
            Response.Write "Invalid Account Number. Click " & _
                " the Back button on your browser to continue."
            Response.End
        End If
        Set R = conn.Execute("SELECT * FROM Transactions " & _
            "WHERE AccountNumber='" & URLData & "' ORDER " & _
            "BY TransactionDate DESC", , adCmdText)
        With Response
            .Write "<html><head><title>Account History " & _
                "</title></head>"
            .Write "<body><center>"
            .Write "<table width='90%' align='center' " & _
                "border='1'>"
            .Write "<tr><td align='center' bgcolor=" & _
                "'#80FFFF'><font size='5'><b>Account " & _
                "History</b></font><br>Account: " & _
                dAccount("AccountType") & "  " & _
                dAccount("AccountNumber") & "</td></tr>"
            .Write "<tr><td align='left'>This report " & _
                "shows your entire account history, " & _
                "beginning with the most recent " & _
                "transactions.</td></tr>"
            .Write "</table>"
            ' display a table
```

```
                s = RecordsetToTable(R, "90%", "center", 1, _
                    True,TransactionID,TransactionDate, _
                    TransactionType,Amount,Balance")
                s = Left$(s, Len(s) - Len("</table>"))
                s = s & "<tr><td colspan='5' align='right'>" & _
                    "Starting Balance: " & "  " & _
                    Format$(dAccount("StartingBalance"), _
                    "Currency") & "</td></tr>"
                s = s & "</table>"
                .Write s
                R.Close
                Set R = Nothing
                Set d = Nothing
                .Write "</body></html>"
            End With
    Exit_AccountHistory_Respond:
            Exit Sub
    Err_AccountHistory_Respond:
            Err.Raise Err.Number, Err.Source & _
                methodName, Err.Description
            Resume Exit_AccountHistory_Respond
    End Sub
```

When you run the program, the reports look similar to Figures 7.6 and 7.7.

**FIGURE 7.6:**

Balance Inquiry Report page

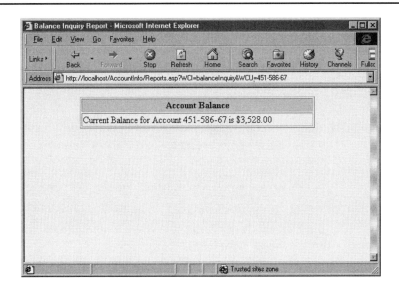

**FIGURE 7.7:**

Account History Report page

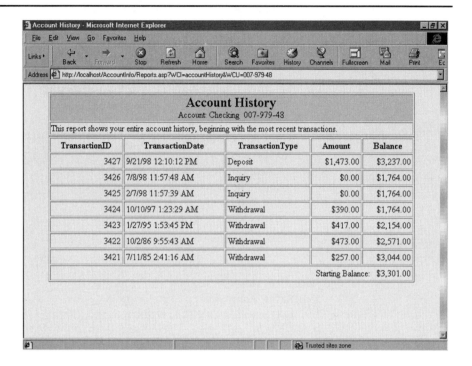

Despite the convenience of URLData, it isn't a complete replacement for QueryString-formatted data, and it doesn't stop you from using QueryString data if you desire—even in conjunction with the URLFor method. It's perfectly acceptable to write code like this:

```
Response.Write <a href='" & URLFor("AccountOptions") & _
    "&AccountNumber=" & AccountNumber & "'>" & _
    AccountNumber & "</a>"
```

If you were to look at the result of that code by selecting View Source in the browser, the href parameter of the anchor tag would look something like the following:

```
'Reports.asp?WCI=AccountOptions&AccountNumber=110-67-4459'
```

Back on the server, you can retrieve all the QueryString parameters by using the Request.QueryString collection. Note that you can retrieve the URLData using WCU as the variable name, for example:

```
myVar=Request.QueryString("WCU")
```

After you've run the program and seen how it works, remember that there are several ways that users can get to a URL. Try saving one of the pages as a favorite. Then, close your browser, open a new instance of the browser, and try navigating to the favorite. What happens? The program should re-route you to the Signon page. You should also check to see what happens if you sign on as one person, but try to change the URL in the address bar to look at another person's account. You should get an unauthorized message, similar to Figure 7.8.

**FIGURE 7.8**

Unauthorized account access message

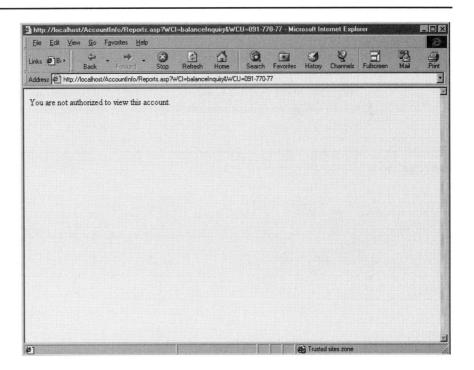

Using the URLData value and some authorization checks, you've controlled the flow in this program. Users cannot reach a report page without moving through the Signon, Account Selection, and Account Options pages. But what if you had a program, like a linear story, in which you wanted people to be able to move only one page at a time, either forward or backward. In other words, if you had 10 pages, a user should always start at page 1, then see page 2. From page 2, the user could either back up to page 1, or move forward to page 2, but could not access page 3.

To create such a program, write the program rules first, then implement them in code. The rules are as follows:

- All users must start on the first page.
- From the first page, users may quit or go to the next page.
- From the last page, users may quit or go to the previous page.
- For all other pages, users may move only to the next or the previous page, or quit.

You can visualize this programmatically as if the user's position were a pointer into an array. The array items are the pages. When the user first begins the program, the array pointer is empty; therefore you redirect to the first page, regardless of which page was requested. Figure 7.9 shows all the possible valid requests for the program.

**FIGURE 7.9**

Valid request diagram

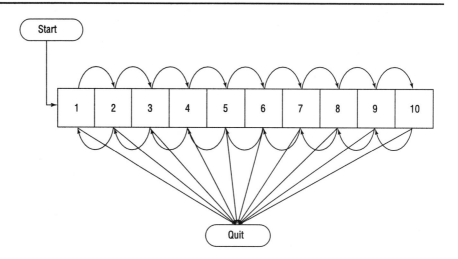

You store the current page in a Session variable, in a cookie, in a URLData or QueryString variable, or in a hidden form field. Each time the user requests a page, you:

1. Find the user's current position in the array, as stored in your variable.
2. Find the position of the requested item in the array.

3. If the two items are not contiguous—that is, if they're not next to one another, and the request is not a `Quit` request, you deny the request.

Exactly what happens when you deny a request is up to you and depends on the requirements of the program. The most likely scenario is that you simply ignore the request and redisplay the current page, but you might decide to display an invalid page message. Alternately, you could determine the direction from the relative positions of the user's current position and the request and move one page in the requested direction.

In this chapter, you've seen how to repurpose WebClasses, use more than one WebClass in an application by redirecting between WebClasses, and find and control the user's progress through your application. In the next chapter, you'll extend and generalize these concepts to maintain a user's state in your application.

# CHAPTER EIGHT

# Maintaining State in IIS Applications

- Selecting a State Maintenance Option
- Exploring the State Maintenance Options
- Caching Information
- Summing Up State Maintenance

**M**aintaining state means keeping track of all the information your application needs to know about a specific user, either during a single session or between multiple sessions. Examples of the kinds of information you may need to know are:

- What is the user's name?
- Has the user signed on?
- Has the user seen the previous page?
- Has the user properly filled out a form at some previous stage?
- Is the user waiting for a response from the application?

Longer term, you might want to be able to answer more complex questions, such as:

- Has this user purchased any other product like <*this*> from us during the past year?
- Which pages in the application has this user *never* seen? How might you best route them there?

In essence, maintaining state is the process of *associating* information with a specific user. This is the biggest single problem you're likely to have with your Web applications, and how you solve it depends, or should depend, on several factors:

- The number of users you expect to access your application simultaneously
- The size and speed of your server
- The efficiency of your pages
- The amount of information you need to store to maintain state for a single user

In this chapter, I'll show you several options for maintaining state in WebClass applications and discuss the advantages and disadvantages of each.

# Selecting a State Maintenance Option

WebClasses have two options for maintaining state. You select which option you want to use by setting the `StateMaintenance` property of the WebClass. The

`StateMaintenance` property takes one of two values, called (not very intuitively) `wcRetainInstance` and `wcNoState`.

The `wcRetainInstance` setting is seductive; when you select it, you can maintain state by setting properties and variable values within your WebClass—just like a standard stand-alone VB program. The `wcRetainInstance` setting tells the WebClassManager object not to destroy your WebClass instance between requests. Therefore, the WebClass maintains values you set until it times out or you explicitly destroy it by calling the `ReleaseInstance` method. The `wcNoState` option doesn't mean you won't maintain state, it just means that you can't maintain state in WebClass variables—you'll have to use one of the other methods explained in this chapter.

You should *never* use the `wcRetainInstance` option unless your site has a small number of simultaneous users. When you select this option, IIS (or the WebClassManager) stores your entire WebClass in a Session variable between requests. That means that IIS must handle all that user's subsequent requests to the WebClass on the same execution thread as the first request. IIS serializes multiple requests that require the same thread, which means that as your user population grows, the chances rapidly increase that people will have to wait while IIS services a prior request that is using the same thread. If you require any degree of scalability, don't use the `wcRetainInstance` method.

When you select the `wcNoState` method, you avoid the thread problem and you still have five ways to maintain state in your application. Each has advantages and disadvantages. You can maintain state by using:

- Session variables
- Cookies
- QueryString variables
- Hidden form variables
- Database tables or files

I'll discuss all these options and show you when each might be appropriate. For each method, I'll use this example: You have a database table containing demographic information about registered users—UserIDs, sign-ons, names, etc. When a user signs on, you use the sign-on value that the user entered to look up the user's information in the database.

Now assume your application needs access to the user's demographic data for each page in the application. The question is, how do you store and retrieve the information? The only information you always know about a user is their SessionID, because the ASP engine stores the `SessionID` cookie on the browser when the session begins. To be able to retrieve the user's information, you need to somehow make—and keep—an association between the user's SessionID and the information related to that user.

## Maintaining State with Session Variables

Using Session variables is the easiest method for maintaining state. You can store any VB data type in a Session variable. You'll recall that the Session object is an associative array much like a Scripting Dictionary object. A Session can hold a practically unlimited number of name-value pairs. Each Session variable name must be unique. The value associated with that name is a Variant; therefore, you can store primitive data types, such as strings or numeric values, and COM objects, such as Dictionary or custom ActiveX objects.

So, you can store the UserID in a Session variable. Now, whenever the user makes a request, you can use the value of the `Session("UserID")` variable to look up the user's information in the database:

```
Set R = conn.execute("SELECT * FROM Users " & _
    "WHERE UserID=" & Session("UserID"), , _
    adCmdText)
```

But wait! Retrieving database data is an expensive operation in terms of time and server resources. You may not want to perform a database lookup for each user request. You retrieved the data once during the sign-on request—you could store the entire row in Session variables during the sign-on operation. That way, you wouldn't need to go back to the database for each subsequent request. Instead, you can create a Session variable for each field in the table row for that user, for example:

```
Session("UserID") = rs("UserID")
Session("UserSignon") = rs("UserSignon")
Session("UserLastName") = rs("UserLastName")
Session("UserFirstName") = rs("UserFirstName")
Session("UserEMail") = rs("UserEmail")
' etc…
```

Now you have access to the user data from anywhere in the application without returning to the database. In essence, you've *cached* the demographic data for this user in the Session object.

This is absolutely the easiest way to cache data for an individual user of your application, and probably the one you'll use most often. There are only a couple of problems with it (you knew this was coming, didn't you?). Think about what the ASP engine must be doing while it retrieves the variable values for each user. Imagine that the Session object is a Dictionary; each key is a SessionID and each value is itself a Dictionary. The keys of this sub-dictionary are the names you give your Session variables, and the values are your Session variable values (see Figure 8.1). I don't know exactly how the Session object stores data, but it must be with a method similar to this.

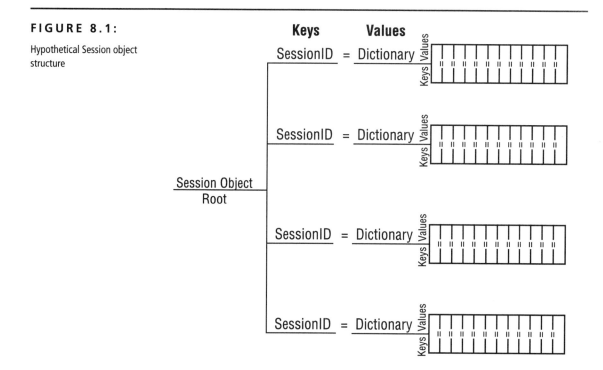

**FIGURE 8.1:**
Hypothetical Session object structure

The point is that using Session variables at all forces the server to access a single object for each request. Therefore, the use of Session variables must force the server to serialize requests, at least during retrieval of the sub-dictionary that contains the Session variables associated with that user's SessionID.

## WebClasses Require Sessions

Why use Sessions at all? You can disable them, either for your entire server, or for a specific site, by using the IIS administration program. Unfortunately, if you disable Sessions, the WebClassManager will be unable to create the WebClass object, and your WebClass will fail to initialize. You *must* leave Sessions enabled for sites that use WebClasses (Sessions are enabled by default when you create an IIS application).

Sessions can be enabled or disabled at either the Web level or the virtual directory level, so you'll need to make sure they're enabled at both levels. To enable Sessions, start the IIS administration program. The check box to enable or disable Sessions is in the Application Configuration dialog box. Right-click the Default Web Site entry in the left-hand pane, select Properties, then click the Home Directory tab. Click the Configuration button, then click the App Options tab (see Figure 8.2). Make sure the Enable Session State check box is checked and then repeat the process to enable Sessions for each virtual directory that uses WebClasses.

**FIGURE 8.2:**

IIS Application Configuration dialog

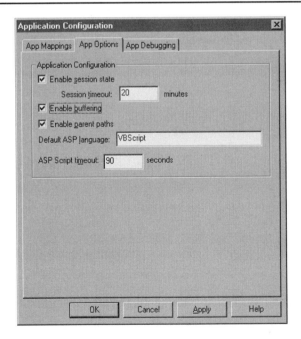

Sessions are a mixed blessing, but they're something you'll have to live with if you want to use WebClasses because WebClasses don't work if you turn off Sessions.

Microsoft recommends that you should use another method besides Sessions to maintain state if you want to build Web sites that will scale to large numbers of users. Why they've made Sessions a requirement for WebClasses is a mystery. You can use ASP without Sessions, but not WebClasses. Maybe in the next version…

Consider a site where you want to use more than one server to service requests. If you use Session variables, you need some method to route requests from one browser to the same server for each request. If you don't have such a method (and the ASP engine doesn't currently provide one), the Session information either won't be available or will be different on each server.

Commercial routers are available that let you use Sessions on sites with multiple servers; you should consider one of these if you build a site with heavy use. For smaller sites, it's relatively easy to write your own multi-server router. Suppose you have a single, publicly available address for your site—for example, http://www.mySite.com. You have four servers, only one of which has a public IP address corresponding to the mySite.com IP address. The other three servers' IP addresses are not mapped to the mySite.com address. Together, all four servers constitute a *Web farm*. The public server receives all initial requests for your site.

The first time a new request arrives, the public server uses a script to route the request to one of the three Web farm servers. That server then provides a SessionID. Subsequent requests by the same browser bypass the public server and go directly to the Web farm server. The script ensures that each server gets an equal number of requests. You do need to use relative paths to ensure that graphics and other resources are available on all the servers. Because you need to balance the load, you may want to ensure that people can't bookmark pages on a specific server by redirecting any users without SessionIDs (new sessions) back to the public server for routing.

Load balancing is beyond the scope of this book, but you could easily write a simple round-robin scheme. Depending on your setup and your application requirements, that may be sufficient, but typically, you'll want to at least poll the servers to find out if they're running, which one currently has the smallest load, etc. You will probably need fail-over protection and may even want to bring additional servers online as needed.

Finally, although it may not always be an issue, you need to be aware of the memory requirements when you use Session variables. Storing a few small strings and numbers for each user won't use much memory, but storing entire recordsets—even as arrays—will use up large amounts of memory in a hurry. If the server runs out of RAM memory, it will begin spooling the data out to virtual memory—and that will definitely adversely affect your application's response time and scalability.

## Maintaining State with Cookies

You don't have to use Session variables at all (but you do have to have Sessions enabled). Instead, you can use the same method that the ASP engine uses to identify users —cookies. Remember that a cookie provides a way to store information on the client. The browser associates the cookie with a given site and sends the cookie information along with each request.

From the ASP server-side scripting point of view, a cookie is a collection of keyed values—much like a Dictionary object. You use the Request object to retrieve cookie values and the Response object to create or alter them. Therefore, in the example, you would store the UserID in a cookie after you have authenticated the user during sign-on:

```
Response.Cookies("UserID") = rs("UserID").Value
```

To retrieve the value in subsequent requests, use:

```
aUserID = Request.Cookies("UserID")
```

Even better, a cookie can have multiple keyed values, called subkeys. You can group the user information in a single cookie:

```
Response.Cookies("User")("UserID") = rs("UserID").Value
Response.Cookies("User")("Signon") = rs("UserSignon")
Response.Cookies("User")("LastName") = rs("UserLastName")
Response.Cookies("User")("FirstName") = rs("UserFirstName")
Response.Cookies("User")("UserEMail") = rs("UserEmail")
' etc.
```

To retrieve a subkey value from a cookie, use this syntax:

```
aUserID = Request.Cookies("User")("UserID")
```

If you're not sure whether a cookie has subkeys, you can check by using the **HasKeys** property. The **HasKeys** property returns **True** when the cookie contains subkeys:

```
If Request.Cookies("myCookie").HasKeys then
    ' do something
End If
```

After the server receives a request, it parses the cookies into some kind of collection object, which understands the For...Next syntax. To process all the cookies in a request, you can use a loop like this:

```
With Request
    For Each aKey in .Cookies
        If .cookies(aKey).HasKeys Then
            For Each subKey in .Cookies(aKey)
            Response.Write subKey & "=" _
                    & .cookies(aKey)(subkey) & "<BR>"
            Next
        End If
    Next
End With
```

If you don't need to store much information between requests, cookies are an excellent way to maintain state because they don't take up any memory on the server. You can even write "permanent" cookies that store data on the client's hard drive. Permanent cookies, also called persistent cookies, make it possible to store state even *between* sessions.

To make a cookie permanent, use the Expires property. When you set the Expires property to a date *later* than the current date, the browser will store the cookie on the user's hard drive. For example, to create a cookie that expires in one week:

```
Dim nextWeek As Date
NextWeek = dateAdd("d", 7, now())
Response.Cookies("User").Expires = NextWeek
```

Unfortunately, the maximum size of cookies differs somewhat from browser to browser. To be safe, you shouldn't count on more than 4,096 bytes (4K) of data. In addition, although cookies don't take up server space, they *do* take up bandwidth. This may not be an issue if you're storing only a few values, but suppose you have 100 clients sending 4K of data for each request, each requesting four pages per minute. If you change the cookie slightly at each request to maintain state, you're sending over 1.5MB of information per minute over the network. With 1,000 clients, that increases to 15MB per minute—and that doesn't even take any other data into account, such as the content of the pages themselves. That may not bring your network to its knees, but remember that your application may not be the only one on the network, or even on the Web server. Also, because cookies are sent as strings, the Web server must parse the strings into the Request.Cookies collection, and that also consumes resources.

By default, the browser sends all cookies set by an application back to that application. If your application has more than one directory, you can specify which cookies the browser should send to each directory in your application by adding a path to the cookie. The browser compares the path of the request to each cookie and sends the cookie only if it matches the path. To add the path, use the `Path` property:

```
Response.Cookies("myCookie").Path = "/myPath"
Response.Cookies("myCookie") = "someCookie"
```

In the preceding example, the browser would send the `myCookie` cookie only to requests for pages in the `/myPath` virtual directory.

For cookies that have an expiration date, you can set the domain as well as the path. This lets you create a cookie in one application that the browser will send to a different application in another domain.

In the background, transparent to developers, the Response object writes an HTTP header to tell the browser to save the cookie. You can use the Response object's `AddHeader` method to bypass the automatic cookie-management and cookie-storage functions. To add a cookie, use this syntax:

```
Response.AddHeader "Set-Cookie", "<name>=<value> " _
    & [; <name>=<value>]...[; expires=<date>][; " _
    & domain=<domain_name>][; path=<some_path>][; secure]
```

Here's an example:

```
Response.AddHeader "Set-Cookie", "myCookie=someCookie"
```

The result is the same as if you had used the Cookies collection—the browser stores the cookie.

The browser stores cookies in a `Cookies` subdirectory of your `Profile` directory. On Windows NT, your profile is in the `Profiles` subdirectory of the `$systemRoot$` path—usually called `WinNT`. On Windows 95/98, your profile is in a single subdirectory of the `$systemRoot$` path—usually called `Windows`. When you add a cookie using the Response.Cookies collection, you can set the `Expires` parameter using any valid date format. When you use the HTTP method, you need to specify the date in the format `ddd, dd-mmm-yyy hh:mm:ss GMT`.

Use the VB `Format` command to format the date properly:

```
Dim GMTDate as string
GMTDate = Format$(Now, "ddd, dd-mmm-yyyy hh:nn:ss") _
    & " GMT"
```

You can look in the appropriate `Cookies` directory to check that your application sent the cookie in the correct format. If it did, the browser will create a file like `username@domain.txt` that stores the cookie information.

The browser stores and transmits cookies as text files, so you need to encrypt the cookie if the information is sensitive, such as sign-on and password information. You can manually encrypt the information or tell the browser to automatically encrypt the data. Cookies have a `Secure` attribute that tells the browser to store the cookies in encrypted form and send them only to sites that use Secure Sockets Layer (SSL) encryption.

## Maintaining State with QueryString Variables

Not all browsers accept cookies. There's been a great deal of press coverage (mostly negative) about how unscrupulous Web operators are stealing your privacy by storing unwanted information on your computer. Therefore, some of the more paranoid individuals have improved their privacy by turning off cookies. For clients that won't accept cookies, you can't store anything in the Session object because the ASP engine won't find the `Session.SessionID` cookie and will try to create a new one for each request. In this case, of course, you can't use cookies to maintain state either. Instead, you can pass information through the QueryString collection.

Remember that the data contained in the QueryString collection is actually a delimited text string appended to the URL. On the server, you receive the data in the Request object as the Request.QueryString collection. As is typical with Web communications, the raw data is in `key=value` form just as it is in cookies, form variables, etc. Ampersands separate the key-value pairs. A question mark separates the entire query string from the URL. The following URL example contains two QueryString values, `LastName` and `FirstName`.

```
http://myServer/mySite.com?LastName=Doe&FirstName=John
```

Most browsers support up to about 1,024 characters in QueryString data. The server parses the QueryString data into a collection, so you can retrieve it using keys or indexes (1 based, not 0 based). The QueryString collection supports standard `For Each...Next` syntax. Using the QueryString from the previous example:

```
Response.Write Request.QueryString("LastName") ' prints Doe
Response.Write Request.QueryString.Count ' prints 2
Response.Write Request.QueryString(2) ' Prints John
```

That makes it extremely easy to retrieve the data sent by the browser. You can add QueryString parameters to HTML you send to the browser in two ways:

- Concatenate strings to produce a valid URL.
- Use the URLData property of the WebClass.

Concatenating strings is a straightforward process—you just need to remember to separate the first key=value pair from the file portion of the URL with a question mark and all subsequent pairs with ampersands. For example, suppose you have a recordset of user names. You want to display the names as links. When an administrator clicks one of the names, you want to display a form to edit the user's information. For each link, you'll want to return the user's ID.

```
While Not R.EOF
    With Response
        .Write "<a href=somepage.asp?ID=" & _
        R("UserID").Value & ">" & R("Name") & "</a>"
```

Now, when the administrator clicks the link, you'll be able to pull the UserID from the QueryString collection to display the form to edit the user's information:

```
Dim anID
anID = Request.QueryString("ID")
' display form based on anID
```

When you show the form, you'll need to keep track of the ID in the form page too, and possibly in several subsequent pages; that's the application user's state—editing the user with the ID called anID. All that concatenation can become painful when you're trying to keep track of multiple variables. Imagine trying to append enough information to keep track of 20 or 30 critical variables in an application!

Luckily, VB can help. As you saw in Chapter 7, "Controlling Program Flow," each WebClass has a URLData property that it can append to every URL generated by the URLFor method. VB also appends the URLData to every link in an HTML template that contains a WCU parameter when you call the WriteTemplate method. Letting VB format the strings is much more convenient than formatting the URL strings yourself.

The URLData can be in any format you desire. Because VB returns the URL, it does not have to follow the key=value format imposed by QueryString data.

Using URLData or QueryString data to maintain state has some undesirable characteristics. First, the user (and other observers) can see the data because it appears in the address bar. Therefore, you should never use these methods to send any private information unless you also apply your own encryption scheme to the data. Second, if you use QueryString data and your data contains spaces or other non-alphanumeric characters, you must apply the Server.URLEncode method to the query string before appending it to a URL. You don't need to do that for URLData; the WebClass method automatically replaces the appropriate characters with their encoded equivalents.

> **NOTE** The Server.URLEncode method replaces characters with a percent sign followed by the hex value of the character. For example, a space (ASCII 32) is %20.

## Maintaining State with Hidden Form Variables

Yet another way of maintaining state on the client is to use hidden form variables. If you do this, you need to create a <form> tag and insert the hidden form variable for *each* page requiring you to pass state back to the server. You also need to ensure that the client submits the form using the Post method. That means that you will either have to have a Submit button for each page or will need to write client-side script to submit the form when a navigation event—such as a click on a link or button—occurs.

For example, to pass a variable called ID with a value of 2817 from one page to another, the first page could contain:

```
<form name="frmHidden" method="Post">
    <input type="hidden" name="ID" value="2817">
    <input type="submit" value="Submit">
</form>
```

When the user clicks the Submit button, the form will send the value ID=2817 to the server. You can retrieve the value by using the Request.Form collection, then use the value in a form on the next page.

To submit the form from a link, use client-side script such as this:

```
<script language="javascript">
    function doSubmit() {
        document.frmHidden.submit();
    }
</script>
```

```
<form action="mypage.asp" name="frmHidden" method="post">
    <input type="hidden" name="ID" value="2817">
    <input type="submit" value="Submit">
</form>
```

Somewhere on the page, you would put a link back to the ASP page that instantiates your WebClass:

```
<a href='mypage.asp' onClick='doSubmit();'>Click Here</a>
```

If you wanted to continue the sequence, you would retrieve the ID value in the WebClass instantiated by the `mypage.asp` script by using `Request.Form("ID")` and then send the ID forward to the next page.

The process of setting and retrieving the ID variable would continue as long as you needed the variable value on the server to maintain state.

Hidden form variables are in some ways better than cookies or QueryString variables. Hidden form variables have no size restriction and they're not visible in the browser's address field; but they are visible to users savvy enough to use the View Source feature of the browser. You should not use hidden form variables for values that you don't want the user to see (for example, answers to test questions).

## Maintaining State in a Database

This method is probably the most scaleable way to maintain state—and it will become especially important if Microsoft changes WebClasses so that they *don't* have to have Sessions enabled. Storing state in a database is definitely slower than the other methods described in this chapter when your application has only a few users, but as the number of users increases, using a database to store state quickly outstrips using Session variables. It's also easier to script than using QueryString or form variables, especially when you have a large application for which you must store many more state variables.

Another major advantage of storing state in a database is that you can maintain state not only *during* a session, but also *across* sessions. The only other way to maintain state across sessions is to use persistent cookies. When you maintain state in cookies, the data resides on the client, whereas when you maintain state in a database, the data resides on the server. Maintaining cross-session state on the server is better. People frequently change computers, delete cookie files, or sign on to their computers using other sign-ons, so client-side state is less certain.

To store state in a database table, you must set up the table properly. By that, I don't mean that you must have a column for every variable, but that you must be able to identify the data row or rows that belong to an individual or session. You do this by setting a single identifying cookie that acts as a primary key to the table, then retrieving the data using that cookie value when each request starts. You can create and set your own cookie value—for secured sites, you will probably want to use the user's unique ID or sign-on. For cross-session state maintenance, you'll need to have each user sign on with an ID and password. For single-session state maintenance, you can use the SessionID cookie as long as you don't care about storing state for an individual *user*, just an individual session.

Here's how to store state in a database on a single-session basis:

1. In the `Session_OnStart` event in the `global.asa` file, you create a new row(s) for the new SessionID or sign-on.

2. In the `BeginRequest` event code for each WebClass in your application, you read the cookie, then retrieve the appropriate row(s) from the database.

3. During page processing, you add or remove state information as appropriate.

4. In the `EndRequest` event code for each WebClass, you update the database with any changed state information.

5. In the `Session_OnEnd` event in `global.asa`, you delete the row(s) from the database.

To store state between sessions, you defer step 1 until after the user has signed on and you create a new row only if the user doesn't already have data. You would eliminate step 5 unless an administrator deletes the sign-on.

You'll need a scheme to delete or archive obsolete state data—data you've stored for individuals who never return to your site. For many public sites, this is the bulk of the data collected; for internal sites, it may occur only when an employee leaves the company. If you use persistent cookies to connect people to their data, you will probably also want a way for a user whose cookie has been lost to reconnect to their data. That's why many sites ask you to provide special personal information—so they can ask you about it if you lose or delete the site cookie.

## Summing Up State Maintenance Options

Unless you're migrating an existing application into WebClass form, there's no particular advantage to using any methods other than Session variables or databases to store state. WebClasses force you to have Sessions enabled; therefore, you may as well take advantage of them—you don't gain anything by ignoring them and moving state information to the client except some free memory on the server. You can use both methods at the same time—database tables to store information between sessions and Session variables to store information during a session. That way, you get the best of both worlds: the persistence of databases and the in-memory access to Session variables.

If Microsoft changes WebClasses so that you can use them *without* having Sessions enabled, you may find that you gain performance and scalability if you expend the effort now to save state entirely in database tables.

# Exploring the State Maintenance Options

All that explanation was interesting, but there's nothing like building a project to show how things really work. In this project, you'll implement all the state maintenance options. After working with them, you'll have a good basis for deciding which to use in your own applications.

## Using Session Variables to Maintain State

Create a new IIS project and rename it **StateMaintenance**. Rename the Designer **WebclassState**, then create a new directory called **StateMaintenance** and save the project. Create a new custom WebItem called **Counter**. Delete the default `WebClass_Start` event code and replace it with this code:

```
Private Sub WebClass_Start()
    Set NextItem = Counter
End Sub
```

Place this code into the `Counter_Respond` event:

```
With Response
    .Write "<html>"
    .Write "<body>"
    .Write "<h1><font face=""Arial"">"
```

```
            .Write "State Maintenance Demo</font></h1>"
            Session("Counter") = Session("Counter") + 1
            .Write "<p>You have visited this page " & _
                Session("Counter") & " times.</p>"
            .Write "</body>"
            .Write "</html>"
        End With
```

This simple application counts the number of times a user visits the Counter page. The application stores the count in the `Session("Counter")` variable. The `Counter` WebItem increments the counter whenever you refresh the page. Go ahead and run the project. Your browser should look like Figure 8.3.

**FIGURE 8.3:**

StateMaintenance Project—Counter WebItem screen

Each time you refresh the page, the counter will increment. You're saving state in a Session variable. That's why Session variables are popular: They're simple to use. Close your browser, restart it, and navigate to the starting URL for your WebClass again. Don't stop the WebClass, though—leave the project running. When you reach the page in the new browser, the counter will have been reset to 1. That's because you lost the Session cookie (and thus the connection to the Session object on the server) when you closed the browser. Closing the browser is a good way to force a new Session. When you did that, you also saw how the WebClass maintains a separate Session value for each active Session. If that's not clear to you yet, open three more (or ten more) browsers simultaneously and navigate to the same page in each one. Start refreshing the browsers randomly. What happens?

## Using Cookies to Maintain State

You aren't limited to storing state in any one method. Let's add a cookie and use that as a second Counter variable. Change the code in the `Respond` event for the `Counter` WebItem as follows:

```
Dim iCookieCounter
If Request.Cookies("Counter") = "" Then
    iCookieCounter = 0
Else
    iCookieCounter = CInt(Request.Cookies("Counter"))
End If
iCookieCounter = iCookieCounter + 1
Response.Cookies("Counter") = CStr(iCookieCounter)
With Response
        .Write "<html>"
        .Write "<body>"
           .Write "<h1><font face=""Arial"">"
        .Write "State Maintenance Demo</font></h1><br>"
        Session("Counter") = Session("Counter") + 1
        .Write "You have visited this page:<br>"
        .Write "Session counter: " & Session("Counter") & _
            "<br>"
        .Write "Cookie counter: " & CStr(iCookieCounter) _
            & "<br>"
        .Write "</body>"
        .Write "</html>"
End With
```

## Using QueryString/*URLData* Variables to Maintain State

If you didn't have Session variables or cookies, you'd need to maintain state using QueryString/URLData or hidden form variables. These aren't quite as convenient as either cookies or Session variables. Change the code in the `Counter _Respond` event to append a `URLData` value to the URL and add a link that refreshes the page. Each time you click the link, the server will retrieve the QueryString counter value, increment it, then redisplay the page with the new value. The easiest way to implement this is to use the `URLData` property of the WebClass to format the QueryString data.

I'm not going to list the entire `Respond` event this time, just the code you need to add. Stop the WebClass and add the following code into the `Respond` event. Dimension another integer variable to hold the QueryString count:

```
Dim iQueryStringCounter As Integer
```

Retrieve or initialize the value:

```
If URLData = "" Then
    iQueryStringCounter = 0
Else
    iQueryStringCounter = CInt(URLData)
End If
iQueryStringCounter = iQueryStringCounter + 1
URLData = CStr(iQueryStringCounter)
```

Display the value:

```
.Write "QueryString counter: " & _
    CStr(iQueryStringCounter) & "<br>"
```

Write the anchor tag for the link:

```
.Write "<a href=" & URLFor(Counter) & _
    ">Increment QueryString Counter</a><br>"
```

Start the WebClass again and click the link a few times. Refresh the page without clicking the link. Note that the values are independent—the Session and cookie values increment no matter which method you use to refresh the page. You're storing different values in different places.

## Using Form Variables to Maintain State

At the beginning of this event, the code either retrieves the cookie value or sets a default counter value of zero. It then creates or overwrites the cookie and displays the two counters. Both counters should display the same number as you refresh the page—and they do if you refresh the page slowly. If you refresh quickly, however, the client-side cookie counter gets behind. I suspect this is because the browser doesn't bother parsing the cookie header if you tell the browser to refresh before the previous response arrives.

Let's add a hidden form variable counter to the page as well. I won't list the entire `Respond` event this time either, just the code you need to add. Stop the

WebClass and add the following code into the `Respond` event. Dimension another integer variable to hold the form count:

```
Dim iFormCounter As Integer
```

Each time you submit the form, retrieve the value from the Request.Form collection and increment it.

```
iFormCounter = Request.Form("FormCounter")
iFormCounter = iFormCounter + 1
```

Display the counter:

```
.Write "Form counter: " & CStr(iFormCounter) & "<br>"
```

Redisplay the form with the incremented value.

```
.Write "<form name='frmCounter' method='post' action=" _
    & WebClass.URLFor(Counter) & ">"
.Write "<input type='hidden' name='formCounter' _
    & "value='" & CStr(iFormCounter) & "'>"
.Write "<input type='submit' value='Increment _
    & "Form Counter'>"
.Write "</form>"
```

Note that the Form counter returns to 1 if you click the Increment QueryString Counter link, but that the QueryString counter increments when you click the IncrementForm Counter button. That's because the browser sends the QueryString data when you post the form, but the browser does *not* send the form data when you click the link. This should reinforce the hardest part of using form variables to maintain state: *You have to submit the form* to have access to the form values on the server.

## Using Database Tables to Maintain State

Now that you've seen the Session variable and client-side (cookies, QueryString/URLData, and form) options for maintaining state, you should implement state in databases as well. I saved this option until last not only because it's the most complicated, but because the concepts in this section are also the most useful.

You'll need a database and a table for storing the information. If you download the code for this project, you'll see an Access database called `StateMaintenance.mdb` that you can use, but if you want to create your own, create a new database called **StateMaintenance** and create one table, called **SessionState**.

The table has three columns, all of which are required:

**ID**   A 50-character varChar field that holds an ID you'll generate for the current Session—not null

**Position**   Holds an integer value that tells you the sequence of that row for that ID—not null, default 0

**State**   A 255-character text field in Access (varChar field in SQL Server)—not null, default is an empty string

You won't use the Position field in this example. I've included it just so you can see how easy it would be to extend this concept to any reasonable number of strings, as long as no single string exceeds the maximum length of the field. Using this method, you aren't limited to 255 characters for state information even if you're using a database (such as Access or SQL Server 6.*x*) with a maximum string length of 255 characters. I've excluded the use of long binary or memo fields for performance reasons.

## How to Create a DSN

You'll need to create a Data Source Name (DSN) for the database so that you can access it easily. DSNs are the easiest (but not the best) way to connect to a database source. You use the ODBC Data Source Administrator program to create a DSN. This program is a wizard, so you'll find it easy to use. To find the ODBC Data Source Administrator program, click Start ➢ Settings ➢ Control Panel, then double-click the ODBC32 icon. You'll see the screen in Figure 8.4.

Any DSN you use through an Anonymous connection must be a System DSN. Click the System DSN tab on the dialog, then click the Add button. You'll see a list of ODBC drivers installed on your system (see Figure 8.5).

Select the appropriate ODBC driver for your data source, then click Finish. What happens next depends on the type of driver you select:

**Microsoft Access**   You need to select the database. For file-based databases such as Microsoft Access, make sure that the `IUSR_MachineName` and `IWAM_Machine-Name` accounts have Change (RWXD) access to the directory in which the database file resides.

*Continued on next page*

> **SQL-Server or other ODBC database**  You must select or enter the server name and the database name, and provide a sign-on and password. Follow the steps in the Wizard until you see a Finish button. Be sure to click the Test button to test the connection.

**FIGURE 8.4:**

ODBC Data Source Administrator

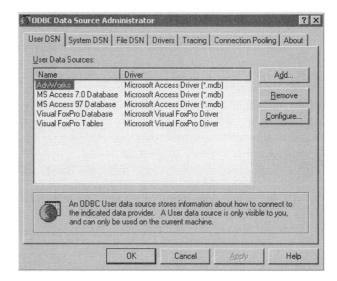

**FIGURE 8.5:**

ODBC Create New Data Source dialog

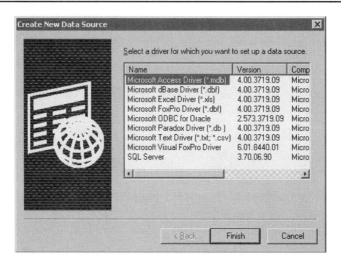

The rest of this project uses the steps outlined in the "Maintaining State in a Database" section earlier in this chapter. Recall step 1: In the `Session_OnStart` event in the `global.asa` file, you create a new row(s) for the new SessionID or sign-on.

Note that the code for this step isn't part of the WebClass; it's code that you place into the `global.asa` file. Find the `global.asa` file for the StateMaintenance project—IIS creates the file in your project directory.

The code in the `global.asa` file runs on the server, so the first line in the file is

```
<script language="vbscript" runat="server">
```

And the last line is

```
</script>
```

The rest of the code in the file goes between the `<script>` tags. You'll need access to the connection string for your database (in this case, the StateMaintenance DSN) throughout the project, so a good place to store it is in an Application variable. You can create this variable when the application starts.

```
Sub Application_OnStart()
    Application.Lock
    Application("DB") = "StateMaintenance"
    Application.Unlock
End Sub
```

Now you can write the `Session_OnStart` code:

```
Sub Session_OnStart()
    dim conn
    set conn = Server.CreateObject("ADODB.Connection")
    conn.ConnectionString=Application("DB")
    conn.mode=3
    conn.open
    conn.execute "INSERT INTO SessionState " _
        & "(ID, Position, State) VALUES " _
        & "('" & Session.SessionID & "', 0, '')"
    conn.close
    set conn = nothing
End Sub
```

Next write the code for step 2: In the `BeginRequest` event code for each WebClass in your application, you read the cookie, then retrieve the appropriate row(s) from the database.

For now, you're using the `Session.SessionID` value as the cookie. In the `WebClass_BeginRequest` event, you want to open the connection and retrieve the rows of data associated with the SessionID. After you retrieve the recordset, you need to decide how to represent the data inside the WebClass.

I elected to store the data in a comma-delimited string. Each item in the string consists of a key and an associated value, separated by an equals sign. Here's an example:

```
Counter=1,LastName=Jones,FirstName=Bill
```

So to retrieve the data, you need to concatenate the records, then parse the resulting string into a Dictionary object so you can use the data easily during the request. The `BeginRequest` event calls a `getState` function, which retrieves the recordset:

```
Private Sub WebClass_BeginRequest()
    Call getState(Session.SessionID)
End Sub

Private Function getState(anID As String)
    Dim conn As ADODB.Connection
    Dim R As Recordset
    Dim s As String
    Set conn = New Connection
    conn.ConnectionString = Application("DB")
    conn.Mode = adModeReadWrite
    conn.Open
    Set R = New Recordset
    R.Open "SELECT Position, State FROM SessionState " _
        & "WHERE ID='" & anID & "' ORDER BY Position", _
        conn, adOpenForwardOnly, adLockReadOnly, adCmdText
    While Not R.EOF
        s = s & R("State")
        R.MoveNext
    Wend
    Set R = Nothing
    Call parseStateString(s)
End Function
```

The `parseStateString` function parses the string into a Dictionary dimensioned as a module-level object variable. You'll need to add a project reference to the Microsoft Scripting Runtime Library before you can use the Dictionary object from VB.

```
' in Declarations section
Dim dState as Dictionary

Private Function parseStateString(s As String)
    Dim arr As Variant
    Dim i As Integer
    Dim association As Variant
    Set dState = New Dictionary
    dState.CompareMode = TextCompare
    If Len(s) > 0 Then
        arr = Split(s, ",")
        For i = 0 To UBound(arr)
            association = Split(arr(i), "=")
            If UBound(association) = 1 Then
                dState.Add association(0), association(1)
            End If
        Next
    End If
End Function
```

You'll need two additional functions to set a state variable and retrieve a state variable:

```
Private Function getStateValue(aKey As String) As String
    If dState.Exists(aKey) Then
        getStateValue = dState(aKey)
    End If
End Function
Private Function setStateValue(aKey As String, Optional aValue As String = "")
    dState(aKey) = aValue
End Function
```

Now, step 3: During page processing, you add or remove state information as appropriate.

So, just like with all of the other state maintenance options, you retrieve the `dState("Counter")` variable, increment it, store the new value, and display that value. Place the following code in the `Counter_Respond` event.

```
    ' Dimension variables at start of routine
    Dim aVal As Variant
    Dim iDBCounter As Integer
    aVal = getStateValue("Counter")
```

```
        If aVal <> "" Then
            iDBCounter = CInt(aVal)
        Else
            iDBCounter = 0
        End If
        iDBCounter = iDBCounter + 1
        Call setStateValue("Counter", CStr(iDBCounter))
        ' display code for other state options
        .Write "Database counter: " & CStr(iDBCounter) & "<br>"
```

Step 4: In the `EndRequest` event code for each WebClass, you update the database with any changed state information.

To update the database, you need to reverse the parsing process—taking the updated values out of the Dictionary and concatenating them into an array of strings, none of which may be more than 255 characters long. Then it deletes all the existing state rows for the SessionID and inserts the new state strings into the database. Because you wouldn't want to lose state, wrap the process of deleting and inserting the data in a transaction. If any error occurs, you can roll back the transaction. The `EndRequest` method calls a function called `saveState`. The code is in Listing 8.1.

```
Private Sub WebClass_EndRequest()
    Call saveState(Session.SessionID)
End Sub
```

### LISTING 8.1  The SaveState Function Saves Session State in a Database

```
Private Function saveState(anID As String)
    Dim conn As Connection
    Dim R As Recordset
    Dim sArr() As String
    Dim sArrCount As Integer
    Dim V As Variant
    Dim s As String
    Dim i As Integer
    Dim association As String
    Dim recordCounter As Integer
    On Error GoTo Err_SaveState
    For Each V In dState.Keys
        association = CStr(V) & "=" & CStr(dState(V))
        If Len(s) + Len(association) < 255 Then
            s = s & association & ","
```

```
            Else
                ReDim Preserve sArr(sArrCount) As String
                sArr(sArrCount) = s
                sArrCount = sArrCount + 1
                s = ""
            End If
        Next
        ReDim Preserve sArr(sArrCount) As String
        sArr(sArrCount) = s
        sArrCount = sArrCount + 1
        s = ""
        Set conn = New Connection
        conn.ConnectionString = Application("DB")
        conn.Mode = adModeReadWrite
        conn.Open
        conn.BeginTrans
        conn.Execute "DELETE FROM SessionState WHERE ID='" & anID & "'"
        Set R = New Recordset
        R.Open "SELECT ID, Position, State FROM SessionState WHERE ID='" &
    anID & "' ORDER BY Position", conn, adOpenStatic, adLockBatchOpti-
mistic, _
        adCmdText
        For i = 0 To sArrCount - 1
            R.AddNew
            R!ID = anID
            R!Position = i
            R!State = sArr(i)
            R.Update
        Next
        R.UpdateBatch
        R.Close
        Set R = Nothing
        conn.CommitTrans
        conn.Close
        Set conn = Nothing
Exit_SaveState:
        Exit Sub
Err_SaveState:
        conn.RollbackTrans
        Set R = Nothing
        conn.Close
```

```
        Set conn = Nothing
        Err.Raise Err.Number, "saveState", Err.Description
End Function
```

Step 5: In the `Session_OnEnd` event in `global.asa`, you delete the row(s) from the database.

You want to delete all the records that belong to the Session by deleting all records where the ID is equal to the `Session.SessionID` value.

```
Sub Session_OnEnd()
    dim conn
    set conn = Server.CreateObject("ADODB.Connection")
    conn.ConnectionString=Application("DB")
    conn.mode=3
    conn.open
    conn.execute "DELETE FROM SessionState " & _
        "WHERE ID='" & Session.SessionID & "'"
    conn.close
    set conn = nothing
End Sub
```

Save and run the WebClass. You should see the database counter increment just like the other counters. Try storing some other state values in the database. That is a lot of work for a counter, but there is a point to it. By this time, you should have a good idea of which type of state maintenance you want to use for simple values such as counters. You should also recognize that only the Session variable loses its value if you start and stop the WebClass, not the cookie, QueryString, form, or database values. It's obvious why the cookie, QueryString, and form values don't lose their data, but it's less obvious why the database value remains constant. The reason is that the browser retains a Session cookie. The ASP engine recognizes that and creates a new Session with the same SessionID, thus the data exists in the database and therefore remains constant.

One more interesting quirk: Click a dozen or so times on the Increment QueryString Counter link. Now use your browser's History list to step backward several pages. The browser pulls the page from its cache, so all the values appear to decrease. Now refresh the page. Notice that the QueryString and form values increment only by one when you do that, whereas the other values immediately return to their previous values. That's because the QueryString and form values increment based on data they receive from the *client*, whereas the other counter values are stored on the server. Using the browser's History list does not affect the server counters, but it resets the client counters. Make sure you understand why this behavior occurs because it should definitely affect where you store state. In general, the rule is: Store state on the server unless the state data is specifically associated with the current page of the browser.

## Storing State across Sessions

You can easily extend the database method to store state between sessions, but you'll need to use an ID other than the SessionID. Whenever you need unique values in an application, think GUID. A GUID is a *Globally Unique Id*entifier. Here's an example of a GUID:

```
{05589FA1-C356-11CE-BF01-00AA0055595A}
```

You've probably seen plenty of GUIDs already; if not, look in the Registry— Microsoft uses them to uniquely identify classes and other objects, because they're practically guaranteed to be unique across all computers in the world. This unique property makes them ideal for many situations in which you need to ensure that values in disparate locations don't collide when you merge the values.

**WARNING**  Don't change the Registry unless you're sure you know what you're doing.

As an example, suppose you have a large group of local databases from which you periodically send new and updated data to a central database. You need to be able to identify the rows to update and you also need to ensure that new rows don't collide with any existing rows. Unless you can guarantee control of the local database, you can't use numeric (such as AutoNumber or Identity) values, because there's no way to ensure that the locally generated value won't conflict with a value generated on some other local database. You could generate random values, but again, you can't be absolutely sure that the value generated on one computer won't conflict with the value generated on another computer. If you use GUIDs, you can be as sure as it is currently possible to be that the values won't conflict.

You create a GUID with two API calls, one to create the GUID (`CoCreateGUID2`) itself, which is a 16-byte value, and a second (`StringFromGUID2`) to transform it into the familiar string form.

```
Private Declare Function CoCreateGuid Lib _
    "ole32.dll" (buffer As Byte) As Long
Private Declare Function StringFromGUID2 Lib _
```

```
"ole32.dll" (buffer As Byte, ByVal lpsz As Long, _
    ByVal cbMax As Long) As Long
```

I've wrapped the two calls in a single, easy-to-use function called getGUID:

```
Private Function getGUID() As String
    Dim buffer(15) As Byte
    Dim s As String
    Dim ret As Long
    s = String$(128, 0)
    ret = CoCreateGuid(buffer(0))
    ret = StringFromGUID2(buffer(0), StrPtr(s), 128)
    getGUID = Left$(s, ret - 1)
End Function
```

The function returns a GUID in string form. You'll use the GUID returned from this function as a unique identifying cookie value. By providing an expiration date, you tell the browser to store the cookie on the local computer's hard drive. Until the cookie expires (or the user deletes it), the browser will retrieve and send the cookie to your application even if the user closes the browser. You will use the GUID cookie as the key to store and retrieve the information from the database.

To test the GUID cookie, you'll need to change the WebClass_BeginRequest and EndRequest subroutines to retrieve the database row with a GUID key rather than the Session.SessionID key used in the previous section of this chapter.

```
Private Sub WebClass_BeginRequest()
    ' get the GUID cookie
    Dim GUID As String
    GUID = Request.Cookies("GUID")
    If GUID = "" Then
        GUID = getGUID()
        Response.Cookies("GUID") = GUID
    End If
    Call getState(GUID)
End Sub

Private Sub WebClass_EndRequest()
    Dim aGUID As String
    aGUID = Request.Cookies("GUID")
    Call saveState(aGUID)
End Sub
```

Finally, the original `Session_OnEnd` event in `global.asa` deletes the database rows associated with the `Session.SessionID` for that session. Although the code will no longer work (because you're storing information with a GUID rather than a `SessionID` key), you should still clean up the code. To do so, you can delete the entire subroutine.

## Eliminating Obsolete Data

Another problem associated with storing state data across sessions is that it's difficult to know when the data you're storing is obsolete. For example, suppose a person visits your site one time and never returns. You may not want to keep that data forever. One way to solve the problem is to update an expiration date whenever you access a row. At the beginning or end of the application, you can delete the rows that have an expiration date earlier than the current date. I haven't included the code to do that, both because it requires a change to the database and because there are many other valid solutions. Other possible solutions when the data expires include sending e-mail to the user asking whether you should delete the data (assuming you obtain an e-mail address), moving the obsolete records to archive tables, and storing the data outside the database in a file.

# Caching Information

So far in this chapter, I've concentrated on storing user state, but there's another side to state maintenance—application state. The requirements for storing user state are often very small, but some applications require quick access to large amounts of data. Some application state needs are shared between all sessions; others are specific to a given session.

For example, suppose you have an inventory database. One of the tables in the database contains parts information and descriptions. Every person using the application needs to see and interact with the parts list. Assume that the users are distributors, who typically order dozens or hundreds of parts at once. For each distributor, you'll also need to display and maintain the state of the order they're building in the current session. The volume of data makes it impractical to store state on the client; therefore, you'll need to use a database. The volume of information and the infrequent changing of some tables also makes it inefficient to retrieve the parts list and the current order records from the database for each request. In such cases, you need a way to cache information on the server. You want to store the information such that:

- You don't have to make a database query for each request.
- You don't have to store ActiveX objects in a Session variable.
- You have robust programmatic access to the data just as you would with recordset-based data.
- You can retrieve and (sometimes) update information easily.

In the rest of this chapter, I'll show you several options for caching larger amounts of data on the server. You'll see how to use each one and the advantages and disadvantages of each option.

You can't store VB ActiveX objects as Session or Application variables. I know I've said that before, but you need to remember it. Well, OK, you *can*, but it's a bad idea because when you do that, you force the server to use the same thread to service all requests from the client, which severely impacts scalability. That leaves two options for storing multiple values in memory: strings and arrays. Both work quite well for storing multiple values. In the preceding section, you saw how easy it is to store a string, retrieve it, turn it into a Dictionary object, change the values, then re-store the string. You can do the same thing with arrays. Before we go any further, you need to remember that the Session object doesn't actually store anything except Variants. No matter which type of data you save in a Session variable, it's saved as a Variant.

Luckily, ADO Recordset objects have two methods that can help you store them easily: the `getString` method and the `getRows` method. The `getString` method, by default, returns a string with the fields separated by tabs and the rows separated by carriage returns. You can alter the separator characters in the call to `getString` if you wish. For example, if you create a connection and retrieve a recordset of all the authors in the `pubs` sample database, then call the `getString` method, you get a listing that looks like this:

```
712-45-1867 del Castillo    Innes    615 996-8275    2286 Cram Pl. #86   Ann Arbor    MI    48105    -1
722-51-5454 DeFrance        Michel   219 547-9982    3 Balding Pl.       Gary         IN    46403    -1
etc...
```

The `getString` method is convenient, but data in the form of a raw string has several problems:

- Getting to any particular record is difficult—you have to count the carriage returns to find a record.
- After finding a record, you have to parse the string into fields.
- The method doesn't store the field names in the first "row," which makes it easy to think you're accessing one field when you're actually accessing another one.

> **NOTE** The Microsoft **pubs** database comes with SQL Server. If you don't have SQL Server, you can download a Microsoft Access database containing the tables of the **pubs** database from the Sybex Web site.

> **NOTE** To download code, navigate to `http://www.sybex.com`. Click the Catalog button and search for this book's title. Click the Downloads button and accept the licensing agreement. Accepting the agreement grants you access to the downloads page for the book.

The `Recordset.getData` method returns data in a two-dimensional array, which solves the first two problems, but still doesn't deliver the field names.

One solution to these problems is to create a data structure that provides the information you need, while still using Variants that you can store in a Session or Application object. Consider the problem: You need programmatic access to individual data fields by name in a two-dimensional array of records. To get that, you need a list of the field names—in sequence, the data itself, and the number of records. Given those three pieces of information, you should be able to get any individual value.

## Writing a StoredRecordset Class

The answer to storing recordsets in usable form is to store the data as a Variant array that contains:

- A Variant array of the field names

- The two-dimensional data array obtained by the call to `getData`
- A third array containing other meta-information you want to store about the recordset, for example, the number of rows, the last activated row, etc.

I call this structure a *StoredRecordset*. A StoredRecordset DLL encapsulates this structure and has properties and methods to retrieve the data easily. The DLL exposes one public object, called CStoredRecordset.

Here's the code to create a StoredRecordset:

```
' assume you have a populated Recordset object (rs)
dim SR as new CStoredRecordset
call SR.StoreRecordset(R)
```

To store the structure as a Session variable, you call the `StoredRecordset` property:

```
Session("SR") = SR.StoredRecordset
```

To reconstitute the CStoredRecordset object from the data stored in the Session object, use the following:

```
dim SR as new CStoredRecordset
SR.StoredRecordset = Session("SR")
```

The code is too long to include in its entirety, but you can download it from the Sybex Web site. Table 8.1 contains a list of the properties and methods of the CStoredRecordset class.

**TABLE 8.1:** CStoredRecordset Class Methods and Properties

| Name | Type | Description |
| --- | --- | --- |
| StoredRecordset | Property Get | Retrieves the Variant structure containing the stored recordset data. Call this method to obtain the structure you store in an Application variable or in a Session variable between requests. |
| StoredRecordset | Property Let | Initializes the CStoredRecordset object from a Variant containing a stored recordset structure. Call this method when you want to reconstitute a CStoredRecordset object from data stored in an Application or Session variable. |

*Continued on next page*

**TABLE 8.1 CONTINUED:** CStoredRecordset Class Methods and Properties

| Name | Type | Description |
| --- | --- | --- |
| StoreRecordset (R as Recordset) | Sub | Stores the field names and data from a Recordset object into a Variant structure suitable for storing in an Application or Session object. |
| Fields | Property Get | Returns a list of field names as a Variant array. |
| Data | Property Get | Returns the data from the Recordset object. Essentially the same as **getData**, except null values have been transformed to null strings. |
| RecordCount | Property Get | Returns the number of records in the stored recordset. |
| FieldCount | Property Get | Returns the number of fields or columns in the stored recordset. |
| HTMLTableString | Property Get | Returns the stored recordset formatted as an HTML table. |
| FieldNumber (fieldName as string) | Property Get | Returns the integer index of the field that matches the **fieldName** parameter. |
| Value (fieldNameOrNumber as variant, aRecord-Number as long) | Property Get | Returns a Variant containing the value of the column matching the **fieldNameOrNumber** parameter from the record corresponding to the value parameter **aRecordNumber**. |
| Find (fieldsAndValues-Dictionary As Dictionary) | Function | Returns **True** if a record is found that matches the field names and values passed in the fieldsAndValuesDictionary Dictionary object, **False** otherwise. |
| IsStoredRecordset (anSR As Variant) | Property Get | Returns **True** if the Variant parameter **anSR** contains a valid stored recordset structure, **False** otherwise. |
| Rows (rowNumberArray As Variant) | Property Get | Returns a new CStoredRecordset object containing the rows corresponding to the row numbers contained in the **rowNumberArray** parameter. |
| FindRowNumbers (fieldname As String, fieldValue As Variant) | Property Get | Returns a Variant array of the row numbers where the value of the field specified by the **fieldname** parameter matches the value specified in the **fieldValue** parameter. |
| Filter (fieldname As String, fieldValue As Variant) | Property Get | Returns a new CStoredRecordset object containing the rows where the value of the field specified by the **fieldname** parameter matches the value specified in the **fieldValue** parameter. |

*Continued on next page*

**TABLE 8.1 CONTINUED:** CStoredRecordset Class Methods and Properties

| Name | Type | Description |
| --- | --- | --- |
| `Column (fieldname As String, allowNulls As Boolean)` | Property Get | Returns a Variant array of the values in the column specified by the `fieldname` parameter. If `allowNulls` is `True`, the method returns all the values. If `allowNulls` is `False`, the method returns only those rows that do not have a null-string value. |
| `RowToDictionary` | Function | Returns a Dictionary object containing the data for the current row of the stored recordset. The keys are the field names and the values are the field values. |
| `MoveFirst` | Sub | Moves the stored recordset index to the first row (row 0). |
| `MoveLast` | Sub | Moves the stored recordset index to the last row (`RecordCount`). |
| `MoveNext` | Sub | Moves the stored recordset index to the next row. |
| `MovePrevious` | Sub | Moves the stored recordset index to the first row. |
| `MoveTo (aRowNumber As Long)` | Sub | Moves the stored recordset index to the specified row. |
| `Move(offset as long)` | Sub | Moves the stored recordset index pointer by the number of rows specified in the `offset` parameter. |
| `EOF` | Property Get | Returns `True` if the recordset index has moved past the last record. |
| `BOF` | Property Get | Returns `True` if the recordset index has moved in front of the first record. |
| `AbsolutePosition` | Property Get | Returns the current recordset index. |

You can see from the methods and properties available in Table 8.1 that much of the functionality of a recordset is available through the CStoredRecordset class—and it's relatively easy to extend the class methods to enable searching and sorting. The most data-intensive work is all done when you initially load the recordset—iterating through the recordset to find the field names and change null values to empty strings. The class changes the nulls to empty strings because I originally created it for displaying data with ASP pages. If you need the null values or you'd prefer to write code to test for null values, you can easily eliminate part of the initial processing as well.

Once initialized, the CStoredRecordset class is fast because it works directly from the data stored in the arrays. That's not to say that the class methods are completely optimized—with a little work I'm sure you can make the class even more efficient. Shuttling the reference to the Variant containing the arrays back and forth between the Session object and the class is fast because it's just a variable reference—there's no data copying to do.

## Writing a StoredDictionary Class

A stored recordset works well for multiple records, but often you need to store multiple single values. Of course you can store them directly in Session variables, but often such values are grouped. This leads to problems because Session variable names must be unique.

For example, suppose you have three people for whom you want to store data in each Session variable. Each person has a first and last name. To store the six values directly in Session variables, you would have to make up unique names, like `Person1LastName`, `Person2LastName`, etc. It would be much more convenient (and extensible) to store each person's information as values of a Dictionary object. Then you could retrieve the data as `Session("Person1").LastName`.

Unfortunately, as you probably have realized by now, you shouldn't store a Dictionary object in a Session or Application variable. You can, however, use the same principles you saw in the preceding section to create a Dictionary-like object that you can load and store easily. Just like the CStoredRecordset class, you use arrays to store the data, then load the arrays into an ActiveX object called CStoredDictionary when you need to access the data. The goals are:

- Create a class with properties and methods that are similar to those of the Dictionary object.
- Create methods to store and load instances of the class from arrays stored in Session or Application variables.
- Once initialized, the object should load very quickly.

The CStoredDictionary object contains a list of names (the Dictionary keys) and values (the Dictionary items). Each name corresponds to a single value. The keys are strings and the items are Variants. The class needs to be fast; therefore, it sacrifices a small amount of memory to avoid re-dimensioning the arrays each time you add an item. Instead, it creates space for 10 items (by default) at a time. When you add an item, the class re-dimensions the arrays only if adding the item would exceed the current array size. You can set the increment with the `ExpandIncrement` property.

VB can quickly scan strings for the position of substrings —much more quickly than it can iterate through an array and make comparisons—so the class stores the keys as a comma-delimited list of fixed-length strings. By default, the maximum key length is 30 characters. You can expand this if necessary, but only before you add values. To find a given key, the class pads the requested key with spaces and adds a comma, then calls VB's `Instr` function. If the key exists, the index of the value will be the integer value of the position returned from the call to `Instr` divided by the maximum length of the keys, plus one for the comma. For example, if there are two keys, and the maximum key length is 20 characters, the key string looks like

```
",key1               ,key2               ,"
```

Therefore, to find the string `"key2"`, the class would pad the string to

```
"key2                ,"
```

A call to the `Instr` function for the padded string will return 22. The integer value of 22 divided by 21 (length of the key plus the comma) is 1, which is the proper zero-based array index for the second item.

As with all collections, there are trade-offs depending upon the requirements for the collection. This collection is extremely fast for small collections—up to 100 items. It's reasonably fast up to about 500 items. After that, the performance drops off due to VB's problems with concatenating large strings. You can expand this performance limit somewhat by reducing the size of the keys (see the `MaxKeySize` property in Table 8.2). Adding items is already relatively fast, but you can improve that as well by changing the `ExpandIncrement` property, thus limiting the number of times the class needs to re-dimension the data array.

Table 8.2 lists the properties and methods of the CStoredDictionary class.

**TABLE 8.2:** CStoredDictionary Class Properties and Methods

| Name | Type | Description |
| --- | --- | --- |
| Add | Sub | Adds a key-value pair to the CStoredDictionary object. The key must be a string; the value may be any data type, including Object. |

*Continued on next page*

**TABLE 8.2 CONTINUED:** CStoredDictionary Class Properties and Methods

| Name | Type | Description |
|---|---|---|
| AsVariant | Property Get | Returns the CStoredDictionary as a single Variant, suitable for storage as an Application or Session variable. |
| CompareMethod(aMethod As VbCompareMethod) | Property Let | Controls whether the CStoredDictionary keys are case sensitive. Valid values are vbBinaryCompare and vbTextCompare. |
| CompareMethod | Property Get | Returns the current case-sensitivity setting, either vbBinaryCompare or vbTextCompare. |
| Count() as Long | Property Get | Returns the number of items in the CStoredDictionary object. |
| Exists(aKey As String) As Boolean | Property Get | Returns True if the specified key exists, False otherwise. |
| ExpandIncrement(expandValue As Integer) | Property Let | Sets the increment value for re-dimensioning the data array. |
| InitFromVariant(V As Variant) | Sub | Initializes the properties of a StoredDictionary from a Variant. Typically, you store the StoredDictionary in a Session or Application variable using the AsVariant method, then restore it using InitFromVariant. |
| Item(anIndex As Variant) As Variant | Property Get | Retrieves the value associated with a specific key or numeric index position. |
| Items() As Variant | Property Get | Retrieves all the values in the CStoredDictionary as a Variant array. |
| Key(index As Variant) As String | Property Get | Retrieves the key at the specified numeric index position. |
| Keys() As Variant | Property Get | Returns all the keys in the StoredDictionary as a Variant array. |
| MaxKeyLength() As Integer | Property Get | Retrieves the maximum length of a CStoredDictionary key. |
| MaxKeyLength(aLength As Integer) | Property Let | Sets the maximum length of a CStoredDictionary key. |
| StoreRecord(R As Recordset) | Sub | Stores the contents of the current record from the Recordset parameter R. The method uses the field names as keys and the field values as values. |
| Remove(aKey As Variant) | Sub | Removes the key and value pair associated with the parameter aKey from the CStoredDictionary. |

## Using the CStoredRecordset and CStoredDictionary Classes

As an example of how to use the StoredRecordset and StoredDictionary DLLs, you'll build a short project called DataCache. You'll need to download the Stored-Recordset and StoredDictionary projects from the Sybex Web site to build this project. Start a new IIS project and rename it **DataCache**. Name the WebClass Designer **DataCacheTest**. Add the CStoredRecordset and CStoredDictionary classes to the project.

> **WARNING** If you don't add the CStoredRecordset and CStoredDictionary classes to your project, you can still run the DataCache project in design mode by adding references to the StoredRecordset and StoredDictionary DLLs. However, it (probably) won't work in compiled mode. You'll see why in Chapter 11, "Using ActiveX DLLs from WebClasses," when you build ActiveX DLLs for use with WebClasses. For now, add the class files to your WebClass project.

The project retrieves a list of authors from the Authors table in the pubs sample database. If you don't already have one, you'll need to create a DSN using the ODBC Data Source Administrator applet (see directions earlier in this chapter, in the "How to Create a DSN" sidebar). Put the code in Listing 8.2 into the Start event of the WebClass.

**LISTING 8.2**  Sample Code for the StoredRecordset and StoredDictionary Classes (*DataCacheTest.dsr*)

```
Private Sub WebClass_Start()
    Dim sr As CStoredRecordset
    Dim sd As CStoredDictionary
    Dim conn As Connection
    Dim R As Recordset
    Dim vField As Variant
    Dim i As Integer
    With Response
        .Write "<html>"
        .Write "<body>"
    End With
    Set sd = New CStoredDictionary
    Set sr = New CStoredRecordset
```

```
If IsEmpty(Session("SR")) Then
    Response.Write "Retrieving data from database<br>"
    ' if the recordset is not already stored,
    ' get a recordset
    Set conn = New Connection
    conn.Open "dsn=Pubs;uid=sa;pwd="
    Set R = conn.Execute("SELECT * FROM Authors", _
        , adCmdText)

    ' store the first record in a StoredDictionary
    Call sd.RecordToStringDictionary(R)

    ' set a session variable to cache the data
    Session("SD") = sd.StoredDictionary

    ' store the entire recordset in a StoredRecordset
    Call sr.StoreRecordset(R)

    ' set a session variable to cache the data
    Session("SR") = sr.StoredRecordset
Else
    Response.Write "Retrieving data from " _
        & Session variables<br>"
    ' reconstitute the classes from the stored variant
    sd.StoredDictionary = Session("SD")
    sr.StoredRecordset = Session("SR")
End If
' print the data
With Response
    .Write "<h3>StoredDictionary</h3>"
    For i = 0 To sd.Count - 1
        .Write sd.Key(i) & "=" & sd.Item(i) & "<BR>"
    Next
    .Write "<p>"
    .Write "<center>"
    .Write "<h3>StoredRecordset</h3>"
    .Write sr.HTMLTableString()
    .Write "</center>"
    .Write "</body>"
    .Write "</html>"
End With
End Sub
```

Save the project and run it. You should see the screen shown in Figure 8.6.

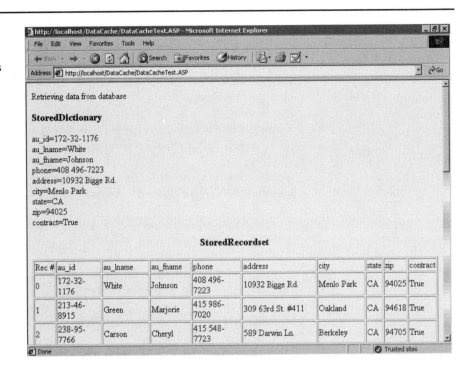

**FIGURE 8.6:**

DataCache Project—Start Event results

The first time you run the project, the code creates a CStoredDictionary and a CStoredRecordset, retrieves the data from the `pubs` database, initializes the objects, then stores them as Variants in Session variables. Set a breakpoint at the top of the `Start` event code, then refresh the page. This time, you'll see that the method retrieves the data from the Session object, initializes the CStoredDictionary and CStoredRecordset objects, then displays the data again.

You could just as easily store either the data from these objects in Application variables. Just remember, always use the methods that return the data as Variants; don't store the objects themselves directly in Session or Application variables.

## Summing Up State Maintenance

In this chapter, you've seen several ways to maintain state information for single users or the entire application. You've also seen ways to cache data on the client browser and on the server. The caching mechanisms available to you range from single values to complete tables.

You can easily overuse these methods. My advice is, don't store any more information than you have to. Although caching all the data is tempting, with practice you'll find a good balance between caching data in memory and storing/retrieving data from a database. Often, it's useful to cache data during specific page sequences. There may be several such sequences, each of which comprises only a part of your application, and each may require that you cache different information. You should use the Session and Application `Contents` methods to find and remove data that you no longer need.

# CHAPTER NINE

# Dealing with Multiple Browsers

- Understanding Differences between Browsers
- Determining Browser Type
- Writing Browser-Specific Code
- Writing Code with Code

**N**ot everyone uses the Internet Explorer browser. I know that's hard to believe, but it's true. Somewhat less than half the world uses the Netscape Navigator browser. Fewer than 5 percent use less well known browsers such as Opera or Mosaic.

In this chapter, I'm going to concentrate on the differences between Netscape Communication Corporation's Netscape Navigator and Microsoft's IE, but the principles you'll see here apply to any browser. You'll learn how to:

- Determine the type of browser accessing your application
- Find detailed information about that browser type
- Use several approaches to writing browser-specific code

# Understanding Differences between Browsers

Not all browsers are the same, but they have some base-level capabilities that you can count on. For example, all modern browsers can display HTML version 3.2, and all modern browsers can display frames. Frames became available when Netscape released version 2 of its Navigator browser.

I'm not going to discuss browsers earlier than Netscape/IE version 2, although you might find a few still active on the Web. A few stubborn souls still surf the Web in text mode, but most people have realized that they're missing a large part of the Web experience by sticking to obsolete browser technology. I've found that most people upgrade relatively quickly when new versions become available.

Despite the universality and standard syntax of HTML, browsers differ in the quality of the HTML that they will accept and in the way that they display the information. Although important, the HTML differences in browsers through version 3.*x* were relatively small—Netscape and IE had a few proprietary tags. But starting with version 4.*x* browsers, the differences became huge—primarily because IE 4 included a much more complete implementation of dynamic HTML and cascading style sheet technology.

In addition to HTML tags, major differences exist in the capabilities of the two companies' browsers. Table 9.1 shows some of the most important differences in the version 4.*x* browsers.

**TABLE 9.1:** Comparison of Netscape and Internet Explorer Browser Features

| Feature | Netscape | Internet Explorer |
| --- | --- | --- |
| Inline frames | No | Yes |
| JavaScript | Yes | Yes (ECMAscript, JScript) |
| VBScript | No | Yes |
| ActiveX DLLs | No native support—available through third-party plug-ins | Yes |
| Java applets | Yes | Yes |
| Absolute positioning | Yes (with layers) | Yes |
| Functional buttons outside of forms | No | Yes |
| Viewing of documents other than HTML | No | Yes, all ActiveX documents (most Microsoft Office documents) |
| Script binding | No | Yes |
| Data binding | No | Yes |

As you can see—and as you would expect—Microsoft's implementation is tightly bound to Windows and COM technology. IE can directly display almost any Microsoft Office document in the browser. The appropriate application merges its menus and toolbars with the IE menus and toolbars. This lets you browse Word, Excel, and PowerPoint files in the same way that you browse HTML files. You also need to be aware of the client browser's capabilities if you begin sending client-side script, dynamic HTML, or, in general, any code that executes on the client rather than on the server.

Fortunately, WebClasses, like ASP files, execute entirely on the server. If the client browser is IE, you can use ActiveX technology or Java; if it's Netscape, you can use Java. The main point is that *whichever browser the client is using won't directly affect your WebClass code*. The browser type affects only what happens with the response that your WebClass returns.

Consequently, the job of the WebClass is to determine which browser the client is using, then to format a response appropriate for that browser.

Before you go any further, I should warn you that one part of WebClass development is directly related to browser type—the HTML templates. Unless you're delivering to a specific browser type, you should use a platform-neutral HTML editor. Failing that, write the HTML as strings concatenated with VB code. It's difficult to write code to parse the HTML template text and reformat it for one browser or another at runtime. You can select a template based on browser type, but you'll have to write two sets of separate-but-identical methods in your WebClass or put all the logic into subroutines and functions. You can't just substitute one template for another in the current implementation.

# Determining Browser Type

Browsers send an identifying string along with each request. The ASP page parses that into the ServerVariables collection under the key HTTP_USER_AGENT. For Internet Explorer 5, the string is:

```
HTTP_USER_AGENT=Mozilla/4.0 (compatible; MSIE 5.0; Windows NT 5.0)
```

For Netscape Communicator 4 for Windows 95, it is:

```
Mozilla/4.0b1 (Win95; I)
```

The string has plenty of information; how much of it you'll need depends on what you need to do. Differences exist not only between browsers and versions, but also between minor versions of each of the browsers (3, 3.1, 3.2, etc.). To make matters even worse, the capabilities of a specific version or sub-version differ between platforms: IE for the Macintosh is not exactly the same as IE for Windows 95, which is not the same as IE for Windows 3.1. Sometimes you need to know the exact browser version number, platform, and capabilities; other times you need to know only whether it's Netscape or IE. If you stick to standard HTML 3.2, you won't care at all as long as your HTML is well formed.

At the most basic level, you can search the HTTP_USER_AGENT string to determine whether a browser is IE or Netscape.

```
If instr(1, Request.ServerVariables("HTTP_USER_AGENT", _
    "MSIE", vbTextCompare) > 0 Then
......' browser type = IE
ElseIf instr(1, Request.ServerVariables _
    ("HTTP_USER_AGENT", "Netscape", vbTextCompare) > 0 Then
......' browser type = Netscape
```

If you need to know more than just the browser type, you can use the MSWC Browser Capabilities component (`browscap.dll`) delivered and installed with Active Server Pages technology. The MSWC.BrowserType object maps the HTTP_USER_AGENT string to a set of entries in an .ini file (`browscap.ini`) that must exist in the same directory as the `browscap.dll` file. Microsoft maintains this file with help from many developers. You can download the latest copy of the `browscap.ini` file from many sites on the Web. The official Microsoft version is now at `http://www.cyscape.com/browscap/`, but other sites have `browscap.ini` files that are much more complete.

When a BrowserType object finds one or more browser entries that match the string sent by the browser (more on that in a minute), the component finds the matching string in the `browscap.ini` file. The .ini file contains an associated list of properties for that browser, which the component then makes available to you as properties. Here's a sample entry from `browscap.ini` for an early version of Internet Explorer:

```
[Mozilla/1.22 (compatible; MSIE 2.0c; Windows 95)]
parent=IE 2.0
platform=Win95
version=2.0c
```

**NOTE** An .ini file is a text file. It contains strings in brackets called *sections*. Each section contains zero or more *entries*. Each entry consists of a key and a value. Comment lines begin with a semicolon. In Windows 3.*x*, .ini files held application initialization and settings, hence the name .ini. Microsoft abandoned .ini files (mostly) starting with Windows 95. Windows now stores most application settings in the Registry. Nonetheless, Windows still contains the API functions to read and write data to .ini files.

The section entries (in square brackets) correspond to the text sent by the browser in the HTTP_USER_AGENT variable. When the `BrowserType` object finds a matching string, it reads the parent entry if one exists—in this case, IE 2.0. The parent entry contains the list of base properties for that browser:

```
[IE 2.0]
browser=IE
version=2.0
majorver=2
minorver=0
frames=FALSE
```

```
tables=TRUE
cookies=TRUE
backgroundsounds=TRUE
vbscript=FALSE
javascript=FALSE
javaapplets=FALSE
beta=False
Win16=False
```

Individual browser sections can override or extend the base properties. For example, the base property named `Win16` is `False`. There is a 16-bit Windows version of IE 2, though, so the entry for that browser overrides the base property value:

```
[Mozilla/2.0 (compatible; MSIE 2.1; Windows 3.1)]
parent=IE 2.0
platform=Win16
Win16=True
version=2.1
minorver=#1
frames=True
```

If the BrowserType object can't find an exact match, it looks for wildcard matches. A wildcard section contains an asterisk. These sections are useful for matching browsers with only minor differences. For example, there were several minor differences between various NT versions of IE 3, so `browscap.ini` contains an entry that will match all of them:

```
[Mozilla/2.0 (compatible; MSIE 3.0; Windows NT;*)]
parent=IE 3.0
platform=WinNT
```

If the BrowserType object can't find *any* match, it looks for a default entry—a single asterisk that matches any browser. Here's a partial default entry listing:

```
;Default browser
[*]
browser=Default
Version=0.0
majorver=#0
minorver=#0
frames=False
tables=True
```

The BrowserType object searches the .ini file from top to bottom. It stops searching at the first match. Therefore, wildcard entries must appear after all other entries for that browser; otherwise, the BrowserType object will always find the wildcard entry first. Similarly, the default entry must be the final entry in the file.

Almost all the entries expose these properties:

- Major and minor version numbers
- Cookies
- Frames
- VBScript
- JavaScript

Other properties are exposed on a per-browser basis. You query the BrowserCap object's `Capabilities` property to find out whether the requesting browser supports these other capabilities.

## Using the Browser Capabilities Component

In this project, you'll use the Browser Capabilities component to determine the capabilities of your browser. You can't add a reference to the MSWC.BrowserType component from VB, and you can't create a new BrowserType object in a normal way from inside a WebClass (although I'll show you how to do that in Chapter 11, "Using ActiveX DLLs from WebClasses"). For now, the easiest way to take advantage of the component is to use it in an ASP page. This requires mixing VB WebClasses with ASP pages—something that you haven't done yet in the projects in this book. Fortunately, you can mix ASP pages and WebClass "pages" with impunity because the WebClass (as you'll recall from Chapter 4, "Introduction to WebClasses") is just a COM component called by an ASP page. WebClasses and ASP pages share the same ASP objects (Session, Response, etc.) so you can pass information from ASP pages to WebClasses and back again in Session variables.

The capability to mix ASP pages and WebClasses provides you the opportunity to put code that may change often (such as decisions about browser types) into a form that you can change easily. There's no code in the world that you can change more easily than an ASP page, because it's a text file, not a compiled and registered DLL.

In this project, you'll call an ASP page that will instantiate the Browser Capabilities component and store browser properties in Session variables. Your WebClass can then read the properties from the Session variables.

Start a new WebClass project. Name it **BrowserCapProj**. Rename the default WebClass to **BrowserCapTest** and set the `NameInURL` property to **BrowserCapTest** as well.

Enter this code into the `WebClass_Start` event:

```
Private Sub WebClass_Start()
    If Session("Browser") = "" Then
        Response.Redirect "getBrowserCapabilities.asp"
        Exit Sub
    End If
    Response.Write "<html><head></head><body>"
    Response.Write Request.ServerVariables _
        ("HTTP_USER_AGENT") & "<br>"
    Response.Write "Browser=" & Session("Browser") _
        & "<br>"
    Response.Write "Version=" & Session _
        ("BrowserVersion") & "<br>"
    Response.Write "Cookies=" & Session _
        ("BrowserCookies") & "<br>"
    Response.Write "VBScript=" & Session _
        ("BrowserVBScript") & "<br>"
    Response.Write "JavaScript=" & Session _
        ("BrowserJavaScript")
    Response.Write "</body></html>"
End Sub
```

The `WebClass_Start` event code writes the HTTP_USER_AGENT header string, then checks the value of `Session("Browser")`. If the variable is empty, then it redirects the browser to an ASP page called `getBrowserCapabilities`. The ASP page creates an MSWC.BrowserType component and saves five values in Session variables. Here's the VBScript code for `getBrowserCapabilities.asp`.

```
<% @ LANGUAGE = VBScript %>
<%
Response.Expires=-1
Dim objBrowsCap
Set objBrowsCap = Server.CreateObject("MSWC.BrowserType")
Session("Browser") = objBrowsCap.browser
Session("BrowserVersion") = objBrowsCap.version
```

```
Session("BrowserCookies") = objBrowsCap.cookies
Session("BrowserVBScript") = objBrowsCap.VBScript
Session("BrowserJavaScript") = objBrowsCap.JavaScript
Set objBrowsCap = Nothing
Response.redirect "BrowserCapTest.asp"
%>
```

The last line of the ASP script redirects back to the original WebClass page, which will then run the `WebClass_Start` event again. If you step through the project with the debugger, that's exactly what you'll see. Figure 9.1 shows the output of the program for Internet Explorer version 5.

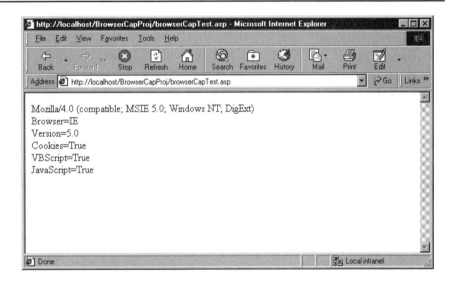

**FIGURE 9.1:**

Output from the BrowserCapTest WebClass_Start Event

Whether you need to use the Browser Capabilities component depends on how many types of browsers you expect to access your site and how polite you want to be. For many sites, searching the HTTP_USER_AGENT string tells you all you need to know. For example, if you only want to know whether the client browser is Internet Explorer, look for MSIE in the string:

```
Dim isIE As Boolean
isIE = InStr(1, Request.ServerVariables _
    ("HTTP_USER_AGENT"), "MSIE", vbTextCompare) > 0
If isIE Then
    Response.Write "You're using Internet Explorer."
End If
```

Now that you know how to determine *which* browser is accessing your application, you can determine how to respond.

# Writing Browser-Specific Code

As I mentioned at the beginning of this chapter, there are three ways to include browser-specific code in WebClasses. I'll show you all of them, and you can decide which method is best for you. The methods are:

- Writing browser-specific HTML templates
- Writing browser-specific HTML from a WebClass
- Using replaceable markers to create browser-specific pages

In the preceding section, you created a project that determined the browser type in the `WebClass_Start` event. In this section, you'll create two simple HTML templates—one for Netscape and one for IE. If you don't have both browsers, you can still run the code and see how the two differ.

## Writing Browser-Specific HTML Templates

Create a new HTML file. In the first file, enter this code:

```
<html><head><title>Internet Explorer Template</title></head>
<body>
<h2 align="center">Internet Explorer</h2>
<script language="VBScript">
...msgBox "This message box was created in VBScript",,"Message Boxes Have Titles!"
</script>
</body>
</html>
```

Save the file as **IETemplate.htm**. Create another HTML file and place this code in it:

```
<html><head><title>Netscape Navigator Template</title></head>
<body>
<h2 align="center">Netscape Navigator</h2>
<script language="JavaScript">
```

```
...alert("This message box was created in JavaScript");
</script>
</body>
</html>
```

Save the file as **NetscapeTemplate.htm**.

> **TIP** Did you remember to save the .htm files in a directory *other* than your WebClass project directory?

Create a new project directory and call it **MultipleBrowsers**. Create a new IIS project, rename it **MultipleBrowsers**, and save the project in the `Multiple-Browsers` directory. Rename the default WebClass to **WhichBrowser** and set the `NameInURL` property to **WhichBrowser** as well. Add both files as HTML templates. When the WebClass imports HTML files as templates, it does not retain the original filenames, so rename the IE template **IETemplate** and rename the Netscape template **NetscapeTemplate**.

Place this code into the `WebClass_Start` event:

```
Private Sub WebClass_Start()
    Dim isIE As Boolean
    isIE = InStr(1, Request.ServerVariables _
        ("HTTP_USER_AGENT"), "MSIE", vbTextCompare) > 0
    If isIE Then
        Set NextItem = IETemplate
    Else
        Set NextItem = NetscapeTemplate
    End If
End Sub
```

The `Start` event code determines which template to write based on the value of the Boolean variable `isIE`.

In the `Respond` event for each template, return the template with the `Write-Template` method:

```
Private Sub IETemplate_Respond()
    IETemplate.WriteTemplate
End Sub

Private Sub NetscapeTemplate_Respond()
    NetscapeTemplate.WriteTemplate
End Sub
```

Save the project. If you have a Netscape browser and an IE browser, navigate to the WebClass URL with each browser. You should see a message box in IE and an alert (which looks identical to a VB message box, but doesn't have a programmable title) in Netscape. If you don't have both browsers, use IE and add this code to the `WebClass_Start` event:

```
Private Sub WebClass_Start()
    Dim isIE As Boolean
    isIE = InStr(1, Request.ServerVariables _
        ("HTTP_USER_AGENT"), "MSIE", vbTextCompare) > 0
    If IsEmpty(Session("incr")) Then
        Session("incr") = 0
    Else
        Session("incr") = Session("incr") + 1
    End If
    isIE = (Session("incr") Mod 2 = 0)
    If isIE Then
        Set NextItem = IETemplate
    Else
        Set NextItem = NetscapeTemplate
    End If
End Sub
```

The changed code creates and increments the `Session("incr")` variable each time it runs. If the value is evenly divisible by two, the code returns the IE template with the VBScript message box; otherwise, it returns the Netscape template with the JavaScript alert. You can do this because IE supports both VBScript and JavaScript.

The advantage of putting browser-specific HTML in separate templates is that you can use an HTML editor to create and maintain the files. The disadvantage of putting the code in templates is that you now have two more files to maintain, vs. only one when you write the HTML from inside the WebClass.

## Writing Browser-Specific HTML from a WebClass

You can easily accomplish the same result without the templates. Change the `WebClass_Start` event code as follows:

```
' Change this
If isIE Then
    Set NextItem = IETemplate
```

```
Else
    Set NextItem = NetscapeTemplate
End If

' To this
If isIE Then
    Call IEStart
Else
    Call NetscapeStart
End If
```

Create a new subroutine called **IEStart**. Copy the HTML out of the IETemplate HTML template and paste it into the IEStart routine. Select the pasted HTML and replace the double quotes with single quotes; then add Response.Write commands to the beginning of each line.

```
Private Sub IEStart()
    With Response
        .Write "<html><head><title>Internet " _
            & "Explorer Template</title></head>"
        .Write "<body>"
        .Write "<h2 align='center'>Internet " _
            & "Explorer</h2>"
        .Write "<script language='VBScript'>"
        .Write "MsgBox ""This message box was created " _
            & "in VBScript""", ," _
            & """Message Boxes Have Titles!"""
        .Write "</script>"
        .Write "</body>"
        .Write "</html>"
    End With
End Sub
```

Do the same thing for Netscape, but call the routine **NetscapeStart**.

```
Private Sub NetscapeStart()
    With Response
        .Write "<html><head><title>Netscape " & _
            "Navigator Template</title></head>"
        .Write "<body>"
        .Write "<h2 align='center'>Netscape Navigator</h2>"
        .Write "<script language='JavaScript'>"
            .Write "alert(""This message box was " & _
```

```
                    "created in JavaScript"");"
            .Write "</script>"
            .Write "</body>"
            .Write "</html>"
        End With
    End Sub
```

Save and run the project. You'll see exactly the same screens and message boxes/alerts that you saw with the template-based method.

## Using Replaceable Markers to Create Browser-Specific Pages

The third method combines the two approaches by using WebClass tags for the parts of the template that are browser specific. You then substitute the appropriate content during the `ProcessTag` event. This approach is suitable for simple files but difficult to maintain for files that are more complex. Part of the HTML resides in the templates, part in the WebClass. Neither the person editing the HTML nor the programmer can see how the file will look or act until after it is rendered by the WebClass.

You've had plenty of practice with tag replacement at this point, so I'm not going to write out the code. If you want to test the third method, insert a WebClass tag in place of the script in one of the templates, then write out either the VBScript or the JavaScript code during the `ProcessTag` event.

# Writing Code with Code

You did add one new tool in the last two projects; you're using server-side code to write client-side code. The message box and the alert scripts run entirely on the client.

The ability to write code with code is not only interesting, but also powerful. If you've ever written a Visual Basic add-in, then you'll immediately understand the time you can save by automating common tasks. One common task is writing client-side scripts, many of which are repetitive and lend themselves to automation. You can write dynamic scripts easily by using tag replacement or by wrapping the code to generate the scripts in a function. You can pass parameters to these script-automation functions to create page-specific scripts. This capability is especially useful when your project work is split between HTML/layout artists and programmers, who can then insert scripts as needed to act on the various objects on the page.

You should be aware that you can write not only client-side code with WebClasses, but also server-side code in the form of ASP or HTML files. You've already seen how to create an ASP file that rewrites itself. You can extend this capability with WebClasses. If certain portions of your application need to change often, you can write the ASP files by using information collected by the WebClass.

For example, suppose your application generates a complex report. The database queries may take several minutes. Unless the report needs to be up to the minute, you can cache it by writing an HTML or ASP page that contains the result of the first report request. Having generated the page for one request, you can simply return the generated page for subsequent requests. You can use a hidden date field or a database query to determine when you need to refresh the report.

# CHAPTER TEN

# Retrieving and Storing Data in Databases

- Understanding ADO
- Introducing the ADO Object Model
- Retrieving Data with ADO

An entire book in this set of VB Developer's Guides is devoted to explaining ADO in detail, so you can see that it's a topic too large to cover completely in a single chapter. Nevertheless, you should be able to find enough information here to cover most of your data access needs.

I'm going to assume that you understand how to move around and create objects (tables, queries, indexes, etc.) in your database of choice. I've written the examples in this chapter so they'll work in both Access and SQL Server.

The purpose of this chapter is to show you how to use ADO in WebClasses. If you've used ADO from Active Server Pages or other types of Visual Basic projects, you won't find much that's new in this chapter. In other words, there's no syntactical difference between using ADO from ASP or from standard projects in VB and using ADO from WebClasses. But there's a big difference in the way you *approach* data access from a Web application.

Those of you who have not used Data Access Objects (DAO) yet should find this a quick and practical introduction. By the end of the chapter, you will be able to retrieve and store data via ADO, use stored procedures, and use DDL and ActiveX Data Object Extensions (ADOX) to create and modify objects in your database.

I am—reluctantly—going to write most of the code so you can use it from either Access or SQL Server. I will warn you in advance that Access is suitable for developmental and learning purposes only; you should not use it for production-quality applications. If you're using Access 2000, you can use the new Microsoft Data Engine (MSDE) to experiment with stored procedures. For MSDE databases, use the SQL Server examples in this chapter.

# Understanding ADO

ADO is a flexible method of retrieving and storing data not only in relational databases, but also in text files, spreadsheets, directories—any type of data store for which someone has written an Object Linking and Embedding Database (OLEDB) driver, called a *provider* in ADO-speak. Microsoft introduced ActiveX Data Objects (ADO) version 1 with IIS 3 and ASP pages. They have continued to extend the technology, which is now at version 2.1, soon to be 2.5.

Microsoft is committed to ADO. I expect that ADO will gradually supplant other methods of database access, because it's easy to learn and to use.

The main advantages of ADO are that it has:

- A simple and relatively flat object model
- Consistent syntax across all data stores
- The capability for disconnected and persistent recordsets

Many programmers—especially those using Access and FoxPro databases—avoided ADO until recently. Earlier versions of ADO provided SQL Server programmers with access to the database objects through DDL but did not provide easy ways to program Access database objects. That's changed with version 2.1, which includes the ADOX that contain the equivalents of Table, QueryDef, Index, and other intrinsic database objects.

# Introducing the ADO Object Model

You need to worry about only four ADO objects for retrieving and storing data (see, it's already easier than DAO). These are:

**Connection object**  Connections are pipelines to data. You can't get data until you tell ADO where the data is. You also need to tell ADO which driver (called *provider* in ADO) you want to use to retrieve the data. The Connection object provides the properties and methods to open and close database connections.

**Recordset object**  The ADO Recordset object is a two-dimensional array that holds data that you retrieve from a data store. The Recordset object provides the methods and properties to access any single data element and to navigate between data rows.

**Field object**  This object contains data for a single column in one row of a recordset.

**Command object**  You use ADO Command objects to get data from queries or stored procedures. Queries and stored procedures are pre-compiled SQL stored in the database. You can use Connection objects and recordsets with queries and stored procedures that don't require parameters. You need to use Command objects only when you're performing the same query or stored procedure multiple times, or when you need to supply or retrieve parameter values to or from a query or stored procedure.

> **NOTE** To use ADO from Visual Basic, you must set a reference to the Microsoft ActiveX Data Objects library.

## Opening and Closing Connections

To open a database connection, you create a Connection object, then use its Open method to create an open connection through which you can retrieve and update data.

```
Dim conn as new ADODB.Connection
conn.Open  "Provider=SQLOLEDB;" & _
"SERVER=myServer;DATABASE=pubs","sa",""
```

> **NOTE** The Microsoft **pubs** database comes with SQL Server. If you don't have SQL Server, you can download a Microsoft Access database containing the tables of the **pubs** database from the Sybex Web site.

> **NOTE** To download code, navigate to http://www.sybex.com. Click Catalog and search for this book's title. Click the Downloads button and accept the licensing agreement. Accepting the agreement grants you access to the downloads page for the book.

The Open method takes up to four arguments. ADO passes any additional arguments through to the provider. The four arguments are:

**ConnectionString** The ConnectionString can be a DSN (for example, pubs), or it can be a semicolon-separated string containing the provider, database, server, remote provider, and remote server. The remote provider and remote server parameters are required only for connections opened remotely (such as the client browser). You can't specify the provider with a DSN. If you don't specify a provider, ADO uses the default ODBC driver

(MSDASQL). You should avoid DSNs unless you're happy with the default ODBC driver.

**UserID**  The ID of the person you want to connect to the database. Usually, you can use the same `UserID` for every connection unless you need multiple levels of permissions.

**Password**  The password that matches the specified `UserID`.

*Optional*  A `ConnectOptionEnum` value. The only current valid values are none (leave the parameter blank) and `adConnectAsync`. The Connection object will notify you via a `ConnectComplete` event when the connection is available if you use the `adConnectAsync` value.

Get used to writing the connection string. If you aren't sure how to write one, create a DSN, open a connection, then print or use the debugger to view the `ConnectionString` property. For example, after opening a connection using the pubs DSN, my connection string looks like this:

```
Provider=MSDASQL.1;User ID=sa;Data Source=pubs;Connect
Timeout=15;Extended Properties="DSN=pubs;Description=Pubs
database;SERVER=myServer;UID=sa;APP=Visual
Basic;WSID=myServer;DATABASE=pubs;Network=DBMSSOCN;
Address=myServer,1433;Regional=Yes;UseProcForPrepare=0";
Locale Identifier=1033
```

After you see the connection string, you can copy the appropriate parts and change the provider:

```
Provider=SQLOLEDB;SERVER=myServer;DATABASE=pubs
```

By default, ADO opens connections in an unknown state, which is effectively read-only. If you need to update or insert data via a connection, you need to set the `Connection.Mode` property *before* you open the connection.

```
Dim conn as new ADODB.Connection
Conn.Mode = adOpenReadOnly
conn.Open  "Provider=SQLOLEDB;" & _
"SERVER=myServer;DATABASE=pubs","sa",""
```

After you have an open connection, you are ready to access the data. Databases are capable of only two types of operations: They can retrieve data, and they can alter the data and objects in the database. You'll see how to do both in the rest of this chapter.

# Retrieving Data with ADO

You retrieve data from a data store into a Recordset object. In ADO, there are often several ways to accomplish the same task. For example, you can retrieve data by using a Connection object, a Command object, or the Open method of a Recordset object. Sometimes, to accomplish your goals you must use only one of these methods. Other times, you may freely choose between any of them. The principal difference lies in how much code you want to write.

In general, you want to minimize the number of objects you have to create and you want to specify exactly what data you want to retrieve, how you want to retrieve it, and how you want the recordset to act. This leads to the rather odd fact that the more code you write in ADO, the faster your data access is likely to be.

## Retrieving Data with the ADO Connection Object

The simplest way to retrieve data from a database is to create a Connection object, open it, then use it to retrieve the data into a Recordset object. For example, to retrieve all the book titles from the pubs sample database:

```
Dim R As ADODB.Recordset
Dim conn as new ADODB.Connection
conn.Open  "Provider=SQLOLEDB;" & _
"SERVER=myServer;DATABASE=pubs","sa",""
Set R = conn.Execute("SELECT * FROM Titles")
```

When you open a recordset in this manner, you get a read-only, forward-only recordset. This is the most efficient type of recordset, and you'll use it more than other types in Web applications. However, it has several deficiencies that make it unsuitable for many purposes. For example, you can't update the records, you can't determine how many records were returned (without looping through the recordset), you can only move forward through the recordset, and you can't control whether or how the server locks the retrieved records. If you want to access earlier records again, you have to retrieve a new copy of the recordset.

## Using ADO Cursor Types

Each recordset that you open contains a pointer to the current record, assuming the query returned any records. By default, when you open a recordset, the pointer points to the first record. ADO allows several types of record pointers (called *cursors*, because you can move through the data with them). Many people call the read-only, forward-only type of cursor a *firehose cursor*, or sometimes, a cursorless recordset. The firehose cursor is the fastest type of cursor.

There are four types of cursors. All except the adForwardOnly cursors allow both forward and backward movement; however, the keyset cursor provides the best level of backward movement performance. The four types are described in the following list:

**adOpenForwardOnly**   This is the firehose cursor. You use this type of cursor when you want to display records.

**adOpenStatic**   This cursor takes a "snapshot" of the records at the time when you retrieve the recordset—you can't see any changes that other people make to the records. You use this type of cursor when you need to cache records.

**adOpenKeyset**   Each record has a unique key. When you use this cursor type, the recordset retrieves the set of keys to the requested records and buffers the first few records. As you request more records, the cursor retrieves the data from the database. You can see changes that others make to the records in the recordset, but you can't see new or deleted records. You use this type of cursor when you need to make multiple updates or when the retrieved recordset is large.

**adOpenDynamic**   This cursor is like adOpenKeyset, but you can see new and deleted records. Dynamic cursors use lots of resources and aren't particularly useful in a Web environment. You should not usually need to use dynamic recordsets with WebClasses.

## Retrieving Data with the Recordset Object

If you need anything other than a forward-only cursor, if you want to know how many records were returned, or if you want to control how the server locks records, you can't use the Connection object's Open method. You must use the Recordset.Open method instead. To do this, set the Recordset's CursorType property to the cursor type you need, then open it using the Recordset.Open method. For example, to obtain the list of titles from the pubs database using a static cursor, you would write

```
Dim R As ADODB.Recordset
Set conn = New ADODB.connection
conn.Open "Provider=SQLOLEDB;" & _
"SERVER=myServer;DATABASE=pubs","sa",""
```

```
Set R = new ADODB.Recordset
R.Open "SELECT * FROM Titles", conn, adOpenStatic
```

The `Recordset.Open` method accepts several arguments, most of which are optional:

**Source** Required. An SQL query, name of a table, name of a query/stored procedure, or name of a Command object

**ActiveConnection** Optional. An open Connection object

**CursorType** Optional. An ADO `CursorTypeEnum` constant

**LockType** Optional. An ADO `LockTypeEnum` constant

**Options** Optional. An ADO `CommandTypeEnum` value (may require combined values)

Don't worry about `LockType` and `Options` right now; we'll get to those soon.

Most of the ADO properties and arguments have default values. ADO often lets you substitute one type of value for another. For example, rather than opening a Connection object, you can substitute a connection string for the second parameter of the `Recordset.Open` method.

```
Dim R As ADODB.Recordset
Set R = new ADODB.Recordset
R.Open "SELECT * FROM Titles", "Provider=SQLOLEDB;" & _
"SERVER=myServer;DATABASE=pubs;UID=sa;PWD=", adOpenStatic
```

If you do this, ADO creates and opens a connection for you. As soon as you close the recordset, the connection closes as well. However, it's not a good idea to open recordsets this way because ADO will create a Connection object anyway and use that to retrieve the data—and ADO does not pool connections created in this manner. In general, despite the availability of default values, you're much better off if you specify all the properties and methods. When you don't provide them, ADO makes the decision for you—and it doesn't always make the best decision.

## Using Disconnected Recordsets

Since ADO 2, you can "disconnect" or disassociate recordsets from the connection with which you opened them. To disconnect a recordset, you must set the `CursorLocation` property to `adUseClient`. Both the Connection object and the Recordset object support the `CursorLocation` property. The default value is adUseServer, which places the burden of cursor movement on the server rather than the client (the recordset). The adUseClient setting is better. If you set the Connection object's CursorLocation property, recordsets that you open using that connection inherit the setting. You can override the setting for individual recordsets by setting the CursorLocation property for the Recordset object.

Disconnecting a recordset frees its associated connection to the pool so that the freed Connection object can be reused. Freeing connections is a major performance enhancement when you are likely to keep a recordset open for any significant length of time. For example, when you're formatting a large table with data from a recordset, you should disconnect the recordset first, to free the connection. If you cache Recordset objects by storing them in Session variables (which I don't recommend), the associated connection is unavailable to any other user unless you first disconnect the recordset.

When you open and disconnect a recordset by using the adLockBatchUpdate locking option, you can update the disconnected records, then save the data to the database later by reconnecting the recordset to a valid connection. If you plan to do this (which is convenient), you need to be aware of two issues:

- ADO cannot update values from multiple tables. If your recordset contains data from multiple tables, you should update the data yourself.

- You must include the key field(s) from the table in order to update the data properly. ADO cannot match the disconnected records to their proper rows if the key values are missing.

## Using ADO Record-Locking Options

ADO provides four record-locking options. The result they provide depends on the database you're using. Some databases lock rows, others lock pages. The options are as follows:

> **adLockReadOnly**   Database does not place locks on data
>
> **adlockOptimistic**   Database locks data only during actual updates
>
> **adLockPessimistic**   Database locks data until you explicitly release the locks
>
> **adLockBatchOptimistic**   Like adLockOptimistic, but you use this flag to batch updates rather than to perform single record updates

In general, you want to use the locking scheme that will place the least restrictions on other people using your application. The least restrictive option is `adLockReadOnly`. I highly recommend that you use this option exclusively if possible. That means that you should not use recordsets to update data—use stored procedures instead. If you follow that recommendation, you won't need to worry about locks. Use timestamp fields to determine whether the underlying data has changed since you retrieved it.

If you insist on using recordsets to update data, try to use the `adLockOptimistic` option or `adLockBatchOptimistic` option whenever possible—preferably with disconnected recordsets. The reason you should avoid `adLockPessimistic` is that the data is unavailable to other users while you have the record locked. The data stays locked until you have finished updating it. Sometimes it's convenient to lock the data exclusively, but you don't ever have to; you can use timestamp fields instead.

## Understanding ADO's Unfortunate *Options* Argument

Most areas of ADO are well thought out, but not all. One area that needs some work is the ubiquitous `Options` argument.

For example, the `Connection.Execute` method takes three arguments: an SQL statement or query, a variable to hold the number of rows affected, and an `Options` argument. When calling `Connection.Execute`, the `Options` argument is a `CommandTypeEnum` value. The `CommandTypeEnum` value isn't required, but leaving it out affects how quickly the ADO can interpret the command. The possible values of the `Options` argument are:

**adCmdText**   Interprets the `CommandText` argument as an SQL statement.

**adCmdTable**   Interprets `CommandText` as a table name.

**adCmdTableDirect**   Interprets `CommandText` as a table name whose columns are all returned.

**adCmdStoredProc**   Interprets `CommandText` as a stored procedure name.

**adCmdUnknown**   Default. If you don't specify the `CommandType`, ADO sets it to `adCmdUnknown`. For unknown command types, ADO checks `CommandText` against the names of stored procedures and tables. If it finds a match, it executes `CommandText` as a table or stored procedure; if not, it attempts to parse `CommandText` as a SQL statement.

**adCommandFile**   Use this value when you're reconstituting a persisted recordset from a file.

**adExecuteNoRecords**  When you execute a command that doesn't return records, or for which you don't want the returned records, use this value. Unlike all the other values, you combine this with `adCmdText` or `adCmdStoredProc`.

In other cases, the `Options` argument requires a different value. For example, the `Connection.Open` method (which the MSDN documentation says takes three arguments) can actually take four; the fourth one, `Options`, accepts a `ConnectOptionEnum` value. Currently (up to ADO 2.1) the `ConnectOptionEnum` has only one value: `adAsyncConnect` (16).

It's easy to confuse the required `Option` type values because of the common name. Using the Object Browser to find the required values is also easier (and more accurate) than using the documentation.

## Retrieving Data with the Command Object

You've seen how to open recordsets from connections and how to use the `Recordset.Open` method. You can also use the Command object to retrieve data. You don't typically need to use a Command object unless you want to perform a query multiple times or unless your query has parameters. Remember, creating unnecessary objects carries a performance penalty.

To use a Command object, you:

1. Create the Command object
2. Set its `CommandText` property to a table name, query/stored procedure name, or an SQL statement
3. Set its `ActiveConnection` property to an open Connection object
4. Use the `Execute` method to retrieve a recordset

Here's an example:

```
Dim conn as Connection
Dim cm as Command
Dim R as Recordset
Set conn = New ADODB.connection
conn.Open "Provider=SQLOLEDB;" & _
"SERVER=myServer;DATABASE=pubs","sa",""
Set cm = New Command
```

```
cm.CommandText="SELECT * FROM Titles"
set cm.ActiveConnection = conn
set R = cm.Execute
```

Setting up and executing a Command object takes more code, but when you need to run a query multiple times, it's much faster than retrieving data via a Connection object. The initial execution is no faster than using the `Execute` method of a Connection object with an SQL statement. However, like a stored procedure or Access query, subsequent executions contain pre-compiled SQL and, therefore, they execute very quickly.

When you specify SQL as a string, it's called *dynamic SQL*. Dynamic SQL is relatively slow compared to queries or stored procedures because the server has to parse and compile the SQL, create a query execution plan, then retrieve the data. In contrast, when you use queries and stored procedures, both the SQL and the query execution plan are pre-compiled and immediately ready for execution—all the database server has to do is retrieve the data.

I've been using the terms *query* and *stored procedure* interchangeably so far, but they're not the same at all. The generic term *query* means any SQL statement that returns data. For most VB programmers, a query means a Microsoft Access pre-compiled SQL statement. Access queries can contain only a single SQL statement. A stored procedure is a term used with ODBC databases such as SQL Server and Oracle. Stored procedures can contain not only multiple SQL statements but also *code*. This feature is extremely important because it can mean the difference between a successful and unsuccessful application.

> **NOTE** For the rest of this book, I'm going to use the term *stored procedure* to mean either an Access query or a stored procedure. This is partly to avoid having to write *query/stored procedure* whenever I need to use the term and partly to encourage you to move away from Access and toward an ODBC database as quickly as possible. I'll use the term *query* generically to mean any dynamic SQL request to the database server except stored procedures.

Executing code on the database server results in three benefits for your application:

- You can move program logic into the database where you can update it easily by replacing the text of the stored procedure. You don't have to recompile your application.

- Code compiled in the database acts directly on the data without moving that data back and forth through the network. Not only does this reduce network traffic, it also frees your Web server from performing routine database updates.

- You can partition your program to take advantage of the database's built-in security—restricting access to data and stored procedures based on a person's identity.

In SQL Server, you use a Basic-like language called Transact SQL to write stored procedures. Transact SQL has a full set of operators, built-in functions, and If... Then...Else, For...Next, Case, and looping constructs that let you write complex programs that execute within the context of the database server.

Besides running queries multiple times, the other reason to use a Command object is to retrieve data by using stored procedures that require parameters. Often, these two needs go hand in hand. For example, to retrieve a single record from the Authors table in the pubs database, you need to specify a *condition* that determines which record to select. In SQL, you specify conditions in a WHERE or HAVING clause:

```
SELECT * FROM Authors WHERE au_ID = '238-95-7766'
```

The query will select a single record (not all fields are shown here):

| au_id | au_lname | au_fname | phone |
|---|---|---|---|
| 238-95-7766 | Carson | Cheryl | 415 548-7723 |

Now suppose you have a need to run that same query, but with a different author ID, once for every request to your Web site. You can't store the SQL as written because it will always return a specific record. Instead, you store it as a parameter query or stored procedure. The following stored procedure returns a single Author record. To use the stored procedure, you must specify one parameter: the Author ID (au_id).

In Access the stored procedure looks like this:

```
PARAMETERS au_id Text;
SELECT Authors.* FROM Authors
WHERE (((Authors.au_id)=[au_id]));
```

To create the stored procedure in Access, click the Queries tab, then click New. Click OK to accept Design View, then click the Close button without selecting any tables from the Show Table list. Click the SQL button on the toolbar and select the SQL view. Paste the text of the procedure into the SQL window to define the stored procedure. Save it as **getAuthor**.

In Transact SQL, the stored procedure looks like this:

```
CREATE PROCEDURE getAuthor @au_id varChar(11)
AS SELECT * FROM Authors WHERE Authors.au_id = @au_id
```

To create the stored procedure in SQL Server, paste this script into the iSQL window and run it.

```
if exists (select * from sysobjects where id = object_id('dbo.getAu-
thor') and sysstat & 0xf = 4)
    drop procedure dbo.getAuthor
GO

CREATE PROCEDURE getAuthor @au_id varChar(11)
AS SELECT * FROM Authors WHERE Authors.au_id = @au_id
GO
```

Despite the difference in the procedure's definitions in the two databases, you use them from ADO as if they were identical. Assume you have an open connection called **conn**. You create the Command object and assign the name of the query or stored procedure to the `CommandText` property, set the `ActiveConnection` to your open connection, then use the `Execute` method to fetch the data.

```
Dim cm as Command
Dim R as Recordset
Set cm = New Command
cm.commandText="getAuthor"
set cm.ActiveConnection = conn
set R = cm.Execute(Set R = cm.Execute _
    (reccount, Array("238-95-7766"), adCmdStoredProc)
```

The `Command.Execute` method takes several arguments. The first argument is a long integer value called `RecordsAffected` (the variable `recCount` in the fragment). You pass the variable in by reference and the database server fills it with the number of records affected by the query.

> **NOTE** The `RecordsAffected` argument always receives a value of –1 for queries that return records. It's only useful for queries that alter data (such as UPDATE, INSERT, and DELETE queries).

The second argument to the `Command.Execute` method is a Variant array of parameter values—in this case, the `au_id` of the record to retrieve. The third argument, `Options`, contains an ADO `CommandTypeEnum` value. The database server substitutes the values in the Variant array for the declared parameters in the stored procedure. The type and sequence of the parameter values in the array *must match the declared type and sequence of the expected parameters declared in the query definition.*

Getting the types and sequences to match by using Variants is not only difficult, it's an invitation to disaster. Luckily, the Command object has an alternate syntax that, while longer, is faster and unambiguous. When you use a Variant array to pass parameters, the Command object converts the array into individual Parameter objects and appends them to its Parameters collection. (OK, there is *one* more ADO object type that you need to know about, but it's very simple.)

To create a Parameter object, use the Command object's `CreateParameter` method, then append the new Parameter to the Parameters collection:

```
Dim cm as Command
Dim R as Recordset
Set cm = New Command
cm.commandText="getAuthor"
set cm.ActiveConnection = conn
cm.Parameters.Append cm.CreateParameter _
    ("au_id", adVarChar, adParamInput, 11, "238-95-7766")
Set R = cm.Execute(reccount, , adCmdStoredProc)
```

To create a Parameter object, you specify the name, data type, direction (input or output), defined size, and value of the parameter. Typically, you'll create and append Parameter objects in one statement, as shown.

The difference in speed between dynamic SQL and stored procedures can be dramatic. It's always best to experiment with such issues yourself to get a feel for the difference. After you've done this, you'll probably agree that the extra effort required to create and call stored procedures is worthwhile. The best way to experiment is to create a noncritical project that isolates the problem. In the next section, you'll create a project that illustrates the speed difference between dynamic SQL and stored procedures.

## Investigating Stored Procedures

For this project, you'll build a database with a large number of rows and populate the rows in code, using SQL statements. You will measure how long it takes to fill the table. Next, you will delete the data and populate the table again using a stored procedure, measuring how long that method takes.

Create a database and call it **WebData**. If you're using SQL Server 6.5 or earlier, you'll need to create the database on a device with at least 20MB of free space. Create the database log with a minimum of 10MB of free space. If you're creating the database in Access, you don't have to worry about the database size (yet). The Access database is available for download from the Sybex Web site. If you purchased this book in a set, the Access database is on the set's CD.

> **NOTE** To download code, navigate to `http://www.sybex.com`. Click Catalog and search for this book's title. Click the Downloads button and accept the licensing agreement. Accepting the agreement grants you access to the downloads page for the book.

Create one table in the database, called Products, that contains these fields:

**Microsoft Access**

| FieldName | FieldType | Size |
| --- | --- | --- |
| ID | AutoNumber | 4 |
| Name | Text | 100 |
| Description | Text | 255 |
| Price | Currency | 8 |
| Quantity | Long Integer | 4 |

**SQL Server/MSDE**

| FieldName | FieldType | Size |
| --- | --- | --- |
| ID | Identity | Integer |
| Name | VarChar | 100 |
| Description | VarChar | 255 |
| Price | Currency | 8 |
| Quantity | Integer | 4 |

Here's an SQL Data Definition Language (DDL) statement to drop and re-create the database. Load this script into the iSQL utility in SQL Server Enterprise Manager and run it to create the Products table.

```
if exists (select * from sysobjects where id =
   object_id('dbo.Products') and sysstat & 0xf = 3)
   drop table dbo.Products
GO

CREATE TABLE dbo.Products (
   ID int IDENTITY (1, 1) NOT NULL ,
   Name varchar (100) NOT NULL ,
   Description varchar (255) NOT NULL ,
   Price money NOT NULL ,
   Quantity int NOT NULL
)
GO
```

Create a new IIS project and rename it **WebDataAccess**. Rename the default WebClass to **WebData**. Add a reference to the Microsoft ActiveX Data Objects 2*x* Library (not the ActiveX Data Objects Recordset Library or the multi-dimensional library). Enter the code from Listing 10.1 into the `WebClass_Start` event procedure (overwriting the default `Start` event code), and run the project.

**LISTING 10.1**    **Code for Investigating Stored Procedures (*WebDataAccess.dsr*)**

```
Private Sub fillProductsSQL(whichDB As String, _
   withTran As Boolean)
   Dim SQL As String
   Dim conn As Connection
   Dim i As Integer
   Dim aName As String
   Dim aDescription As String
   Dim aPrice As Currency
   Dim aQuantity As Long
   Randomize
   Set conn = New Connection
   conn.Mode = adModeReadWrite
   If whichDB = "Access" Then
       conn.Open "WebData", "Admin", ""
       conn.Execute "DELETE FROM Products"
```

```
            Response.Write "Started Access Dynamic SQL Loop " _
                & "at: " & FormatDateTime(Now(), vbGeneralDate) _
                & "<BR>"
        Else
            conn.Open "Provider=SQLOLEDB;SERVER=Russell;DATABASE=WebData", _
"sa", ""
            conn.Execute "TRUNCATE TABLE Products"
            Response.Write "Started SQL Server Dynamic SQL " _
                & "Loop at: " & FormatDateTime _
                (Now(), vbGeneralDate) & "<BR>"
        End If
        If withTran Then
            conn.BeginTrans
        End If
        For i = 1 To 1000
            aName = "Product" & CStr(i)
            aDescription = "This is a test description " _
                & "of a non-existent product."
            aPrice = CCur(100 * Rnd)
            aQuantity = Int(1000 * Rnd) + 1
            SQL = "INSERT INTO Products "
            SQL = SQL & "(Name, Description, Price, Quantity) "
            SQL = SQL & "VALUES ('" & aName & "', '" & _
                aDescription & "', " & aPrice & ", " & _
                aQuantity & ")"
            conn.Execute SQL
        Next
        If whichDB = "Access" Then
            Response.Write "Finished Access Dynamic SQL " & _
                "Loop at: " & FormatDateTime _
                (Now(), vbGeneralDate) & "<BR>"
        Else
            Response.Write "Finished SQL Server Dynamic " _
                & "SQL Loop at: " & FormatDateTime(Now(), _
                vbGeneralDate) & "<BR>"
        End If
        If withTran Then
            conn.CommitTrans
        End If
        conn.Close
        
    End Sub
```

```
Private Sub fillProductsSP(whichDB As String, withTran As Boolean)
    Dim SQL As String
    Dim conn As Connection
    Dim cm As Command
    Dim i As Integer
    Dim aName As String
    Dim aDescription As String
    Dim aPrice As Currency
    Dim aQuantity As Long
    Randomize
    Set conn = New Connection
    conn.Mode = adModeReadWrite
    If whichDB = "Access" Then
        conn.Open "WebData", "Admin", ""
        conn.Execute "DELETE FROM Products"
        Response.Write "Started Access Stored " _
            & "Procedure Loop at: " & FormatDateTime _
            (Now(), vbGeneralDate) & "<BR>"
    Else
        conn.Open "Provider=SQLOLEDB;SERVER=Russell;" & _
            "DATABASE=WebData", "sa", ""
        conn.Execute "TRUNCATE TABLE Products"
        Response.Write "Started SQL Server Stored " _
            & Procedure Loop at: " & FormatDateTime(Now(), _
            vbGeneralDate) & "<BR>"
    End If
    Set cm = New Command
    cm.CommandType = adCmdStoredProc
    cm.Parameters.Append cm.CreateParameter _
       ("Name", adVarChar, adParamInput, 100, "")
    cm.Parameters.Append cm.CreateParameter("Description", _
       adVarChar, adParamInput, 255, "")
    cm.Parameters.Append cm.CreateParameter("Price", _
       adCurrency, adParamInput, , 0)
    cm.Parameters.Append cm.CreateParameter("Quantity", _
       adInteger, adParamInput, 4, 0)
    Set cm.ActiveConnection = conn
    cm.CommandText = "InsertProduct"
    cm.CommandType = adCmdStoredProc
    If withTran Then
        conn.BeginTrans
    End If
```

```
        For i = 1 To 1000
            cm.Parameters(0) = "Product" & CStr(i)
            cm.Parameters(1) = "This is a test description of " _
                & "a non-existent product."
            cm.Parameters(2) = CCur(100 * Rnd)
            cm.Parameters(3) = CLng((1000 * Rnd) + 1)
            cm.Execute
        Next
        If whichDB = "Access" Then
            Response.Write "Finished Access Stored Procedure Loop " _
                & "at: " & FormatDateTime(Now(), vbGeneralDate) & "<BR>"
        Else
            Response.Write "Finished SQL Server Stored Procedure " _
                & "Loop at: " & FormatDateTime(Now(), vbGeneralDate) & "<BR>"
        End If
        If withTran Then
            conn.CommitTrans
        End If
        conn.Close
End Sub
Private Sub WebClass_Start()
    ' call the dynamic SQL version with no transaction
    Call fillProductsSQL("Access", False)
    Call fillProductsSQL("SQLServer", False)
    ' call the stored procedure version with no transaction
    Call fillProductsSP("Access", False)
    Call fillProductsSP("SQLServer", False)

    ' call the dynamic SQL version with a transaction
    Call fillProductsSQL("Access", True)
    Call fillProductsSQL("SQLServer", True)
    ' call the stored procedure version with a transaction
    Call fillProductsSP("Access", True)
    Call fillProductsSP("SQLServer", True)
End Sub
```

The `WebClass_Start` event calls each function four times: twice for Access and twice for SQL Server, once with `withTran` (the second parameter) set to `False` (no transaction), and once with it set to `True` (use a transaction). If you have both Access and SQL Server, you will see something interesting—the Access version is over twice as fast as the SQL Server version when no transaction is in effect!

When you use a transaction, however, the SQL Server version is over twice as fast as Access!

On my computer, which has a Pentium II 400Mhz processor, it takes roughly five seconds to insert a thousand records into Access without a transaction, and twelve seconds to insert the same number of records into SQL Server. With a transaction, it still takes five seconds in Access, but less than two seconds in SQL Server.

When you run the code, you will notice that there is little (if any) difference between the dynamic SQL version and the stored procedure version. That's because the insert operation takes so much time that the process of parsing and compiling the SQL is not apparent. Retrieving data is a different story, though.

Listing 10.2 contains the code for another test that retrieves records from the table data you just created. To run the test, you'll need to create a stored procedure called **getProduct** in both Access and SQL Server. The stored procedure requires one argument: the ID of the product row to retrieve. It returns all the fields in that row. In Access the procedure (query) definition is

```
PARAMETERS ID Long;
SELECT Products.*, Products.ID
FROM Products
WHERE (((Products.ID)=[ID]));
```

In SQL Server, the stored procedure definition is

```
CREATE PROCEDURE getProduct @ID int AS
SELECT * FROM Products WHERE ID=@ID
```

Create another WebClass and set it as the start-up object, or replace the code from the previous test. On the Sybex Web site (or the CD, if you purchased this book in a set), the `WebData.dsr` contains a combination of the code from Listing 10.2 and Listing 10.1. Enter the code from Listing 10.2, then run the project.

> **NOTE** If you ran the insert procedure in Listing 10.1 more than once, you'll need to adjust the random ID generation code inside the Access loop in Listing 10.2, because the AutoNumber ID in Access won't start at 1. Use the formula `Int((upperbound - lowerbound + 1) * Rnd + lowerbound)` where **upperbound** is the highest ID value and `lowerbound` is the lowest ID value in the Products table.

**LISTING 10.2**     **More Code to Investigate Stored Procedures (*WebData.dsr*)**

```vb
Private Sub WebClass_Start()
    ' call the dynamic SQL version for each server
    Call getProductSQL("Access")
    Call getProductSQL("SQLServer")

    ' call the Stored Procedure version for each server
    Call getProductSP("Access")
    Call getProductSP("SQLServer")
End Sub
Private Sub getProductSP(whichDB As String)
    Dim SQL As String
    Dim conn As Connection
    Dim anID As Long
    Dim s As String
    Dim i As Integer
    Dim R As Recordset
    Dim cm As Command
    Randomize
    Set conn = New Connection
    conn.Mode = adModeReadWrite
    Set cm = New Command
    cm.CommandText = "getProduct"
    If whichDB = "Access" Then
        conn.Open "WebData", "Admin", ""
        Set cm.ActiveConnection = conn
        Response.Write "Started Access SQL Retrieval Loop " _
            & "at: " & FormatDateTime(Now(), vbGeneralDate) & "<BR>"
        For i = 1 To 1000
            anID = CLng((1000 - 1 + 1) * Rnd + 1)
            Set R = cm.Execute(, Array(anID), adCmdStoredProc)
            R.Close
        Next
    Else
        conn.Open "Provider=SQLOLEDB;SERVER=Russell;" & _
            "DATABASE=WebData", "sa", ""
        Set cm.ActiveConnection = conn
        Response.Write "Started SQL Server SQL Retrieval Loop " _
            & "at: " & FormatDateTime(Now(), vbGeneralDate) & "<BR>"
        For i = 1 To 1000
            anID = CLng((1000 - 1 + 1) * Rnd + 1)
            Set R = cm.Execute(, Array(anID), adCmdStoredProc)
```

```
            R.Close
        Next
    End If
    If whichDB = "Access" Then
        Response.Write "Finished Access SQL Retrieval Loop " & _
            "at: " & FormatDateTime(Now(), vbGeneralDate) & "<BR>"
    Else
        Response.Write "Finished SQL Server SQL Retrieval Loop " & _
            "at: " & FormatDateTime(Now(), vbGeneralDate) & "<BR>"
    End If
    Set R = Nothing
    conn.Close
    Set conn = Nothing
End Sub
```

This time, the results are a little different. Each procedure generates a random value between 1 and 1,000, then retrieves the record from the Products table that corresponds to the random ID. The procedure getProductSQL retrieves the records by using dynamic SQL. The getProductSP retrieves the records by using a stored procedure. Each procedure loops 1,000 times, so each retrieves 1,000 records.

On my computer (a 400Mhz Pentium II running NT Workstation), the get-ProductSQL procedure takes about five seconds running against Access and about two seconds running against SQL Server. The stored procedure version still takes five seconds running against Access (no improvement) but takes less than one second running against SQL Server.

The results of these two tests should show you several things:

- You're better off running SQL Server in Web applications.
- Use transactions when inserting data.
- Use stored procedures when retrieving data.

# Accessing Databases from WebClasses

There are some specific differences between accessing databases from standard client-server programs and accessing databases from Web applications.

> **WARNING** Don't use WebClasses to access databases directly; use data access components instead.

OK, that's not a commandment, but you violate it at your peril. You should usually place your database access code in a separate component and run it as an MTS (or COM+) component. If you don't do that, you limit the scalability of your application because all your code must run on one computer. Later in this book, you will build an application that uses multiple components and MTS, but so far, I've violated that rule, purely because it's more expedient to do so in order to create understandable examples. In other words, do as I say, not as I do.

## Get In, Get the Data, Get Out

Your goal, in the server portion of a Web application, is to service the client's request as efficiently as possible while using as few server resources as possible. You can translate that goal to "Get in, get the data, and get out." Keep that goal in mind as you access databases. This section lists a few rules that apply to all Web applications that use databases:

- *Only retrieve the fields you need*. Granted, writing an SQL statement such as "SELECT * ..." is much easier than writing all the fields. Taking SQL shortcuts such as leaving out the table names for unique fields (for example, writing au_id rather than Authors.au_id) is also tempting. Each time you take a shortcut, though, somebody else's code needs to fill in the missing pieces.

- *Minimize locks*. Open connections and cursors in read-only mode whenever possible. The database does not have to apply table, page, or record locks to retrieve data in read-only mode. For single queries, you'll never see the difference. Under heavy use, you will.

- *Use firehose cursors*. Whenever possible, use a forward-only, read-only cursor. This type of cursor has the least overhead and is the fastest type of cursor, thus saving resources and time.

- *Use connections lavishly*. This is directly opposed to your natural inclination to open a connection early in a program, leave it open by caching it in a variable, then use it whenever you want to. When you do that, you avoid the overhead (and the extra code) of closing the connection, but it's the wrong approach in a Web environment. Instead, you want to open connections as late as possible and release them as early as possible. This works because IIS and MTS can pool connections. The pooled connection doesn't actually close when your application closes it; the connection is released to the pool instead, so some other thread can use it.

- *Disconnect recordsets when possible*. Since ADO version 2, you can disconnect recordsets from their connections. To disconnect a recordset, set its `ActiveConnection` property to `Nothing`. Doing so frees the connection for use by another thread or application. You may disconnect Recordsets only with static cursors and with their `CursorLocation` property set to `adUseClient`.

- *Cache data in files when possible*. As you saw earlier in this book, you can cache preformatted table data in files. When the data values are static or don't change often, retrieving a file is much more efficient than accessing a database.

- *Don't cache ADO objects*. You should never store any ADO object in Session or Application variables. This is one of the first things most new WebClass and ASP programmers want to do, and it has an immediate deleterious effect on their applications. Store the data as individual variables, strings, or arrays, or use the StoredRecordset and StoredDictionary classes to cache data.

- *Use Command objects and stored procedures*. Writing all your SQL as dynamic SQL is tempting because it's so easy to change, but it's highly inefficient. Create stored procedures instead. Not only will you get an immediate performance boost, but you also will help isolate your application from changes if the database changes. That means you won't have to recompile and reinstall your application just because someone changed a field name on the server. Use Command objects and pass parameters to the stored procedures to obtain the recordsets.

- *Use output parameters*. Although you haven't seen any examples in this book (because using output parameters is beyond its scope), when you want to retrieve individual values from the database, you can—and should—use output parameters rather than returning recordsets. An output parameter is essentially the same as a return value from a function. You pass a variable in to hold the value, SQL Server fills the variable with the return value, and you retrieve the value when the stored procedure call returns. Output parameters save resources, time, and code.

- *Don't concatenate long strings*. As you saw in Chapter 4, "Introduction to WebClasses," when formatting table data, building short strings and periodically adding them to a longer return string is much more efficient than continually appending data directly to the return string.

## Write Functions to Simplify ADO

One of the problems with most data access models is that because they're powerful, they can also require a good deal of repetitive code. To alleviate this problem, you can write wrapper functions for ADO that eliminate most of the code. The key is to make the wrapper functions sufficiently flexible so that you can open connections and recordsets of various types by using the same syntax for all calls.

To do this, you must first realize that there are really only two types of database operations: those that retrieve data, and those that change either data or database objects. Therefore, it should be possible to construct a small number of methods to access the data. In fact, you can wrap ADO in only three functions, with minimal loss of functionality. They are:

**OpenConnection**   Opens connections

**GetRecordset**   Retrieves recordsets and/or values of output parameters

**ExecuteSQL**   Updates/inserts/deletes data, or alters database objects

The `OpenConnection` function isn't absolutely necessary, but it does simplify development by trapping errors associated with opening connections. How many times have you seen another developer (not you, of course) write code like this:

```
Set conn = New Connection
Conn.Open "myConnection", "sa", ""
```

I suspect we've all seen (and written) code like this numerous times. The code is technically perfect—but it won't always work. At some point in the life of your application, the connection will be unable to open. Maybe the network's down, maybe the database server is down, maybe someone changed the database name or DSN reference—who knows? That's the point: You don't know, so you must anticipate and plan for the unexpected. Therefore, in the real world, the code you must write looks more like this:

```
Function myFunction()
    On Error Goto connectionError
    Set conn = New Connection
    Conn.Open "myConnection", "sa", ""
    On Error goto otherError
    ' do something
myFunctionExit:
    Exit Function
```

```
ConnectionError:
    Select Case Err.Number
        ' handle errors
    End Select
    Resume myFunctionExit
OtherError:
    ' handle errors here
    ' Resume myFunctionExit
End Function
```

I don't know about you, but I certainly don't want to handle errors in each and every individual function. Instead, the idea is to centralize error handling by isolating specific operations in functions that are both easy-to-use and have robust error-trapping.

The functions do require parameters, but most of them are optional, and all of them have default values. For example, to retrieve a read-only, forward-only recordset, you would write code like this:

```
Set conn = openConnection(myConnectionString)
If not getRecordset(R, conn, "myStoredProc", _
    adCmdStoredProc, ALLOW_EMPTY) then
    ' show error here
End If
'   display results
```

One function is not only easier to remember than multiple methods for retrieving recordsets, but also easier to teach to others and to maintain.

You can write similar code to execute database commands and stored procedures that don't return recordsets. The `ExecuteSQL` function accepts parameters in a Dictionary object. The function builds ADO Parameter objects using the Dictionary keys as the names of the parameters. The Dictionary values are the parameter values. It uses the variable subtype (for example, String, Currency, Long, etc.) of the Dictionary values to translate Visual Basic data types into their corresponding ADO parameter type value constants. I've included the code for these and other useful functions on the Sybex Web site.

So far, you've had to include classes in your projects to use objects. In the next chapter, you'll see how to use compiled ActiveX DLLs to extend the functionality of your applications. Although I'm sure you've built and referenced DLLs in standard projects many times, they won't work with WebClasses at runtime unless you run them under Microsoft Transaction Server. In the next chapter, you'll see how to set up external DLLs so you can use them from WebClass-based applications.

# CHAPTER ELEVEN

# Using ActiveX DLLs from WebClasses

- Thinking of WebClasses as Glue
- Accessing ActiveX DLLs from WebClasses
- Using the ObjectContext Object from WebClasses
- Testing ActiveX DLLs from a WebClass
- Persisting ActiveX Objects
- Building a Browser-Based Code Repository

In this chapter, you'll see how to create and use external DLLs that expose ActiveX objects. Using external DLLs from a WebClass can result in permissions problems and object reference problems, and this chapter will show you how to solve these problems. You'll also see how to persist objects and how to extend your command of state maintenance to objects. At the end of the chapter, I've included a project that uses almost every technique that you've seen in this book. You'll be happy to know that—unlike the other projects in the book—I don't expect you to make continual changes to the code.

# Thinking of WebClasses as Glue

In Chapter 4, "Introduction to WebClasses," I said that WebClasses act as the glue between the user interface (HTML) and back-end databases or middle-tier business objects. So far, you haven't seen this in action—we've put all the business rules and class objects directly into the WebClass project. Including business and database logic inside a WebClass project is useful for training purposes, for small sites, and for initial development, but it's not the best approach for several reasons.

Consider what happens when a user makes a call to your WebClass. The server must ask the WebClassManager to create an instance of your WebClass. Obviously, the larger the WebClass, the longer it takes to load and the more resources it uses on the server. Remember, the whole point of a Web application is to get in, get the data, and get out as fast as possible.

Another problem with using WebClasses as part of the business objects or the data-access layer is that you can't replace a DLL while IIS holds a reference to it without stopping and starting the application, or in some cases, the server itself. However, you can replace individual COM DLLs called by the WebClass without stopping the application—as long as the COM DLLs run in an MTS package.

If you want a fast and scaleable site, you need to plan your code so that the WebClass obtains data from back-end business objects and formats that data to feed HTML and script to the browser. You should not access databases directly or perform complex logical processing within your WebClass.

# Accessing ActiveX DLLs from WebClasses

WebClasses do not participate in transactions—in other words, they don't automatically run under MTS. WebClasses don't recognize the design-time MTSTransactionMode setting available from other VB ActiveX DLLs. Nevertheless, IIS applications (those you create via the Internet Service Manager) run under MTS whether you run them as part of the IIS root application or whether you set them up to run in an isolated process.

The inability of WebClasses to run natively as MTS objects leads to permissions problems when you attempt to access external ActiveX DLLs from WebClasses. These are complex problems; you may want to visit the following explanation more than once.

When a WebClass tries to create a new instance of an external ActiveX DLL, NT creates the object via distributed COM (DCOM). For security reasons, DCOM requires that each object must run in a defined *context*. A context in NT is the set of permissions associated with a user or an *impersonation* of a valid user. For example, when you sign on to your computer, you acquire the context associated with your sign-on. That context gives you permission to do certain things and access specific directories.

Registered objects that do not explicitly write their context in the Registry run under a default context that you can set by using the program dcomcnfg.exe that comes with Windows NT. By default, users in the Administrators group, the System account, and the Interactive User account (called INTERACTIVE ) have permission to read the appropriate Registry keys and launch applications. When you install the NT 4 Option Pack with IIS 4, the installation adds the same permissions for the IUSR_MachineName and IWAM_MachineName accounts.

The whole system works well when *you're* the person signed on to the NT computer. Whenever you (or a program you're running) launch an object, NT checks to see whether you have permission to launch that object, which—as the interactive, signed-on, and authenticated user—you generally do.

Unfortunately, the system doesn't work as well for WebClasses. IIS launches an anonymous request for a WebClass in the context of IUSR_MachineName or IWAM_MachineName, depending on whether the application runs under the root application or an isolated process. But those two accounts aren't authenticated users—they belong to the Guest account. Also, although the anonymous accounts have a password, they don't have the ability to supply the password security identifier (SID) to DCOM when it tries to authenticate the launching user. This is the primary reason that many people have trouble accessing their SQL database from ASP pages and WebClasses. Therefore, when IIS allows anonymous requests, any calls made to external DLLs from a WebClass may fail.

You never see this happen when you're developing a WebClass and running it in the VB environment. Inside VB, the WebClass runs under your context, but when you compile the WebClass DLL, it runs under the IIS default user context. When you launch an ActiveX DLL from a WebClass, DCOM asks IIS for the proper authorization credentials. When IIS is unable to supply them, the launch fails. When an object fails to launch, the WebClass method will also fail. You should check the Application event log for error messages if you see `permission denied` errors.

# Using the ObjectContext Object with WebClasses

One of the most common problems you may face when creating ActiveX DLLs for use with WebClasses is that there's no ObjectContext object available to your WebClass. By default, although WebClasses are instantiated from an ASP page that *does* have access to the MTS ObjectContext object, WebClasses do *not* have access to the ObjectContext object. You can't obtain a reference to the ObjectContext with a call to `getObjectContext`. The WebClassManager object passes references to the other ASP variables when it launches a WebClass, but it does not pass a reference to either the ScriptingContext object or the (obsolete) ObjectContext object.

What is the ScriptingContext object and why would you want to obtain a reference to it? Let me give you a little history. The first version of ASP did not include a public ScriptingContext object. Instead, the ASP engine called `OnStartPage` and `OnEndPage` methods on external DLLs. ASP still supports these methods in all versions.

Just after instantiating each ActiveX object created on a page, ASP calls the `OnStartPage` method for that object and passes the ScriptingContext object as the only argument. Any ActiveX object that implements the method can gain references to the intrinsic ASP objects. For example:

```
Public Sub OnStartPage(sc as ScriptingContext)
    Set mApplication = sc.Application
```

```
        Set mSession = sc.Session
        Set mResponse = sc.Response
        Set mRequest = sc.Request
        Set mServer = sc.Server
    End Sub
```

Just before destroying the object when the page ends, the ASP engine calls the OnEndPage method. When the OnEndPage event fires, the object can release the references:

```
    Public Sub OnEndPage()
        Set mApplication = Nothing
        Set mSession = Nothing
        Set mResponse = Nothing
        Set mRequest = Nothing
        Set mServer = Nothing
    End Sub
```

Objects that implement these two methods have an automatic way of gaining references to the ASP objects. Thus, you could write code in an ActiveX DLL that used the values stored in Session objects and could write output back to the browser, via the Response object.

In the second version of ASP, released with the NT 4 Option Pack and IIS 4, Microsoft directly exposed the ScriptingContext object. Web applications in IIS 4 and later all run under MTS; therefore, Microsoft now recommends that apartment-threaded ActiveX objects no longer use the OnStartPage and OnEndPage methods. Instead, you should add two project references: one to the Microsoft Transaction Server Type Library and one to the Microsoft Active Server Pages Object Library. You can then use the getObjectContext method to obtain the ASP ObjectContext object reference, then use that to gain access to the other intrinsic ASP objects:

```
    Public Function TestResponse()
        Dim objContext As ObjectContext
        Dim mResponse as Response
        Set objContext = GetObjectContext()
        Set mResponse = objContext("Response")
        mResponse.Write "Hello World"
        set mResponse = Nothing
    End Function
```

That's enough history. Here are the problems: The code shown in the Test-Response function works fine as long as you create the object from an ASP page, but the same code doesn't work inside a WebClass. This is surprising—you would expect that the WebClass would run under MTS because the ASP page that launches a WebClass runs under MTS.

Microsoft's explanation for this behavior is that WebClasses don't run under MTS because they needed to be compatible with IIS 3. As you'll soon see, that was an unfortunate choice because it causes additional problems.

When you create an ActiveX DLL object from a WebClass that's not running under MTS, you cannot get a reference to the ObjectContext object by creating the object with the `New` keyword. Luckily, you can solve this problem in two ways:

- Use the Server object's `CreateObject` method from inside the WebClass to create the ActiveX object. ActiveX objects created in this manner do have access to the ObjectContext, even though the WebClass does not.

- Because the compiled WebClass is also an apartment-threaded ActiveX DLL, you can run it in a package under MTS with no problems. After your WebClass is running in a package, you can get an ObjectContext, add other ActiveX DLLs to the package, and everything works fine.

**NOTE** In Chapter 9, "Dealing with Multiple Browsers," I promised to tell you how to use the MSWC.BrowserType component from WebClasses. Here's the answer: Use the `Server.CreateObject` method to instantiate the component, and it will work exactly as it does from an ASP page.

# Testing ActiveX DLLs from a WebClass

At this point, you're probably confused. The best way to understand the problem is to duplicate it. This project uses a simple ActiveX DLL that exposes one class called CHello. The sole purpose of the CHello class is to write the word *Hello* back to the browser.

Create a new IIS project. Rename the project **WCTestCOM**. Rename the default WebClass **WCTest** and set the `NameInURL` property to **WCTest** as well. Save the `WCTestCOM` project.

Copy the following code into the `WebClass_Start` event. If you're typing the code, don't leave out the error-trapping code.

```
Private Sub WebClass_Start()
    Dim ch As CHello
    Set ch = New CHello
    On Error GoTo ErrWebClass_Start
    Call ch.WriteHello(Response)
ExitWebClass_Start:
    Exit Sub
ErrWebClass_Start:
    Response.Write Err.Number & "<br>" & _
        Err.Source & "<br>" & _
        Err.Description
    Resume ExitWebClass_Start
End Sub
```

> **NOTE** You will need to change the code several times to follow along with the text of this section. As I promised, this time you won't need to enter the code yourself—I've provided commented-out versions of the `WebClass_Start` event. Comment and uncomment them as needed to run the tests in this section.

You'll need to create an ActiveX DLL project for the CHello class. Add a new ActiveX DLL project to your workspace and rename it **TestObjContext**. Rename the default class **CHello**.

You'll also need to add some project references before you can run the project. Click the `WCTestCOM` project (the IIS project) in the Project Explorer, click the Project menu, select References, and check the `TestObjContext` project. Similarly, select the `TestObjContext` project, click the Project menu, select References, and add references to the Microsoft Active Server Pages Object Library and to the Microsoft Transaction Server Type Library.

The CHello class has one public method called `WriteHello` that prints a `Hello...` message to the browser, with one optional argument called `mResponse` that accepts a Response object. Inside the `WriteHello` method, the CHello class calls `getObjectContext` in an attempt to get a reference to the ObjectContext object. It then tries to use the ObjectContext object to obtain a reference to the Response object:

```
Public Sub WriteHello(Optional mResponse As Response)
    Dim objContext As ObjectContext
```

```
        Set objContext = GetObjectContext()
        If Not objContext Is Nothing Then
            objContext("Response").Write _
            "Hello from ObjectContext Response"
        Else
            If Not IsMissing(mResponse) Then
                mResponse.Write "Hello from Response argument"
                Set mResponse = Nothing
            Else
                Err.Raise 50000, "CHello.WriteHello", _
                "Unable to obtain a reference to " & _
                "the Response object."
            End If
        End If
        Set objContext = Nothing
    End Sub
```

Save the project and press F8 to step through it line by line. Notice that the WebClass explicitly passes a reference to the Response object in the argument to the `WriteHello` method. When the call occurs, the CHello class tries to get an ObjectContext reference. That attempt fails. Next, it tests to see whether the `mResponse` argument has been set. In this case, it has, so the `mResponse.Write` method executes successfully and you see `Hello from Response argument` in the browser.

The question is, why doesn't the call to `getObjectContext` work? You're running in a WebClass—an ActiveX DLL instantiated from an ASP page running in MTS—which does have an ObjectContext. You have a proper reference set to the ObjectContext object in the `TestObjContext` project. Everything should work, but it doesn't.

You might think (as I did), "OK, the *WebClass* doesn't have an ObjectContext, but the ActiveX DLL should be able to get one if I add it to an MTS package." I'll save you the trouble of trying it—that doesn't work either. You can get an ObjectContext object, but attempting to use that ObjectContext to obtain references to the intrinsic ASP objects fails.

This failure makes sense, because the WebClass doesn't have access to the ASP ScriptingContext object—remember, that's the one ASP object not passed to the WebClass from the launching ASP file.

As further proof that the failure stems from instantiating the CHello class from a WebClass rather than from any problem with the code itself, you can launch the

CHello class from an ASP file and everything works perfectly. Create an ASP file called **ASPHelloTest.asp** containing the following code and save it in the WCTest-COM Web site:

```
<%
dim ch
set ch = Server.CreateObject("TestObjContext.CHello")
call ch.writeHello()
%>
```

When you run the ASP file, you'll see `Hello from ObjectContext Response` in the browser. Knowing that you can call the object from an ASP file makes things easier—just use the `Server.CreateObject` method from inside the WebClass to create the CHello object. Modify your `WebClass_Start` event code as follows:

```
Private Sub WebClass_Start()
    Dim ch As CHello
    Set ch = Server.CreateObject _
        ("TestObjcontext.CHello")
    On Error GoTo ErrWebClass_Start
    Call ch.WriteHello
ExitWebClass_Start:
    Exit Sub
ErrWebClass_Start:
    Response.Write Err.Number & "<br>" & _
        Err.Source & "<br>" & _
        Err.Description
    Resume ExitWebClass_Start
End Sub
```

Objects you instantiate by using the `Server.CreateObject` method from an ASP page are late bound, therefore slow. If you declare your objects in VB, however, they are early bound.

You will have no problems launching ActiveX DLLs that do *not* use the ObjectContext object from a WebClass. To prove this, comment out the `objContext` variable references in the `WriteHello` method as follows:

```
Public Sub WriteHello(Optional mResponse As Response)
    'Dim objContext As ObjectContext
    'Set objContext = GetObjectContext()
    'If Not objContext Is Nothing Then
    '    objContext("Response").Write _
    '        "Hello from ObjectContext Response"
```

```
        'Else
            If Not IsMissing(mResponse) Then
                mResponse.Write "Hello from Response argument"
                Set mResponse = Nothing
            Else
                Err.Raise 50000, "CHello.WriteHello", _
                "Unable to obtain a reference to " & _
                "the Response object."
            End If
        'End If
        'Set objContext = Nothing
    End Sub
```

Change the code in the `WebClass_Start` method so you create the object with the New keyword, then compile the project and run it again.

## How to Replace DLLs in IIS Applications

Before you can recompile a DLL used by an IIS application, you must shut down the application. If the DLL you're replacing runs inside MTS, you must also shut down that package. After compiling, you should refresh all the MTS objects to ensure that the references are correct. To avoid problems, use this sequence:

1. Use the Internet Service Manager to unload the IIS application, then shut down the MTS package.
2. Stop the IIS Administration site using either the Services applet or the IIS Stop icon on the WebClass toolbar.
3. Recompile the WebClass and/or any support DLLs.
4. Refresh the MTS package.
5. Restart IIS.

If you don't follow this sequence, IIS and MTS often get "confused" and your project may not run properly. If this happens to you, my advice is to reboot the server.

You'll see the `Hello from Response argument` message properly printed in the browser. Therefore you *can* use the New keyword to access an ActiveX DLL from a WebClass as long as you don't try to get an ObjectContext reference.

Now let's look at the authentication problem. Uncomment the code from the `WriteHello` method again. You can use either of the `WebClass_Start` versions; it doesn't matter whether you use the one that instantiates the CHello object with `New` or with `Server.CreateObject`. Compile the WebClass project, close VB, and browse to the starting ASP file in a new instance of your browser.

When you launch the compiled WebClass DLL, the CHello object will not instantiate. That's because you don't have permission to use the object. As I said at the beginning of this chapter, the WebClass can't create the object because it can't authenticate with DCOM. You can move the CHello class into the WebClass project, and it will work fine.

The solution to the authentication problem is to move the CHello component into MTS. I'm not going to show you how to do that right now—you can skip ahead to Chapter 12, "IIS Applications and Microsoft Transaction Server," if you want to know—but I wanted to tell you that there is a workaround.

Table 11.1 summarizes the problems discussed in this chapter so far, and their workarounds.

**TABLE 11.1:** WebClass ObjectContext and Authentication Problems and Workarounds

| Problem | Workaround |
|---|---|
| Obtain ObjectContext reference from WebClass | Run WebClass in MTS |
| Use ObjectContext reference in ActiveX object methods to gain access to intrinsic ASP objects | Use `Server.CreateObject` method or pass ASP objects or values explicitly |
| Authenticate DCOM calls successfully | Run ActiveX components in MTS |

Now that you know how to work around the problems, you should be able to use ActiveX classes in separate DLLs freely. Many desirable class functions are not program specific; you can use them in multiple projects, so you wouldn't want to compile them into your WebClass DLL. Also, frankly, isolating these components is a good idea because it usually forces you to make them more generic, thus increasing code reuse.

Be careful of overusing ASP object references inside your ActiveX classes. For example, when you use the Response object inside an ActiveX class, that class is useless outside of a Web application. In contrast, if you pass a string back from the object and use the Response object inside the WebClass to print the string to the browser, you can use the object from ASP pages, from WebClasses, or from stand-alone executables in exactly the same way.

Here's an example: In Chapter 8, "Maintaining State in IIS Applications," the StoredRecordset class exposes an `HTMLTableString` property.

| Name | Type | Description |
| --- | --- | --- |
| HTMLTableString | Property Get | Returns the stored recordset formatted as an HTML table string |

The property returns a string containing an HTML-formatted table. The class works from ASP, from WebClasses, and from stand-alone executables. If, instead, I had used `getObjectContext` to obtain a reference to the Response object with which to print the string from *inside* the class, it would work only with Web applications.

# Persisting ActiveX Objects

I'll start this section with a warning: Don't persist ActiveX objects unless you have to. I've warned you throughout this book that persisting ActiveX objects is a bad idea because of the threading problems associated with storing apartment-threaded objects in Session variables. But now I'm going to show you a way to circumvent the problem. If you don't store the object, just the data required to recreate the object, the threading issue disappears.

## Store Object Data, Not Objects

You've already seen some examples that persist CStoredRecordset and CStoredDictionary objects, but those examples *transform* the ActiveX object rather than storing it with its properties and methods intact. The remainder of this section builds on the idea of transformation for persistence. When you create your own ActiveX objects, you can store them in Session variables as Variants containing byte arrays. You use VB's built-in PropertyBag object to do this. You'll see how to make the whole process of persisting and depersisting objects almost automatic.

In VB 6, you begin the process of persisting ActiveX objects by setting the design-time property called `Persistable` to 1-Persistable. When you do this, VB adds three events to the class: `InitProperties`, `ReadProperties`, and `WriteProperties`. Those of you who have been building ActiveX controls are probably familiar with these events.

The `InitProperties` event fires only when you instantiate the object for the first time. You can, and should, use this event to initialize the values of properties instead of the standard `Initialize` event. The `Initialize` event fires before the `InitProperties` event. If you use the `Initialize` event to initialize property values, the `ReadProperties` event will overwrite those values when you re-instantiate the object. Additionally, you can use the `InitProperties` event to determine whether the object is a "new" instance or a re-created instance.

For example, if you want to count the number of times a new copy of an object is instantiated, you can open a file, read a counter value, increment the value, and assign the result in the `InitProperties` event:

```
Private Sub Class_InitProperties()
    Dim fnum As Integer
    Dim counter As Long
    fnum = FreeFile
    Open "counter.dat" For Binary Lock Read Write As #fnum
    Get #fnum, 1, counter
    counter = counter + 1
    Put #fnum, 1, counter
    Close #fnum
    mCounter = counter
End Sub
```

To see this process in action, create a new IIS project and rename it **WCPersistence**. Rename the default WebClass **WCPersistTest**. Place this code into the WebClass_BeginRequest event:

```
Private Sub WebClass_BeginRequest()
    Dim cpc As TestPersistence.CPersistCounter
    Set cpc = New CPersistCounter
    Response.Write "You have instantiated a " _
    & " CPersistCounter object " & cpc.Counter & _
    " times."
    Set cpc = Nothing
End Sub
```

You must also create the CPersistCounter object. Add a new ActiveX DLL project. Rename the project **TestPersistence**. Rename the default class module **CPersistCounter**. Add this code to the CPersistCounter class:

```
Private mCounter As Long

Public Property Get Counter() As Long
    Counter = mCounter
End Property

Private Property Let Counter(l As Long)
    mCounter = l
End Property

Private Sub Class_InitProperties()
    Dim fnum As Integer
    Dim lCount As Long
    fnum = FreeFile
    Open "hellocounter.dat" For Binary Lock Read _
        Write As #fnum
    If LOF(fnum) > 0 Then
        Get #fnum, 1, lCount
    Else
        lCount = 0
    End If
    lCount = lCount + 1
    Put #fnum, 1, lCount
    Close #fnum
    Counter = lCount
End Sub

Private Sub Class_ReadProperties(PropBag As PropertyBag)
    Counter = PropBag.ReadProperty("Counter", 0)
End Sub

Private Sub Class_WriteProperties(PropBag As PropertyBag)
    PropBag.WriteProperty "Counter", Counter, 0
End Sub
```

Add a project reference in the `WCPersistence` project to the `TestPersistence` project and save both projects. When you run the `WCPersistence` project, you'll see that the count increments each time you refresh the browsers (see Figure 11.1).

**FIGURE 11.1:**

WCPersistence project's initial results

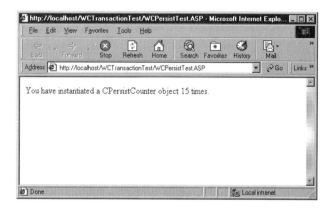

The incrementing count means you're creating a brand new instance of the CPersistCounter object each time you run the `WebClass_Start` method. It's a new instance because persistence isn't automatic. Although the class contains all the code needed to persist and depersist the object, you have to supply the `PropBag` argument to the `ReadProperties` and `WriteProperties` events from outside the class. To do that, you'll need to create a PropertyBag object and call the CPersistCounter's `WriteProperties` and `ReadProperties` methods when you want to save and restore the object.

Add the declaration for the CpersistCounter object to the Declarations section of the WebClass:

```
Dim cpc As TestPersistence.CPersistCounter
```

Replace the `WebClass_BeginRequest` event code so it looks like this:

```
Private Sub WebClass_BeginRequest()
Dim pb As PropertyBag
    Dim b() As Byte
    If IsEmpty(Session("cpc")) Then
        Set cpc = New CPersistCounter
    Else
        Set pb = New PropertyBag
        b = Session("cpc")
        pb.Contents = b
        Set cpc = pb.ReadProperty("CPC")
    End If
    Response.Write "You have instantiated a " & _
```

```
               "CPersistCounter object " & cpc.Counter & " times."
    End Sub
```

The code you just added tests a Session variable called `cpc`. If the variable is empty, the WebClass creates a new CPersistCounter object; otherwise, it creates a PropertyBag object, assigns the value of `Session("cpc")` to the `Contents` property of the PropertyBag object, then re-instantiates the object and assigns it to the variable `cpc` by reading the PropertyBag property called CPC. When you re-create the object this way, it fires the `ReadProperties` method in the newly re-instantiated object, not the `InitProperties` method; therefore, the `Counter` property will acquire its previous value and will not increment on the browser screen.

Of course, you must save the object's data so that you can re-create it. Place this code into the `WebClass_EndRequest` event:

```
Private Sub WebClass_EndRequest()
Dim pb As PropertyBag
    Dim b() As Byte
    If Not cpc Is Nothing Then
        Set pb = New PropertyBag
        pb.WriteProperty "CPC", cpc
        b = pb.Contents
        Session("cpc") = b
        Set cpc = Nothing
    End If
End Sub
```

The `WebClass_EndRequest` code saves the data to re-create the object in the `Session("cpc")` variable. Save and run the project. Be sure to refresh the WebClass several times. I urge you to step through the code with the debugger until you're comfortable with the steps required to save and re-create objects.

Note that you *must* transfer the contents of the Session variable to a byte array before assigning it to the `PropertyBag.Contents` property. The PropertyBag will not accept a Variant, and all Session variables are Variants.

## Automate Object Persistence and Retrieval

Although the preceding code works well for individual objects, it's just too much code to write for each object that you might want to save. A much better method would be to create an object that can then save and re-instantiate any other object. To make such an object, add a new ActiveX DLL project to your workspace. Rename the project **Persistor** and rename the default class **CPersistor**.

The CPersistor class contains two public methods: `Persist` and `Depersist`, which store and save objects. You are responsible for providing a name for each object that you want to persist, and for providing the same name and the correct data when you want to depersist the object. The class returns a Variant containing a byte array when you persist an object, thus enabling you to write the value to disk, to a database, or to store the value in a variable. Place the following code into the CPersistor class:

```
Public Function Persist(aName As String, anObject As Object) As Variant
    Dim pb As PropertyBag
    Dim b() As Byte
    Set pb = New PropertyBag
    pb.WriteProperty aName, anObject
    b = pb.Contents
    Persist = b
End Function
Public Function Depersist(aName As String, varData As Variant) As Object
    Dim pb As PropertyBag
    Dim b() As Byte
    Set pb = New PropertyBag
    b = varData
    pb.Contents = b
    Set Depersist = pb.ReadProperty(aName)
End Function
```

To test the class, change the `WebClass_BeginRequest` and the `WebClass_EndRequest` methods as follows:

```
Private Sub WebClass_BeginRequest()
    Dim CP As CPersistor
    If IsEmpty(Session("cpc")) Then
        Set cpc = New CPersistCounter
    Else
        Set CP = New CPersistor
        Set cpc = CP.Depersist("CPC", Session("cpc"))
    End If
    Response.Write "You have instantiated a CPersistCounter object " & cpc.Counter & " times."
End Sub

Private Sub WebClass_EndRequest()
    Dim CP As CPersistor
```

```
        If Not cpc Is Nothing Then
            Set CP = New CPersistor
            Session("cpc") = CP.persist("CPC", cpc)
        End If
End Sub
```

## Maintain State via Object Persistence

You now have another method for storing state. You can create ActiveX objects and use them to store state by using either files, database tables, or Session variables. Re-creating the objects from files or databases requires exactly the same steps as those shown in this chapter to save the objects in Session variables—instead, just write the Variant data to disk or to a database.

You should notice several things about this method of storing objects. First, you can store objects that hold references to other objects. For example, you can store an entire collection of objects in a single Variant—as long as each object implements the `ReadProperties` and `WriteProperties` events, and the names are unique. To do so, you take the PropertyBag argument passed to the top-level object and pass it on to each referenced object. You must reverse the process to re-instantiate the objects. Also, you must devise a way to store the names of the objects in their proper order; otherwise, you will not be able to restore the object to exactly the same state.

Second, once you know that you can store referenced objects along with their "owners," it becomes obvious that you can store multiple objects in the same PropertyBag. If you want to do this, you'll need to alter the CPersistor class so that it accepts a PropertyBag object as an argument rather than creating a new one each time. You should also know that the names of the objects must be unique. Otherwise, you'll simply overwrite objects whose data has already been stored.

Finally, you can combine this technique with other state maintenance options—for example, you can store the object names on the client, as a cookie, or you can use database key values as the names. Although I hesitate to say so, you can also store disconnected recordsets by making the recordset a property of an object. You can then persist the recordset along with any other property. Note that this is not nearly as efficient as the StoredRecordset class, because persisting the object means you have to copy the data three times: once to the PropertyBag, once to the byte array, and once to the Variant. However, when you re-instantiate the recordset, you have a true Recordset object, with all its properties and methods. In contrast, the StoredRecordset object has only some of the properties and methods of a Recordset object, and only copies data when you call the `StoreRecordset` method; saving the data in a Session variable is just a pointer assignment.

I'll end this section with a warning as well: As with all state maintenance techniques, use persistence sparingly and judiciously. As I stated in Chapter 8, you can easily bog down your server by maintaining more data than you need. For larger sites, you're much better off putting the data in a database rather than using the Session object. Even though databases are slower for a small number of users, they're faster when the server is under load.

# Building a Browser-Based Code Repository

I've included many small projects in this book that show how to use WebClasses. Now it's time to put all this information together. In this project, you'll build a browser-based code repository. The project stores titles and code in an Access database. As always, remember that you can download the code from the Sybex Web site.

> **NOTE** To download code, navigate to `http://www.sybex.com`. Click Catalog and search for this book's title. Click the Downloads button and accept the licensing agreement. Accepting the agreement grants you access to the downloads page for this book.

## Techniques Included in the *CodeRepository* Project

The `CodeRepository` project includes most of the techniques you've seen in this book, including:

- HTML templates
- Custom WebItems
- Custom events
- Frames
- Redirection

- CStoredRecordset and CStoredDictionary
- External ActiveX DLLs
- ADO and the ADO wrapper functions, including stored procedures
- State maintenance
- ActiveX object persistence

There are two tables, called Users and Repository, in the database for this project. Figure 11.2 shows the structure of the database.

**FIGURE 11.2:**

CodeRepository database structure

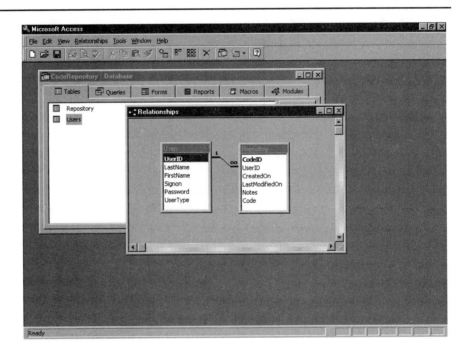

The Users table holds information about the people who use the application. The Repository table holds information about the code and code fragments placed into the repository. You can determine the usefulness of any database by testing whether it can answer the questions you need to know about the data. For example, this program needs to be able to list code entered by date, by user, or that contains a specific word or phrase. Administrators need to be able to find, list, and edit any user.

Each user must register before using the program. After new users register successfully, they receive Guest permissions. There are three levels of user permissions: Guest, Author, and Administrator:

**Guests**   Can view and search for code, but cannot change the code

**Authors**   Can view and search for code, as well as add and edit code

**Administrators**   Have full permissions and can also change any user's permission level

> **TIP**   The database initially contains three sign-ons (you can create your own as well). None of the sign-ons require a password. The sign-ons are `admin`, `author`, and `guest`. They have appropriate permissions assigned. You can use them to explore how to limit program functionality based on permissions levels.

I implemented the project in three imperfectly separated layers:

**WebClass**   Displays and formats data. In some instances, the WebClass retrieves data directly from the data services layer.

**CUser and CCode classes**   Retrieve data from the data services layer.

**CRepositoryData class**   The data services layer. This class handles all database operations for the project.

The WebClass obtains data about individual users and code records from the CUser and CCode classes, which in turn retrieve the data from the CRepositoryData class. The WebClass retrieves lists of users and code directly from the CRepositoryData class. As written, the CUser and CCode classes are part of the main project, but you could easily remove them. If you do that, you should add a CList class to retrieve the lists.

The project uses 10 HTML templates that handle most of the display for the site. The WebClass handles administration functions separately via a custom WebItem.

Users must sign on to enter the application. The WebClass redirects unauthenticated requests to the sign-on page. The sign-on process follows much the same track as you saw in the `SecuredSite` project in Chapter 5, "Securing an IIS Application," with a few alterations due to state maintenance. Figure 11.3 shows the `CodeRepository` project's sign-on page.

**FIGURE 11.3:**

CodeRepository
sign-on page

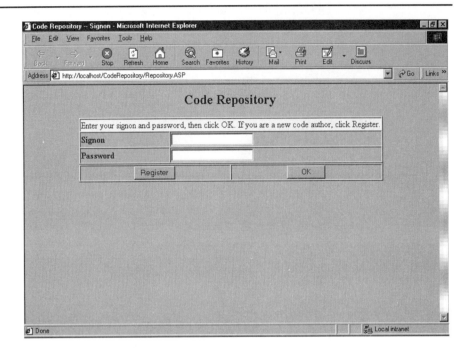

When a user signs on, the sign-on code creates an instance of a CUser object (mUser) that represents the authenticated user. The CUser class contains public properties that correspond to the columns of the Users table in the database.

```
If mUser.InitBySignon(mConnectionstring, _
    Request("Signon")) Then
    If mUser.Password = Request("Password") Then
        Session("SignedOn") = True
    End If
End If
```

The WebClass stores and retrieves the mUser object for each subsequent request, using the CPersistor class you developed earlier in this chapter. The WebClass stores the mUser object during each WebClass_EndRequest event and re-instantiates it during the WebClass_BeginRequest event.

```
Private Sub WebClass_BeginRequest()
    If Not (Session("SignedOn") = True) Then
        If Request.Form("Signon") = "" Then
            Set NextItem = Signon
            Exit Sub
        End If
```

```
        ElseIf Session("SignedOn") = True Then
            Dim cp As CPersistor
            Set cp = New CPersistor
            If Not IsEmpty(Session("User")) Then
                Set mUser = cp.Depersist _
                ("mUser", Session("User"))
            End If
        End If
        mConnectionstring = Session("ConnectionString")
    End Sub
```

> **NOTE**
> If you carefully trace through the `WebClass_BeginRequest` event, you'll notice that one of the problems with using frames is that the browser makes multiple requests to the WebClass—one for each frame. Using the two frames in this application doubles the amount of work the server must do to deliver the first frameset page. After the initial frameset display, the browser makes only one request for each content page. You should take this as a warning, though: Applications with multiple framesets make much heavier demands on the server and generate more network traffic than similar sites that use tables instead of frames.

Note that the WebClass does not attempt to store or retrieve an `mUser` object if the `Session("SignedOn")` variable has not been set to `True`. Therefore, unauthenticated or timed-out users cannot enter the site without signing on. To avoid an endless redirection loop, the WebClass checks the `Request("Signon")` variable. It does *not* redirect users if they are trying to sign on.

```
    Private Sub WebClass_EndRequest()
        If Session("SignedOn") = True Then
            If Not mUser Is Nothing Then
                Dim cp As CPersistor
                Set cp = New CPersistor
                Session("User") = cp.Persist _
                ("mUser", mUser)
            End If
        End If
    End Sub
```

Once authenticated, users see a frames page containing a menu and directions. In a "real" program, you could skip the directions page and jump directly to a code listing. The contents of the menu depend on a user's permission level. Figure 11.4 shows the menu and directions for an administrator.

In contrast, Figure 11.5 shows the menu and directions for a guest.

**FIGURE 11.4:**

Menu and directions for an administrator

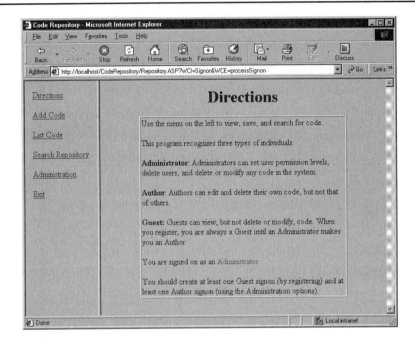

**FIGURE 11.5:**

Menu and directions for a guest

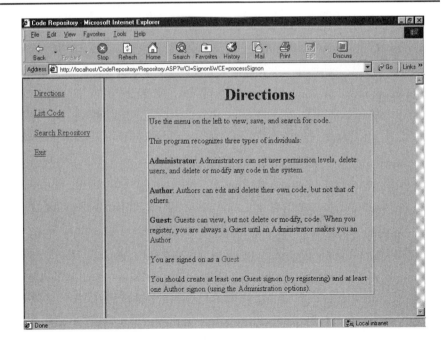

All the links from the menu (left) frame display content in the contents (right) frame. You can't control the window in which content appears from the server; therefore, you must handle those issues on the client. Client-side (browser) code always controls the window in which content appears. Because the number of links in the menu is dependent on a user's permission level, the WebClass creates the links during the `Menu_ProcessTag` event. The Menu template contains a single replacement tag called <wcmenu>. The WebClass replaces that tag with the links appropriate to the authenticated user's permission level. Each link in the menu directs the browser to place the content in the contents frame using the `target=<framename>` syntax.

```
Private Sub Menu_ProcessTag(ByVal TagName As String, _
    TagContents As String, SendTags As Boolean)
    Select Case LCase$(TagName)
    Case "wcmenu"
        TagContents = "<a href='" & URLFor("Directions") _
        & "' target='contents'>Directions</a><br><br>"
        If mUser.UserType <> "G" Then
            TagContents = TagContents & "<a href='" _
            & URLFor("CodeEdit") & _
            "' target='contents'>Add Code</a><br><br>"
        End If
        TagContents = TagContents & "<a href='" & _
        URLFor("CodeList") & "' _
        target='contents'>List Code</a><br><br>"
        ' etc.
    End Select
End Sub
```

When a user clicks the List Code menu link, the WebClass retrieves a list of titles from the database and displays the list in the contents frame. Figure 11.6 shows a sample list.

Determining the interface for displaying large lists is one of the biggest problems in programming. For example, a display like the one shown in Figure 11.6 works extremely well when you have fewer than 50 items. As the list grows, displaying all the items becomes progressively less useful, and it is increasingly difficult for a user to find any specific list entry. Ordering the list can help, assuming the order that you provide is the one the user needs. Imagine that you had 10,000 items in the list. Displaying the title list would not only take a long time, but would make it difficult for a user to find an item. Certainly, you wouldn't want to scroll through thousands of items.

**FIGURE 11.6:**

CodeRepository List Code page

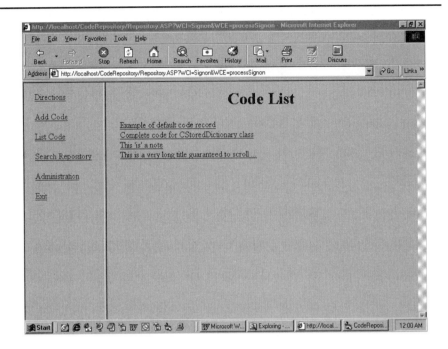

List display problems aren't limited to Web applications—they're common to all applications that deal with large lists. One way to help alleviate the problem is to let users search the list(s) for items that match desired conditions. Users can search the repository by clicking the Search Repository link on the menu frame. Figure 11.7 shows the search page.

Users can search either in the Notes field, the Code field, or in both fields for a single word or phrase. In a production program, you should extend this to allow Boolean and proximity searches as well. The application displays any matching records by title. Figure 11.8 shows the results of a search for the word *complete* in the Notes field. The search found one matching record.

From any code listing, users can click on a title to view the code. Guests view code in read-only mode (see Figure 11.9).

In contrast, authors and administrators view code in edit mode. Figure 11.10 shows the same code in editable form.

**FIGURE 11.7:**

CodeRepository search page

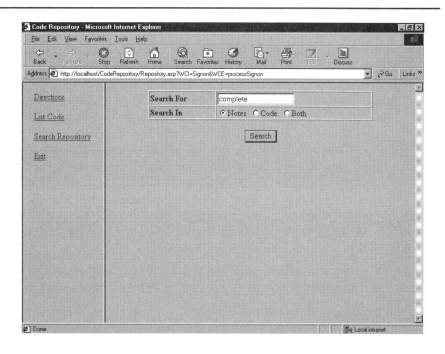

**FIGURE 11.8:**

CodeRepository search results

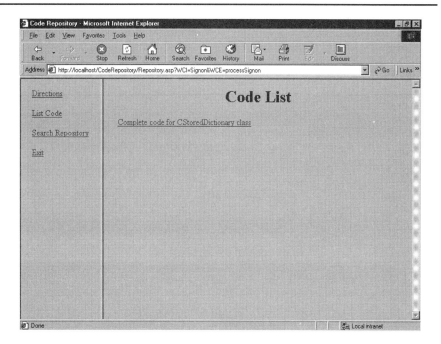

**FIGURE 11.9:**

CodeRepository Guest code view

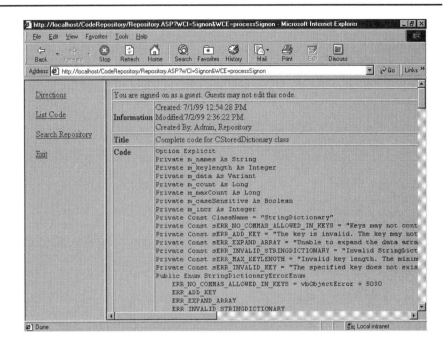

**FIGURE 11.10:**

CodeRepository Author/Administrator code view

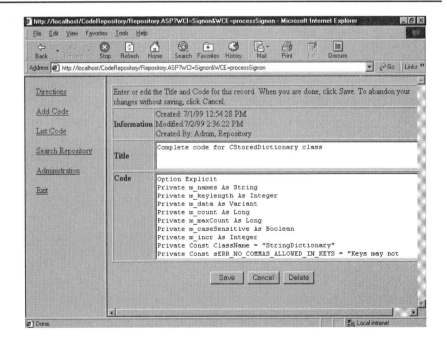

Appropriate buttons to update the changed code, delete the record, or cancel the changes appear below the editable code listing.

Administrators are the only people who can view and edit the registration information for other users. For example, an administrator may need to clear a forgotten password for an author. To edit a user record, an administrator clicks the Administration link in the menu, then selects List Users.

The Administer Users page (see Figure 11.11) shows the names of registered users. The program formats each name as a link. The administrator clicks a name to edit that user's registration information. The Edit User screen is similar to the Registration screen, but allows an administrator to set permission levels and delete users (see Figure 11.12).

**FIGURE 11.11:**

CodeRepository Administer Users page

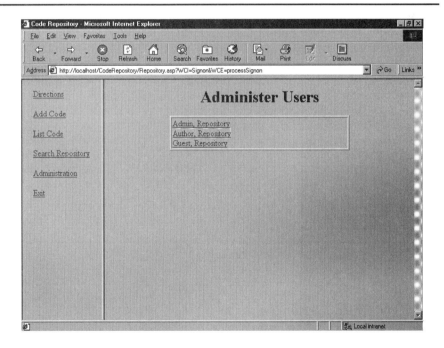

**FIGURE 11.12:**

Code Repository Administration—Edit User

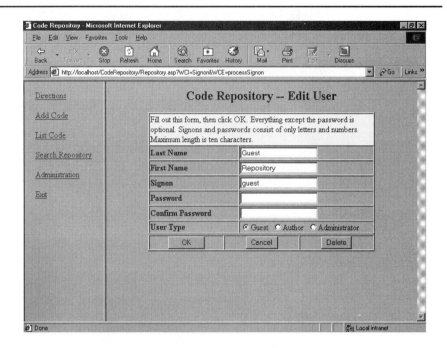

The `CodeRepository` WebClass accesses all data through a CRepositoryData class exposed from an external ActiveX DLL called RepositoryData. Internally, the CRepositoryData class uses the ADO wrapping functions discussed in Chapter 10, "Retrieving and Storing Data in Databases," to open and close connections and retrieve data. Any errors that occur propagate back through the error-handling routines to the WebClass for display. Here are two example routines from the CRepositoryData class:

```
Public Sub deleteCodeByID(aConnectionString As String, _
      aCodeID As Long)
   Dim conn As New Connection
   Dim methodName As String
   Dim sd As CStoredDictionary
   methodName = Classname & "deleteCodeByID"
   On Error GoTo ErrDeleteCodeByID
   Call mADO.openConnection(conn, aConnectionString, _
      adModeReadWrite)
   Set sd = New CStoredDictionary
   sd.Add "CodeID", aCodeID
```

```
        Call mADO.executeSQL(conn, "deleteCodeByID", _
            adCmdStoredProc, sd)
        Call mADO.closeConnection(conn)
ExitDeleteCodeByID:
        Exit Sub
ErrDeleteCodeByID:
        Err.Raise Err.Number, Err.Source & ": " & _
        methodName, Err.Description & vbCrLf & _
        "Unable to delete the code with ID " & aCodeID & _
        " from the repository."
        Resume ExitDeleteCodeByID
End Sub

Public Function getUserBySignon(aConnectionString _
            As String, aSignon As String) As CStoredDictionary
        Dim R As Recordset
        Dim sd As CStoredDictionary
        Dim conn As Connection
        Dim methodName As String
        methodName = Classname & "getUserBySignon"
        On Error GoTo ErrGetUserBySignon
        Set conn = New Connection
        Call mADO.openConnection(conn, aConnectionString, _
            adModeRead)
        Set sd = New CStoredDictionary
        sd.Add "Signon", aSignon
        If mADO.getRecordset(conn, R, "getUserBySignon", _
            adCmdStoredProc, False, , , sd) Then
            Set sd = New CStoredDictionary
            Call sd.StoreRecord(R)
            Set getUserBySignon = sd
            R.Close
            Set R = Nothing
        Else
            Set sd = New CStoredDictionary
            Set getUserBySignon = sd
        End If
        Call mADO.closeConnection(conn)
ExitGetUserBySignon:
        Exit Function
ErrGetUserBySignon:
        Err.Raise Err.Number, Err.Source & ": " & _
```

```
        methodName, Err.Description & vbCrLf & _
        "Unable to retrieve the User with Signon " & aSignon _
        & " from the repository."
        Resume ExitGetUserBySignon
End Function
```

You can see that the routines are similar. The class has one peculiarity that I'll explain more fully in the next chapter; instead of having a `ConnectionString` property, you must pass a valid `ConnectionString` argument to every routine. Each routine opens a connection, performs one task, then returns data (if necessary) in a CStoredDictionary object (for single record results) or in a CStoredRecordset object (for multiple-record results).

Although this technique forces you to write more code, it also limits the number of round-trips to accomplish a task. For example, the WebClass typically calls only one of the methods in the CRepositoryData class for each request. If the class had a `ConnectionString` property, you would need to make two calls to the class, one to set the property and one to execute a method. With the `ConnectionString` argument, you need to make only one call.

In the next chapter, you'll see how to increase the scalability of the project by running the external RepositoryData DLL in MTS.

# CHAPTER TWELVE

# IIS Applications and Microsoft Transaction Server

- What Is MTS?
- How Does MTS Fit into the IIS/Web Application Model?
- How Can MTS Help You?
- When Should You Use MTS?
- How Do You Use MTS Components?
- How Do You Move a Project into MTS?

At the beginning of Chapter 11, "Using ActiveX DLLs from WebClasses," I discussed how WebClasses don't have access to the ObjectContext object or to the ScriptingContext object. You also saw that you have problems accessing objects in external ActiveX DLLs unless they run inside Microsoft Transaction Server (MTS). The *VB Developer's Guide to COM and COM+* by Wayne Freeze (1999, Sybex—part of this series of VB Developer's Guides) explains MTS and COM+ in detail. This chapter focuses only on accessing MTS objects from WebClasses. You'll see how to connect WebClasses to transactional and non-transactional components running inside MTS.

# What Is MTS?

MTS consists of several unrelated capabilities lumped together under a single name. Microsoft, recognizing that MTS is not an accurate name for this collection of features, has renamed MTS to COM+ in Windows 2000.

MTS is an object broker. That means it maintains a list of objects and facilitates other programs' use of those objects. MTS facilitates code reuse. Without MTS, you would have a difficult time sharing objects within your program and between programs. You would have to set up a pool of objects, then devise ways of sharing them without conflict.

MTS is also a transaction monitor. MTS can monitor and manage transactions—work that must either complete successfully or fail totally across multiple components. For example, suppose you want to send e-mail to an administrator each time an employee changes personal income tax deductions. The transaction consists of all the operations required for the employee to make the change in a database and also all the operations required for the program to compose and send the e-mail message to an administrator. If any error occurs when making the database changes, you don't want the program to send the e-mail. If the database changes succeed, you *must* send the e-mail message successfully; otherwise, you need to roll back the changes in the database and inform the employee that the program cannot make the changes.

If you set this up, you would need to write code to ensure that each part of the process completed successfully before committing the transaction. You would also need to write code to roll back the transaction if any error occurred. MTS handles all these issues for you.

MTS uses *components* to perform the units of work involved in a transaction. A component and a class are, to the VB programmer, essentially identical. VB programmers discuss classes and objects. MTS programmers discuss *components*. A component has a specific COM interface, and so does a VB class. A DLL may contain several components or classes, just like in VB. You can't create classes with multiple interfaces in VB (although you can make classes that *use* multiple interfaces).

With Visual Basic 6, Microsoft added a design-time property called MTS-TransactionMode that lets you control whether the classes you create can participate in MTS transactions. The property has five settings, as shown in Table 12.1.

**TABLE 12.1:** The Five MTSTransactionMode Settings

| VB Constant | Value | Description |
| --- | --- | --- |
| NotAnMTSObject | 0 | The class never participates in MTS transactions and does not expect to run under MTS (which doesn't mean it can't run inside an MTS process). |
| NoTransactions | 1 | The class can run under MTS but never participates in transactions. |
| RequiresTransaction | 2 | The class runs under MTS and requires a transaction. If a transaction is already in progress, the class inherits the context for that transaction from the calling object. If no transaction is in progress, the class starts a new one. |
| UsesTransaction | 3 | The class runs under MTS and participates in a transaction if one is in progress, but the class does not start a new transaction. |
| RequiresNewTransaction | 4 | The class runs under MTS and begins a new transaction whenever MTS activates the class. |

WebClasses don't support the MTSTransactionMode property, but standard classes do. That means that although WebClasses don't participate in transactions, they can launch objects that do. Note that components do not *have* to participate in or begin transactions to run under MTS. You can take advantage of some other features of MTS whether you need transactions or not. These features help speed up Web applications:

**Object caching and pooling** Although MTS doesn't support true object pooling for apartment-threaded DLLs such as those you create with VB (although it may in the future), it does cache one or more instances of the class in memory. Usually, each time you create an object instance, the server creates a new instance of the class. In contrast, after MTS has loaded a class, it keeps it loaded and ready, either forever or for a configurable amount of time. That feature alone is worth using, especially for Web applications in which the object creation/destruction cycle happens for every request. To take advantage of this feature, your code needs to tell MTS when you're done with a component.

**State maintenance**   MTS "fools" clients into thinking that they have exclusive use of a component when in fact that component may be shared between multiple clients. That means that you can create a client reference to an MTS component, use the component, do something else, then use the component again. During the time your code isn't using the component, MTS may let another process—or many others—use the component. To the clients, each component acts as if it belongs to them exclusively. MTS creates new instances of components only if none exist or if all the existing components are busy. In other words, you don't have to worry about creating an object, using it, then destroying it as quickly as possible because MTS frees you from those worries. MTS state maintenance saves not only resources, but also a great deal of server time that would otherwise be spent creating and destroying objects.

**Data sharing between components**   MTS lets you share properties between multiple components. In a standard application, you use global variables and constants to share data. Because MTS objects are shared between multiple clients, you can't store state inside the objects themselves. MTS uses an object called a Shared Property Manager to manage data shared between MTS components.

**Process isolation**   MTS isolates your Web server from the effects of misbehaving components. When you run components in the root Web, any component that crashes can also crash the server. Components running inside MTS don't crash the server. You can group components into Packages, each of which can run in a separate process. There's a performance penalty for cross-process object communication. When maximum speed is imperative, you can run components as a Library Package. Library Packages run in the client's process space; therefore, they're faster (but less secure) than components that run in their own process space.

**Security** MTS gives you fine-grained security. You can control security down to the interface level (note that's below the object) in MTS. MTS has role-based security, which means that you create roles, each of which can have different permission levels. You can assign user accounts to those roles, then have MTS manage access to resources based on a user's role.

**In-memory databases** With COM+ in Windows 2000, Microsoft has added support for in-memory database tables. Keeping database tables in memory can provide a huge leap in performance and scalability, because memory access is an order of magnitude faster than disk access. Depending on your needs, this feature alone may be worth upgrading from NT 4.

# How Does MTS Fit into the IIS/Web Application Model?

IIS applications (and by that I mean applications as defined in the Internet Service Manager applet) all run inside MTS. Even the root Web runs in an MTS package. A package consists of one or more components grouped under a package name—in other words, a collection of components. You can use the Microsoft Transaction Server Explorer, which runs as a snap-in to the Microsoft Management Console (MMC) to view the packages and components installed on your system.

## Using Microsoft Transaction Server Explorer

To launch the Transaction Explorer, click the Start button and select Programs ➤ Windows NT 4.0 Option Pack ➤ Microsoft Transaction Server ➤ Transaction Server Explorer (see Figure 12.1). If you're running Windows 2000, the COM+ Explorer provides essentially the same services.

The Transaction Explorer shows you the list of packages installed on your computer. Click the plus signs until you see the Packages Installed entry (see Figure 12.2).

**FIGURE 12.1:**

Finding the Microsoft Transaction Explorer in Windows NT 4

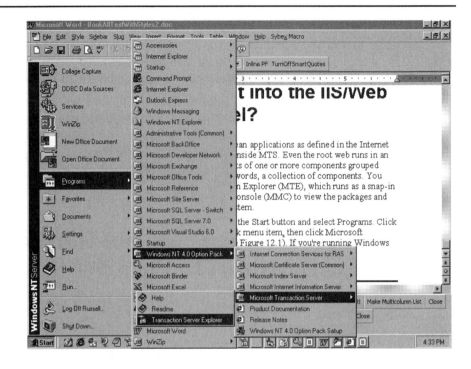

**FIGURE 12.2:**

Microsoft Transaction Explorer—Packages Installed

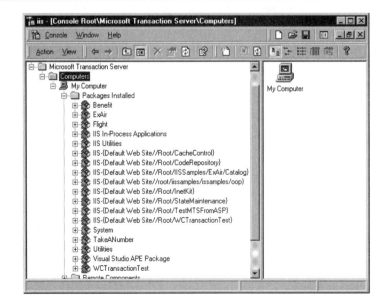

You'll notice that several of the entries begin with *IIS*. Each entry is a separate application. The name of the IIS root application is IIS In-Process Applications. Components that run in the IIS process space appear here. Click the plus sign to expand the IIS In-Process Applications entry, then double-click the Components item to view the components in the right-hand pane (see Figure 12.3).

**FIGURE 12.3:**

IIS In-Process components

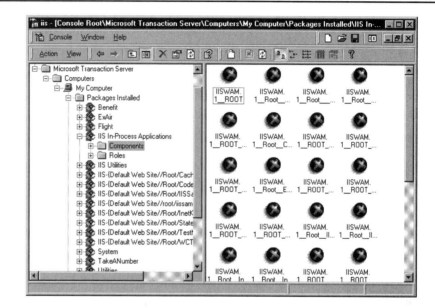

You can change the view in the right-hand pane to a list, which helps when the components have long titles. To show the list, click the View button on the toolbar and select List View (see Figure 12.4).

You can explore the other packages the same way.

**WARNING**   Look, but don't touch! Don't change any of the settings for the IIS packages. Changing the settings can cause the applications or even IIS to fail.

You should spend some time becoming familiar with the various settings and dialogs in MTS. I'm not going to provide details about them in this book other than those necessary to show you how to run components with WebClasses.

**FIGURE 12.4:**

Changing the Transaction Server Explorer view

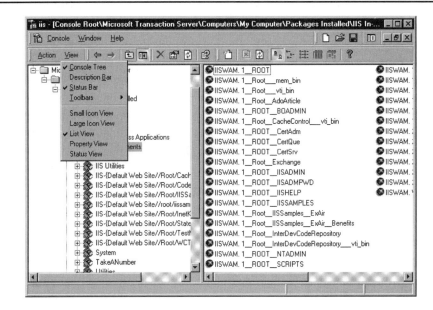

# How Can MTS Help You?

Beyond all the features and advantages already mentioned, possibly the biggest advantage that MTS provides is the capability to update a component without stopping the server. When IIS uses a DLL, it "locks" the DLL into memory. To replace the DLL, you must stop IIS. During development that's no problem at all, but in a production environment it may be impossible to stop the server simply to update one component for your application. Other users may be in the middle of critical operations in other applications running on that server. If you stop the server, you destroy all the sessions.

Using the Internet Service Manager, you can mark your applications so that they run in a separate process space than the root Web application. If you do that, you can release DLL locks on components used exclusively by your application by unloading the application. That helps, but not enough. If any other application is using the DLL, unloading your application won't release all the locks, and you'll still be unable to replace the component. If you run the component under MTS, you can release all references and replace the component without having to stop the applications. Of course, depending on the application's needs, you may still affect the application if you update components while the applications are running.

The second largest advantage is that MTS maintains objects in memory. Throughout this book, I've tried to hammer home the first rule of Web programming: Get in, get the data, get out. Almost anything that can help you do that is worth doing, and you'll see immediate benefits, either in application responsiveness or in application scalability. Unfortunately, few things that you can do will improve both responsiveness *and* scalability. MTS does slow down application initialization, so the first people to reach your application will have to wait longer for the application to load. After it's loaded, though, you'll be able to scale much better with MTS than without it.

Finally, MTS lets you group functionality and control access to functionality through role-based security. In many Web applications, where users access the site anonymously, this kind of security won't do you any good. On intranet sites, where all the people accessing the application can be authenticated through the network, MTS security is a blessing. Instead of having to set individual properties or write code, you can break your application into interfaces and assign permissions to the interfaces.

# When Should You Use MTS?

At first, I thought that MTS should be limited to large sites. After creating several IIS applications (with both ASP and VB WebClasses), I've come to realize that you should *always* use MTS. MTS is much like SQL Server. You think it's overkill—more power than you need—until you deliver your application. When 20 people hit your site at the same time and the server reaches 100 percent usage, you begin to realize that you should have done things differently. I now believe that you should plan for and use MTS in almost all Web applications, whether you think you'll need it or not.

Writing and coding an MTS component is more work than writing a standard ActiveX DLL. Because MTS wants (and for efficiency, requires) stateless components, you need to maintain state elsewhere. It seems as though in the last few years we've moved from an individual client, where you maintained state because that's where your program was running, to a two-tier, then a three-tier, and finally a three-tier-with-MTS application. Each time programming practice adds a layer, you have to write more code. Also, it seems like each added layer wants to shirk the responsibility for maintaining state. For example, you don't want to maintain state on the client—the space available is limited, it's inherently insecure, and it causes too much network traffic. You don't want to maintain state on the Web server—it uses up server resources and slows response time. You don't want to maintain state in the data services components—they need to be stateless so that multiple clients can use them. That puts the burden of state maintenance squarely on the business components. But wait—isn't it more efficient to put the business components in MTS and make them stateless, too? That's right! The answer is, it's just not efficient to maintain state.

State maintenance in Web applications, as you've seen, requires a change in your approach to application programming. Planning an application that uses MTS requires a similar change in mindset. The point is, you need to start approaching all Web applications as though you were unable to maintain state at all. Only grudgingly, when it's absolutely necessary, should you maintain any state information for a client. And when you do, you'll have to decide which will hurt your application's performance the least—to store it on the client, the Web server, or the business component layer. Welcome to the modern world of Web applications, where performance and reusability, but not responsibility, are the watchwords of the hour.

So now that you understand the benefits of using MTS and you know when to use it in your applications, the next section will show you how can you use MTS components with WebClasses.

# How Do You Use MTS Components?

You approach building MTS components differently than components for stand-alone applications. You need to understand how MTS initializes the components and how you tell MTS that you're done with the component. First, you can't create an MTS object by using the New keyword. When you use New (for example, Set myObj = New obj), VB bypasses MTS and provides an object pointer that points directly to the new object. To create an MTS object, you can use either the Server.CreateObject method, which MTS will intercept, or you can use the ObjectContext.CreateInstance method. If you already have an ObjectContext reference, use CreateInstance.

The object reference that you create via `CreateObject` or `CreateInstance` isn't a direct pointer to the object at all (although your program can't tell the difference). Instead, it's a pointer to a context object, which MTS creates as an intermediary. The context object's job is to fool your program into thinking that it can control the target object directly. Therefore, you can treat the object as if you had a "real" object pointer. Behind the scenes, MTS manages one or more instances of the object, but those few instances may be connected to many clients.

Whenever you call a method of your object, MTS looks for the first free instance and passes the call to that instance. That means that the instance that handles your second method call may not be the same instance that handled the first. At this point, you should begin to see why MTS improves scalability. If there were five clients, and each needed to use a certain component, you would normally have five copies of the component in memory. With MTS though, you might only need one or two. MTS uses the time between method calls to recycle a component for many clients.

Because many clients share the components, you can't set a property on a component and then run a method that depends on the component "remembering" the property. For example (and I promised in Chapter 11 that I'd tell you about this), if you set a database access component's `ConnectionString` property, then use that property to make multiple method calls to the database, the property may not be available. That's the primary reason that I set up the CRepositoryData class so that you have to pass the `ConnectionString` with each method call—so it would be easier to move that class into MTS.

A client program can use an MTS object pointer over many method calls and everything will work fine, but the component needs to inform MTS each time it completes a unit of work so that MTS can recycle it. Components do this via the ObjectContext object. Here's a typical sequence:

1. The client requests an MTS component instance—an object.
2. MTS provides a handle to an ObjectContext object instead.
3. The client accepts that handle as a "real" object reference.
4. The client makes a method call to the component.
5. MTS locates an idle instance of the component. If none are available, it creates a new instance.
6. MTS passes the method call to the component.

7. The component uses the `getObjectContext` method to obtain a reference to its object context.

8. The component performs the method. If the method is successful, the component calls the `ObjectContext.SetComplete` method; if the method is unsuccessful, it calls `ObjectContext.SetAbort`.

9. In either case, success or failure, the call to `SetComplete` or `SetAbort` informs MTS that the component has completed its work and is ready to be recycled.

10. When the client calls another method on the component, the cycle begins from step 5, not from step 1. A different instance of the component is likely to perform the method.

You've seen how to use ADO to retrieve data inside a WebClass, and you've seen how to move database method calls out of a WebClass and into an external DLL. If you move the database access component into MTS, what changes must you make?

First, you'll need to isolate the methods. Build the methods of a component so that each one could be a separate component if necessary. Next, add the `getObjectContext` calls for each method. Finally, add the calls to `SetComplete` and `SetAbort`, depending on the outcome of the method call.

Here's an example. In Chapter 11, the CRepositoryData component had a `deleteCodeByID` method:

```
Public Sub deleteCodeByID(aConnectionString As String, _
        aCodeID As Long)
    Dim conn As New Connection
    Dim methodName As String
    Dim sd As CStoredDictionary
    methodName = Classname & "deleteCodeByID"
    On Error GoTo ErrDeleteCodeByID
    Call mADO.openConnection(conn, aConnectionString, _
        adModeReadWrite)
    Set sd = New CStoredDictionary
    sd.Add "CodeID", aCodeID
    Call mADO.executeSQL(conn, "deleteCodeByID", _
        adCmdStoredProc, sd)
    Call mADO.closeConnection(conn)
ExitDeleteCodeByID:
    Exit Sub
```

```
ErrDeleteCodeByID:
    Err.Raise Err.Number, Err.Source & ": " & _
    methodName, Err.Description & vbCrLf & _
    "Unable to delete the code with ID " & aCodeID & _
    " from the repository."
    Resume ExitDeleteCodeByID
End Sub
```

Here's the same method rewritten so it runs in MTS. The highlighted lines show the changes to the code from the non-MTS version:

```
Public Sub deleteCodeByID(aConnectionString As String, _
        aCodeID As Long)
    On Error Goto ErrDeleteCodeByID
    Dim conn As New Connection
    Dim methodName As String
    Dim sd As CstoredDictionary
    Dim oc as ObjectContext
    Set oc = getObjectContext()
    methodName = Classname & "deleteCodeByID"
    On Error GoTo ErrDeleteCodeByID
    Call mADO.openConnection(conn, aConnectionString, _
        adModeReadWrite)
    Set sd = New CStoredDictionary
    sd.Add "CodeID", aCodeID
    Call mADO.executeSQL(conn, "deleteCodeByID", _
        adCmdStoredProc, sd)
    Call mADO.closeConnection(conn)
    oc.SetComplete
ExitDeleteCodeByID:
    Exit Sub
ErrDeleteCodeByID:
    oc.SetAbort
    Err.Raise Err.Number, Err.Source & ": " & _
    methodName, Err.Description & vbCrLf & _
    "Unable to delete the code with ID " & aCodeID & _
    " from the repository."
    Resume ExitDeleteCodeByID
End Sub
```

Note that you do not need to check whether the call to `getObjectContext` returns a valid object. You need to check only when you actually *use* the methods of the ObjectContext object. If `getObjectContext` fails, the object is still set to

Nothing. Therefore, you can easily write a component so that it can run either inside an MTS context or outside a context by checking whether the Object-Context object is Nothing. For example:

```
If Not oc Is Nothing then
    oc.SetComplete
End If

If Not oc Is Nothing then
    oc.SetAbort
End If
```

Writing a `getObjectContext` call in every method quickly becomes tedious. A simpler way is to implement the ObjectControl interface in your class. The ObjectControl interface requires that you support three methods in your class. These methods are explained in Table 12.2.

**TABLE 12.2:** ObjectControl Interface Methods

| ObjectControl Interface Method Name | Description |
| --- | --- |
| Activate | Called just before MTS activates your component. In MTS, this event substitutes for the `Class_Initialize` event. You should remove code from the `Class_Initialize` event if possible. |
| Deactivate | Called just before MTS deactivates your component. In MTS, this event substitutes for the `Class_Terminate` event. You should remove code from the `Class_Terminate` event if possible. |
| CanBePooled | MTS calls this function to determine whether your component can be pooled. Although MTS does not currently support pooling, you must implement the method. Apartment-threaded DLLs like those created with VB cannot be pooled, so you should always return `False`. |

Remember, MTS keeps one or more copies of your components "alive," so your component won't receive `Class_Initialize` or `Class_Terminate` events except when it is truly loaded or unloaded. Instead, MTS fires the `ObjectControl_Activate` event just before it activates a component. You can use the event to perform any required initializations. Similarly, use the `ObjectControl_Deactivate` event to clean up.

The big advantage of implementing the ObjectControl interface is that you can declare a class-level variable to reference the ObjectContext object. That way you don't have to write the `getObjectContext` call in each method. Instead, you obtain the reference during the `ObjectControl_Activate` event and release it during the `ObjectControl_Deactivate` event:

```
Private Sub ObjectControl_Activate()
    On Error GoTo ErrActivate
    Dim methodname As String
    methodname = Classname & ".ObjectControl_Activate"
    Set MTSContext = GetObjectContext()
ExitActivate:
    Exit Sub
ErrActivate:
    Err.Raise Err.Number, Err.Source & ": " _
        & methodname, "Error retrieving an object context."
    Resume ExitActivate
End Sub

Private Sub ObjectControl_Deactivate()
    On Error GoTo ErrDeactivate
    Dim methodname As String
    methodname = Classname & ".ObjectControl_Deactivate"
    Set MTSContext = Nothing
ExitDeactivate:
    Exit Sub
ErrDeactivate:
    Err.Raise Err.Number, "ObjectControl_Deactivate", _
        "Unable to release the object context reference."
    Resume ExitDeactivate
End Sub
```

Even though MTS does not support object pooling, the `ObjectControl_CanBePooled` method is part of the ObjectControl interface specification; therefore, you must implement it. A future version of MTS will manage pools of components, but not apartment-threaded objects such as those you create with VB. You should always return `False` from this function:

```
Private Function ObjectControl_CanBePooled() As Boolean
    ObjectControl_CanBePooled = False
End Function
```

From a WebClass, use the `Server.CreateObject` method to create MTS objects. If you use the `New` keyword, the objects don't run inside MTS. Alternately, you can obtain an ObjectContext object reference and use the `CreateInstance` method to create the MTS object. To obtain an ObjectContext object, you must compile the WebClass and run it inside MTS as well. Either approach works, but the first one works better during the design and debugging phase. Note that you *can* use the New keyword to create objects inside your WebClass project—those objects *do* run inside of MTS if your WebClass runs in MTS.

You cannot perform the following actions without getting fatal errors:

- It doesn't seem possible to persist an object via a PropertyBag object unless you create the object with the New keyword or unless you create the object by instantiating it via the `PropertyBag.ReadProperty` method. This makes sense, because MTS components should be stateless.

- You can't implement the ObjectControl interface on a WebClass. When you do that, MTS shuts down the calling IIS process.

- You can't implement MTS security on objects you want to persist via the PropertyBag.

Other actions seem to work just fine:

- You can run your objects in MTS in either a Library Package or a Server Package.

- You can change the package activation (Library to Server) or security while the application is running with no apparent adverse effects (I haven't tried this under load).

I've rewritten the ADO and CRepositoryData classes so that they run both inside and outside MTS. I've also provided a second MTS-enabled copy of the CodeRepository Web application named `CodeRepositoryMTS` so that you can easily compare the two approaches. You can run both versions on your server to compare response time and scalability.

# How Do You Move a Project into MTS?

The process for moving a project into MTS is involved, but not difficult. The first time you do this, you may find that you have some permissions issues to resolve.

## Make MTS-Specific Code Changes

The CodeRepositoryMTS project is essentially identical to the non-MTS CodeRepository project except that both the WebClass and the RepositoryData data-access classes run inside MTS. I took these actions to move the classes:

- Added the ObjectControl interface to the ADO and RepositoryData classes. Adding the interface is as simple as copying the Activate, Deactivate, and CanBePooled methods into your class and adding a line to implement the interface.
- Changed all New keyword ADO object initializations to ObjectContext.CreateInstance calls.
- Changed all CRepositoryData object initializations to CreateObject calls.
- Set the MTSTransactionMode property for the RepositoryData and ADO classes to RequiresNewTransaction and UsesTransaction, respectively.

You'll find that you can move classes in and out of MTS easily by wrapping object initialization in a function call:

```
Private Function createADO() As ADO
    If Not MTSContext Is Nothing Then
        Set createADO = MTSContext.CreateInstance _
        ("RepositoryData.ADO")
    Else
        Set createADO = New RepositoryData.ADO
    End If
End Function
```

## Compile the Project

To debug a project in VB that runs under MTS, you must have the NT 4 Service Pack 4 installed and you must set binary compatibility for the project. That means that you need to compile at least twice. The first time, compile the project normally. Then, right-click the project name in the VB Project Explorer and select Properties. The Project Properties dialog shown in Figure 12.5 appears.

Check the Unattended Execution and Retained in Memory check boxes, then click the Component tab. You'll see a dialog like the one shown in Figure 12.6.

**FIGURE 12.5:**

VB Project Properties dialog

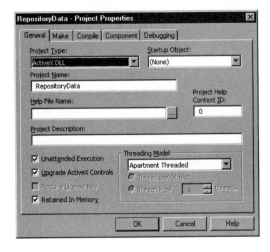

**FIGURE 12.6:**

Component tab on the VB Project Properties dialog

Select the Binary Compatibility option. Type the path and filename to the copy of the DLL you just compiled, or use the browse button to find the file and select it.

The term *binary compatibility*, as applied to a project, is essentially a contract. By checking the Binary Compatibility option, you agree that:

- You aren't going to change the interface. That means that you can't add, remove, or rename methods; add arguments; or change return types for any public function. Depending on how well you plan, that's highly restrictive. I recommend that you avoid adding components to MTS until they're complete and fully debugged.

- VB will no longer change the class ID as you recompile the project. Usually, VB generates a new class ID each time you compile. A consistent class ID is important for MTS because that's how it manages components. If you install a component in MTS, then recompile the component and change the class ID, the new version of the component will no longer run under MTS.

If you do need to change the interface and you have already installed the components in MTS, you should remove the components from the MTS package first. To recompile the component, turn binary compatibility off, recompile, then turn binary compatibility back on and reimport the new components into the MTS package.

## Create and Configure an MTS Package

Launch the MTS Explorer and right-click the Packages Installed entry. Click New Package, then click the Create an Empty Package button (see Figure 12.7).

**FIGURE 12.7:**

MTS Explorer—Package Wizard dialog

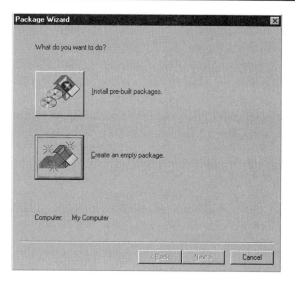

Type a name for your package in the dialog that appears, then click Next. MTS will ask you for the name and password of an account under which it should run the package. Select an account with sufficient permissions to run your objects. Click Finish to save your changes.

The new package appears in the list of installed packages in the MTS Explorer. Expand the Packages Installed entry and find your new package name in the list. Click the plus (+) sign to open it. Right-click Components and select New Component. The Component Wizard dialog in Figure 12.8 appears.

**FIGURE 12.8:**

MTS Explorer—Component Wizard dialog

Click the Install New Component(s) button (don't use the Import Component(s) entry even though your DLLs are already registered). Click the Add Files button and select your DLL, then click the Open button to add the components. MTS adds one entry for each public object in your DLL.

> **NOTE** If you want to delete a component, right-click the component in the MTS Explorer and then select Delete from the pop-up menu.

By default, MTS creates a Server Package with authorization checking disabled, but you can change these settings at any time. To change the settings, right-click the package name in MTS Explorer and select Properties. I strongly urge you to find other sources for MTS information if you plan to work with it often—there's just not enough room in this book to explain all its capabilities.

## Run the Project

You're ready to run the project. Based on my experience, you should plan on a significant block of time to get the project running in MTS until you become familiar with the procedures.

Although you can debug components inside MTS, you should avoid doing so. Debug the components *before* you add them to MTS. The VB debugging environment simulates a single MTS instance on a single thread, so you will not be able to debug components under load from inside the VB integrated development environment (IDE). To test your project after adding the components, don't run the project; instead, launch your browser and navigate to the URL for the starting WebClass.

If you make changes to components running in MTS and called by a WebClass, both IIS and MTS can become "confused." To avoid problems, follow this procedure to make component changes:

1. Stop the WebClass project.
2. Stop IIS by using the Stop button on the WebClass toolbar.
3. Use MTS Explorer to shut down the Package containing your components.
4. Delete the components from MTS (although this step isn't strictly necessary when you have Binary Compatibility turned on, I've found that MTS doesn't always apply changes properly).
5. Alter and recompile the components.
6. Add them back into the MTS package.
7. Start IIS by using the Start button on the WebClass toolbar.
8. Rerun the project.

To run or debug components that require transactions, the Microsoft Distributed Transaction Coordinator (MSDTC) service must be running. The service, as installed, is set to run manually, not automatically. You can start and stop the service from the MTS Explorer by right-clicking the server name under the Computers entry and selecting Start or Stop MSDTC, but it's more convenient to switch the service to start automatically. To do that, click Start ➤ Settings ➤ Control Panel, and then double-click Services to launch the Services dialog.

Select the MSDTC entry from the services list, then click the Startup button to display the Service options dialog (see Figure 12.9). Click the Automatic option, then click OK and Close to close the dialogs. MSDTC will now start automatically when NT starts.

**FIGURE 12.9:**

Service startup options

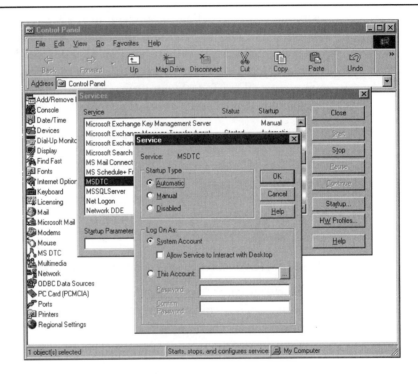

## Change DCOM Permissions

You may find that you have to add or modify permissions (via the Distributed COM Configuration Manager) for the IUSR_MachineName and IWAM_Machine-Name accounts before they can launch the Machine Debug Manager or other classes.

To do that, click Start ➤ Run and type **dcomcnfg** into the Open field. You'll see a list of class IDs (see Figure 12.10). If you scroll down in the list you'll see a list of component names.

**FIGURE 12.10:**

Distributed COM Configuration Properties (dcomcnfg.exe)

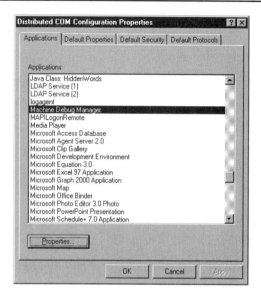

Find the Machine Debug Manager entry in the list and select it. Click the Properties button, then click the Security tab (see Figure 12.11).

**FIGURE 12.11:**

Security tab of the DCOM Machine Debug Manager Properties dialog

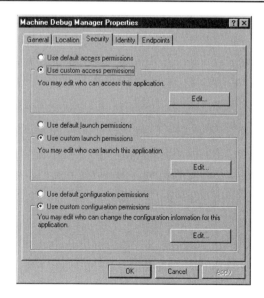

The Machine Debug Manager uses custom access and launch permissions. Click the Edit button for the custom access permissions and add the IUSR_MachineName and IWAM_MachineName accounts to the list with Allow Access permissions (see Figure 12.12).

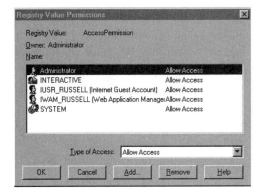

**FIGURE 12.12:**

DCOM Machine Debug Manager Registry Access Permissions

Click OK to save the changes. You take almost exactly the same actions to set the launch permissions. Click the Edit button for the custom launch permissions in the DCOM Machine Debug Manager Properties dialog and add both the IUSR_MachineName and IWAM_MachineName accounts to the list with Allow Launch permissions. Click OK to save the changes.

Permissions issues are the most likely errors you'll encounter as you develop WebClass applications—and they vary from one computer to the next. If you trap all the errors, you'll find that MTS provides reasonably good error entries in the Application event log. For example, Figure 12.13 shows an MTS-generated permissions error.

All the MTS errors I've encountered have shown the class ID and the account that generated the error. Unfortunately, not all class IDs are associated with a name. When the error doesn't show a class name, you need to work backward through the Registry to debug the problem.

You can copy the class ID from the error display and search for it in the HKEY_ CLASSES_ROOT key of the Registry to find the associated class name or executable file. Often that alone provides the information you need to solve the problem.

### FIGURE 12.13:

Application event log MTS error entry

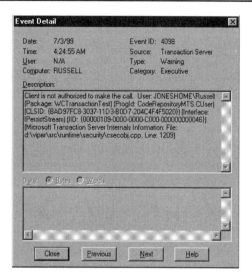

# CHAPTER THIRTEEN

# Deploying WebClass Applications

- Preparing for Deployment
- Creating an Installation Program
- Configuring the Target Server
- Dealing with Permissions Issues

Now that you can design and develop IIS WebClass-based applications, there's only one issue left—deployment. Fortunately, delivering and installing WebClass applications on a new server isn't difficult if you know the problems in advance. In this chapter, you'll see what those issues are and how to solve them. Note that the information in this chapter is a guide, not a reference. The chapter does not contain a comprehensive list of problems or installation issues, just those that you are likely to run into when installing any IIS WebClass application.

# Preparing for Deployment

Deploying a Web application isn't much different from deploying a standard Windows application. There are only three critical differences:

- Compiled WebClass applications run under different permissions from those in the Visual Basic integrated development environment (IDE).

- Compiled WebClasses run on multiple threads. In the IDE, each WebClass runs on one and one thread only. Resource contention that you won't see during development can become an issue after deployment.

- The target server will not be your development server, won't have the same directory permissions that your server does, may not be the same service pack version, and will have different security settings. If you're lucky, you'll have Administrator access to the target server. In both cases, you can help either yourself or the server administrators by following the guidelines in this chapter.

You need a minimum of two servers to test an installation: your development server and a test server. The test server cannot be the development server because all paths, files, DSNs, graphics, virtual directories, permissions, DLLs, and other resources and settings presumably already exist and work on the development server. The point of testing the installation is that the target environment is usually unknown and often uncontrollable. In other words, you may be delivering your application to a server that is radically different from your development server.

## Clean Up the Code

Now's a good time to go through the code and eliminate unneeded methods and variables. It's too early to remove any debugging code, although you should be able to turn the debug output on and off easily for testing. To clean up the code, take the following steps:

1. Check the project references list and remove any unnecessary references. The Visual Studio Package and Deployment Wizard (PDW) includes external DLLs based on the project references list.

2. Delete unused files. Don't forget to delete unused HTML template files—you'll need a clean list to create your installation.

3. Back up the project. As a developer, you're sure (or you should be) that the application runs perfectly right now. You should save that known state in case you make changes during the deployment process and want to undo them later.

4. Make sure that all file references within the project use relative URLs. *Never* include the server name or IP address in any code. The server name will always change. If your root directory name clashes with an existing name, or if, for whatever reason, the clients want to change the root to another name, your program will still work. You can obtain the server name and program root at runtime with the `Server.MapPath` method.

5. Search your program for references to external resources such as log filenames, database DSNs, etc. As you find them, move them to the `global.asa` file and store them as Application-level variables. Change the code so it references the Application variables. That way, you can easily change DSN names, sign-ons, passwords, and external file references, regardless of the resources' locations or names. If security is an issue, put the references in an external file and encrypt the file. The point here is that those filenames, paths, machine resources, and database resources can and will change names and locations. In many cases, these changes are outside your control and will break your application. You want to get the references from a location that you can change easily, preferably without recompiling and reinstalling your application.

6. Try to rename files specific to the application in a consistent manner. That makes it much easier to find and remember files later. It also decreases the risk that a file you're installing will conflict with the name of a file already on the system.

7. Make a version number for your program and provide a method to retrieve it. For example, the About box found on the Help menu in most Windows programs provides that information. Although your browser-based application may not have an About box, you can provide a way to display the version number.

## Test in Compiled Mode

Before you can consider your application ready to deploy on another computer, you need to test it in compiled mode. Compile the project and all the DLLs. Close VB and test the application. Better yet, have someone else test the application. Unless your application runs successfully outside of the VB IDE on your development server, it will never run on someone else's server.

Testing in compiled mode is always important, but it's especially important for WebClass applications. When you run a WebClass in the IDE, it always runs on a single thread and it always runs as "you." In compiled mode, it runs as the IUSR_MachineName or IWAM_MachineName account. In other words, the permissions available to the WebClass in the IDE are different from those out of the IDE.

## Generate Likely Errors

Generate errors for the problems most likely to happen. By likely errors, I mean outside resources and references that your application depends on that tend to change over time. For example, if your application opens connections to a database, shut down the database, then see how your application traps the error. Where do the errors appear? On the browser screen? In the Event Application log? In the Event Security log? You need to know so that you can debug the application remotely on an unfamiliar server.

If your application needs write access to a directory, shut off that access. Delete log files and change DCOM permissions. All these things are out of your control after the application leaves the development stage, but they all happen. Neither you nor anyone else on the development team will remember the information after a few weeks, so write down the exact error messages and the solutions.

If you follow this advice, you'll probably want to go through at least one more testing and revision cycle to beef up the error reporting. I can assure you that this is time well spent if you're deploying to a remote server—one you can't physically reach or on which you don't have Administrator permissions. Review Chapter 6, "WebClass Debugging and Error Handling," for more information about trapping and reporting errors.

I often write "hidden" features into a program that can aid in debugging delivered applications. It's best to isolate these features as far as possible from other program requirements. ASP programs are excellent candidates for these features because they're small and they work as long as the server is working. Some examples are an ASP file that tests database connections, one that lists the contents of the global.asa file, one that checks resources, and one that lets you run SQL code against a database such as iSQL. If you have FTP or FrontPage access to the target server, you can even write and deploy such applets after a problem occurs.

Put the error messages and solutions in an .htm file that accompanies your application and keep a copy for yourself. When you get a support call, you'll be able to tell the caller where to look and what to do to solve the problem.

## Deploy to a Test Server

If possible, install and test the application on a local server—one where you can physically access the machine, start, stop, and even reboot it. Although event logs can be helpful, other server administrators may not want to help you debug your application. Do not install VB on the server unless you can also install VB on all the target servers.

All developers can run programs on their computers; running a compiled, multiuser application on someone else's computer is a different problem. Debugging a compiled application requires its own set of skills. Practice on your server, not your client's server; but practice on a test server, not the development server.

## Beta Test the Application

Many applications run perfectly when tested by the author, but fail miserably when tested by "real" users. By real users, I mean members of the target audience. Real users don't know what input the application expects, so they do unexpected things.

As early as possible, and on an ongoing basis during development, you should try to get several members of your target audience to use or at least critique the application. A decent sample is five to ten people. You'll find that you can catch most bugs, misconceptions, and missing features if you let just a few people use the application.

A real beta test, though, occurs as a next-to-final step. You install the application on a server and let several people use it. They should treat the application as though it were the production version. Fix any problems that arise.

When the application has passed muster in beta form, you can remove the debugging code—it's ready for production. Be sure to recompile and test again without the debugging code.

## Determine the Target Server's Configuration

When you're delivering to a known target server, you may be able to call ahead to find out the configuration of that server. The earlier you can do this in the development process, the better. For example, developing with the latest and greatest version of ADO will do you no good if the target server is still running version 1.5. Similarly, taking advantage of the many convenient features of SQL Server version 7, such as 8,000-character varChar fields, won't work if the target database server is running version 6.5. Server administrators are notoriously "difficult" when you tell them they must upgrade *their* equipment or software to accommodate *your* application.

If you're developing commercial applications, you will need to create more than one version of the application, design for the lowest common denominator, or be willing to give up possible sales to use the latest technology.

In all cases, you'll want to design the application to isolate version-dependent issues so that you can change component versions and databases easily to meet the technical requirements of the customers. For example, if all your database accesses happen via stored procedures, your application will work on any database where you can re-create the set of stored procedures. Moving the application from SQL Server to Oracle may be as simple as creating the stored procedures and copying the data.

I've sometimes found it useful to begin applications by having the program itself check resource availability and versions. Although that may slow down application initialization, it's better than end-user error messages. Alternately, you can write such checks so that they are performed on demand—perhaps via Administrator options or via an unpublished "back-door" URL that runs a method in your WebClass. Using these techniques, you can at least help determine problems after deployment.

When all else fails, you'll want to keep people from accessing your application while you work on it. Create an ASP file with an appropriate message, for example, `This application is temporarily out of service for maintenance`.... You can rename the ASP file that launches your application and substitute the out-of-service message file to temporarily disable the application. When you've solved the problem, restore the original filenames to let people access the application again.

## Creating an Installation Package

You can create an installation program by using the Visual Studio Package and Deployment Wizard. To launch the Wizard, click Start ➤ Programs ➤ Microsoft Visual Studio 6.0 ➤ Microsoft Visual Studio 6.0 Tools and select the Package and Deployment Wizard. Type the path to the project's .vbp file in the Select Project field or select the .vbp file from the Browse dialog (see Figure 13.1).

**FIGURE 13.1:**

Visual Studio Package and Deployment Wizard

Click the Package button to create a new package. Despite the MSDN documentation, select the Standard Setup Package, not the Internet Package. Click Next and select the location for the setup files from the directory dialog. Make sure you do *not* select the same directory as your project. Click Next to continue.

The Wizard checks the project files for dependencies. If it is unable to find the dependency information for one or more files, it shows you a list of those files. At that point, you can mark files that have no dependencies. Your DLLs may appear in this list, but Microsoft DLLs also appear. For example, the file `mtsax.dll` appears if your project references the Microsoft Transaction Server Type Library. It's difficult to know exactly what to do with this information; I've never found it useful. If the Wizard can't find the dependency information, I can't either. I'm sure it's useful to someone, and there's probably a wealth of PDW information available that may help you if you need it. You can probably ignore the dependency dialog without adverse consequences. An obvious exception is if you know that a component makes calls to an external DLL that *isn't* listed next in the PDW process.

Check the list of files carefully. Make sure that all the required components and files appear. For WebClass applications, the file `mswcrun.dll` must appear in the list. You must add HTML template files, image files, and the `global.asa` and ASP files manually—the Wizard never includes any files of those types. To add a file, click the Add button (see Figure 13.2).

**FIGURE 13.2:**

PDW—Included Files list

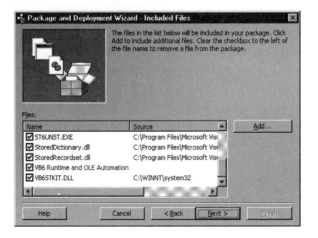

The MSDN information states that the PDW will automatically include .dsr and .dsx files and implies that those must accompany the installation. That is incorrect. You do not have to deliver the .dsr and .dsx files for your WebClasses, just the DLLs. When you have added all the files, click the Next button to continue.

The Wizard typically marks DLLs for installation in the system folder. It also asks you which DLLs to mark as shared. Place shared DLLs in the system folder, application-specific DLLs in the application folder.

The rest of the Wizard is not specific to WebClasses. You can follow the instructions in the Wizard. You should be aware that there are many other Wizard and installation issues. MSDN contains documentation for many of these problems. Microsoft's Web site contains the most up-to-date version of the documentation. The Microsoft newsgroups and information on the many VB Web sites can also help you solve installation problems. I urge you to take advantage of these resources by reading them *before* you undertake a complex installation.

Finally, the PDW is neither the most robust nor the most flexible installation program available. Third-party vendors supply much more powerful and configurable programs. The best of these can install essentially anything. As the programs gain in features, they also gain in difficulty. Each vendor has a set of Wizards. Some have customized scripting languages. The more involved your application installation is, the more difficult it will be to create the installation. Don't let the application installation languish while you tinker with background colors. You'll need a dedicated programmer and a substantial amount of time—two to three days for a simple application, possibly several weeks for a complex application—to create and test a robust installation program. The more you're willing and able to install manually, the simpler your installation will be. Unfortunately, the corollary to that approach is that the more you're willing to install manually, the more difficult it will be for anyone else to perform the installation.

# Configuring the Target Server

In this section, I'll show you what you need to do in addition to creating an installation package. For all IIS applications, you have to change the server configuration somewhat. For the simplest applications, you only need to create a virtual directory; for others, you need to create accounts, assign permissions, create DSNs, and install packages into MTS.

## Capture the Server Configuration Settings

As soon as you create and test the installation package, capture the current settings for IIS and for MTS from your test server. Screen captures work best, but you can write down all the settings as well. Be sure to capture them all.

If you're using an installer other than the PDW, one that can create virtual Web directories and perform MTS installations, you'll need to know the settings to create your package. Otherwise, you or some other server administrator need to know them to configure the target server. There are too many settings to remember, and you won't remember them long-term, so write them down. Put the settings, graphics and all, in the .htm file that accompanies the application and keep a copy for yourself.

## Run the Installation

To configure the server, you'll need to perform some of the following steps, but probably not all of them. Consider this list as a resource only, not as a procedure; I don't know what your applications require, what the server situation is, or whether you're delivering in-house or commercial applications. In general, unless you "own" the server, try to be polite—don't break existing applications just to get your application running.

I've assumed that you're performing the installation, or at least that you are present during the installation. If not, you need to assemble all the documentation and deliver it to the person doing the installation. If you can't be present, have someone else practice the installation by using your documentation on the test server before delivering the application. Follow these steps for installation:

1. Consult with the server administrator before beginning your installation. If you plan to install any system DLLs, make sure the administrator knows the files and versions in advance. Such files usually require a reboot. Therefore, you must often schedule the installation in advance; administrators often must schedule installations that require a reboot during low usage hours. Remember that removing most upgrades is much harder than installing them. Many upgrades aren't perfectly compatible with previous versions. Most servers run multiple applications. You don't want to be responsible for breaking someone else's program.

2. Set up your virtual directory first, using the Internet Service Manager application. Set the directory and applications permissions to the same settings as those from the tested beta version. If you captured those settings as screen shots, this step will be straightforward.

3. Run your installation package to install the files.

4. Create any other required directories—for example, log directories—and set the necessary directory and/or file permissions.

5. Edit the `global.asa` or your external reference file and change the entries so they match the requirements of the server. Such entries include DSNs, file paths, global variables, company names, etc.

6. If your application uses a database, make sure the database has been properly set up. In some cases, that may be as simple as using a Wizard to move the database to a production database server. In others, it's an involved process fully as complex as setting up and creating your IIS application. Database setup is beyond the scope of this book. Just be aware that the database needs to be online and ready, with appropriate permissions set, by this stage of deployment.

7. Check the database connection(s), sign-on(s), and password(s). Many IIS installations break down at this stage because the `IUSR_MachineName` or `IWAM_MachineName` sign-ons don't have permission to access the database server. Test several representative procedures, including procedures with updates, inserts, and deletes to ensure that your application has sufficient permissions. I usually use ASP files to do these kinds of checks because you can alter them quickly based on the immediate needs, conditions, and problems involved. The test ASP files run inside your virtual directory, but more importantly, they run with exactly the same permissions as your application, which can help debug problems.

8. Set up the appropriate packages and import components into MTS. You can do this step manually if you prefer. MTS also provides an export facility that creates an MTS package (.pak) file. The .pak file stores all component names, IDs, and settings. MTS also exports the DLLs themselves. Keep the .pak file and the DLLs together. Don't substitute a later version of a DLL for the version exported by the .pak file or your installation may not work. To re-create the package on another system, right-click the Packages Installed item and select New Package to import the .pak file. Click the Install Pre-Built Packages button and browse to the .pak file for your package.

9. When you create an MTS .pak file, you have the option to include role names and include the NT UserIDs associated with those roles. If you're delivering internal applications, including that information can be useful, but you should not include it if you're delivering to another company or to a location that is not part of your NT network. Make sure that you set up any required roles and users. Bear in mind that you may need to re-create these roles *exactly* as they appeared on the test server if any program code checks a user's role assignment.

10. Check the DCOM default access and launch permissions. Make sure they include the `IUSR_MachineName` and `IWAM_MachineName` accounts if you're delivering an application that uses anonymous access. See Chapter 12, "IIS Applications and Microsoft Transaction Server," for directions on setting permissions for a specific object. Setting the default access and launch permissions is similar; just click the Default Security tab first. You can find detailed directions for changing DCOM permissions in Chapter 12 as well.

11. If you call remote objects, you'll need to repeat the permissions-setting checks on the remote machine also. You may need to set up a trust relationship between your server and the remote computer and add the `IUSR_MachineName` and `IWAM_MachineName` accounts to the remote computer's user account list. Alternately (and this is preferable), you can switch the Web server's anonymous account to a network account with sufficient permissions to run the application on both computers.

# Dealing with Permissions Issues

It's been my experience, unfortunately, that permissions issues arise for almost every IIS application deployment, with both WebClass and ASP applications. Some of these problems you can solve in advance; the rest you'll need to solve during deployment. There's little chance that everything will run perfectly. If you trap the errors properly, practice the installation, and document the settings from your test server, you may have only a few problems. If you haven't done those things, I hope you're a lucky person.

Most permissions errors won't appear on the browser screen or in any log files generated by your application even if you trap them properly. The on-screen or in-log errors typically say something like `Access denied`, which is unhelpful. A better description of most permissions errors appears in the Event log. You need to check both the System log and the Application log if your application isn't running properly.

You don't have to allow anonymous access to your Web server. You can set up IIS so that it requires users to sign on. Internet Explorer users sign on with NT Challenge/Response, which is transparent. Netscape users must manually enter their network sign-on and password (sent via plain text) to gain access to the application. If your server does not allow anonymous access, you can substitute your user's group or account names wherever you see `IUSR_MachineName` or `IWAM_MachineName` throughout this book. Most IIS application permissions errors occur when the `IUSR_MachineName` or `IWAM_MachineName` account requests access or launch permission to a class, component, or file. In some cases, the system or subsystem writes these errors to the System or Application logs; in other cases, they don't. When your error-trapping and the system error-trapping don't provide enough information, you can use NT's auditing feature to help find the problem.

You need to be an administrator to enable auditing for a computer. Document what you do—you'll want to turn it off later, and there's no easy way to turn off auditing without disabling all auditing. To enable auditing, start User Manager for Domains and click the Policies menu, then select the Audit entry. You'll see the System Audit Policy dialog, from which you can select the types of events you wish to audit. You can audit several types of events, but usually you need to audit only File and Object access to debug IIS applications (see Figure 13.3).

**FIGURE 13.3:**

System Audit Policy dialog

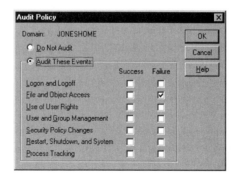

Click the Audit These Events radio button, then check the File and Object Access Failure check box. Click OK to save the changes and close the dialog.

Setting the system audit policy doesn't turn on auditing—it only enables auditing. After setting the audit policy for the server, you turn auditing on and off for individual directories and files by using Windows Explorer. Navigate to a file or directory, then right-click it and select Properties. Click the Security tab and then click the Auditing button. You will see the File Auditing dialog (see Figure 13.4).

**FIGURE 13.4:**

Windows Explorer File Auditing dialog

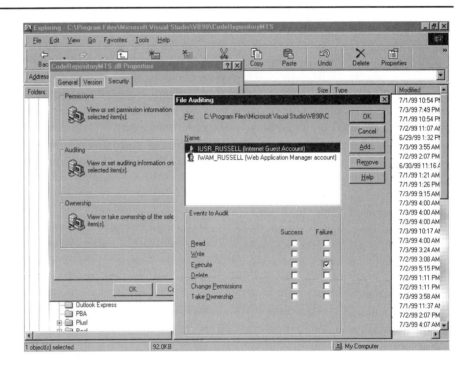

Windows NT audits events for specific sign-ons or groups. Add the IUSR_MachineName and IWAM_MachineName accounts to the list by using the Add button, then click the features you want to audit. The entries in this list don't match the system audit policy list. If you're reasonably sure where the error occurs, audit Execute Failure. If the error occurs during file access, audit Read, Write, or Delete. If you're not sure where the error occurs, auditing successes can help as well, since a success entry can help you eliminate error candidates.

Keep a careful list of the items you audit. When you solve the problem, be sure to turn off auditing. Don't just turn it off using the System Policy Editor—go back to the individual items and disable the auditing by using Windows Explorer. Auditing is a major performance drain because it requires a disk write for every audited action. If another administrator later turns on auditing for another reason, and you leave directory or file auditing turned on, your application may suffer.

Despite all these warnings and error-trapping resources, your application may still have problems. Microsoft's MSDN site and the newsgroups can sometimes provide expert advice. The other books in this Sybex series of VB Developer's Guides also provide expert information on MTS/COM+, ASP, NT, and IIS:

- *Visual Basic Developer's Guide to COM and COM+* by Wayne Freeze
- *Visual Basic Developer's Guide to ADO* by Mike Gunderloy
- *Visual Basic Developer's Guide to Win32 API* by Steve Brown

Maybe Microsoft will provide more power and features in the next version. I can assure you that Windows 2000 will alleviate some of the installation problems you face today—but it will probably introduce others.

# CHAPTER FOURTEEN

# What's Next?

- Where Are Web Applications Headed?

- What about Java and CORBA?

- What about Database Technology?

- What about XML?

You've covered a lot of material in this book, and I hope that it's given you ideas and techniques that help you create and deliver applications. Fortunately (or perhaps unfortunately, depending on your view), changes occur extremely rapidly in this business. While I was writing this book, Microsoft, among other things:

- Delivered Windows 2000, Beta 3—the first-ever occurrence of a pay-to-play beta program
- Released Internet Explorer 5, which may change the way you think about state management
- Released Visual Studio Service Pack 3, which broke many WebClass applications

I love to play with new technology, but I've tried to keep this book aimed squarely at existing technology. Nevertheless, I wanted to mention several issues that might influence the way you develop applications in the future. This chapter is my forum for doing so. The information in this chapter is my opinion; some of it is sheer speculation—you might say it's an awareness chapter. You won't find VB WebClass techniques, tips, or projects here—you've completed all the "real" work earlier in the book—but I hope you'll find some food for thought.

# Where Are Web Applications Headed?

I believe that Web applications are likely to become the dominant form of business applications within the next few years. Although the bulk of program development still occurs for stand-alone and standard client-server applications, Web applications have too many business advantages to ignore. From the point of view of a business, Web applications:

**Centralize administration and security** All the application code, settings, and data reside on centralized servers. Administrators can control and monitor access, solve problems, and perform maintenance without visiting each desktop.

**Lend themselves well to monitoring** That's a scary thought, but it's also a huge advantage to a business to know how much use an application receives and to know who is using it. Without such monitoring, it's difficult to tell whether a program justifies its cost.

**Upgrade easily**   Easily, that is, as compared to upgrading 20,000 desktops. Not only that, but when you upgrade a Web application, you also upgrade all users—simultaneously, which provides tremendous cost savings.

**Provide control over sensitive data**   Not perfect control—people can print files from their browsers (although maybe not for long). But at least administrators have a centralized backup for all the information—no more critical Excel files lost during the weekend vacation.

**Scale as needed**   Employees come and go at businesses. Not all businesses have this problem, but consider a company that provides seasonal employment—tax consultants, for example. During the early part of the year, these companies may swell the employee ranks by several thousand percent. Think of the software costs. If you purchase shrink-wrapped, stand-alone software, you must amortize the cost over a full year—even if you use it only part-time. Software rentals, per-use fees, and timed rentals are inevitable as software becomes centralized. Just as it is easier to upgrade a centralized application, it's also easier to increase the number of users of that application, and for the same reasons.

**Provide global access**   Businesses can provide secure global access to centrally maintained and administered applications.

If only businesses benefited from Web applications, building critical mass would take a long time; but Web applications also provide features that developers like. Developers have traditionally had to work hard to create applications that use data from multiple file formats, have interfaces that adjust to different screen resolutions, and run on widely varying types of equipment. Such applications are now commonplace because of the Web. Incompatible file formats, varying screen resolutions, incompatible equipment—we've all struggled with those issues over the years. These problems haven't gone away, but the Web has ameliorated them. Consider these features; if you've been programming a while, remember how (or if) you used to have to code to provide them:

**Fonts, colors, and graphics**   Sure, they've been available since DOS and they got easier with Windows, but HTML made creating functional and attractive information displays so easy that you don't even need a programmer to create them anymore. Anyone with Word, FrontPage, or any of a few dozen What-You-See-Is-What-You-Get (WYSIWYG) editors can format complex displays, including input controls, with less than a day's training.

**Databases**   Databases used to be a "roll-your-own" affair. DBase and, later, Access gave programmers easy-to-use database power. SQL Server, Oracle, Sybase, and others provided enterprise-level scalability. Today, a great deal of database code (SQL) is portable between many databases. I fully expect eXtensible Query Language (XQL) or a similar syntax to extend that portability to all databases.

**File formats**   The world is moving toward universal file formats. The needs of businesses and governments to store information in ways that are portable—not just from one program version to another, but between all programs— are driving this change. You've already seen display code move from binary form (custom code) to text form (HTML). Just a few years ago, graphics file formats—and their incompatibilities—were a major development issue. When was the last time you worked with anything except .gif and .jpg files? Even the .bmp format, Windows' native graphics format, has become secondary to the popular Web graphics formats. Word processing software, spreadsheets, and even databases are just one step behind. With the release of Office 2000, Microsoft puts the world on notice that eXtensible Markup Language (XML) has become the file format for the future.

**Programming languages**   The choices for programming languages are shrinking rapidly. It's not that there are fewer languages available—there are more; but the number of people who are adept at all but the most popular languages is shrinking because businesses want to use standards. The process feeds on itself. As more businesses standardize on VB, C, and Java, more programmers abandon other languages, such as COBOL and Delphi, to concentrate on those with which they can earn a living. I think this process is far from over. Either the result will be a language that (like XML) has a consistent and extensible syntax, or the various languages will become front ends for a common back-end syntax (which, in a sense, they are already). Perhaps that will be XML; I don't know.

**Multiuser applications**   You used to write custom code to monitor and control multiuser access to files and applications. Now multiuser capabilities are built into every Web server and database server. Scalability is still an important issue, but building scaleable applications is easier than it has ever been before. In the future, as processing becomes increasingly distributed and distributable, scalability issues will become nothing more than cost issues.

Some of the advantages are the same for programmers as for businesses: one (or at least few) copies of the application to maintain, upgrade, and support. Global access means you can create, deploy, and have people using your application within an extremely short time. Although WebClasses themselves won't be a *final* step in the migration of applications to the Web, the time you spend learning about them won't be wasted. The effort you spend learning the art and craft of building Web applications now will put you in a position to lead in the future.

# What about Java and CORBA?

Java is a great language with a lousy syntax. Java's structural heritage is SmallTalk, while its immediate parent is C++. Said another way, Java's genetic makeup is pure SmallTalk, but its vernacular is C++. SmallTalk, for those of you who haven't been around a long time, was the first (and the best, at least in theory) pure object-oriented language.

Java could fulfill the need for a universal programming language, but its implementation ensures that it will fail at that task. I believe that Visual Basic programmers should learn Java, but I also believe that Java programmers should learn Visual Basic. The two languages don't often compete head to head, and I don't believe they're likely to in the near future.

Java has found its niche in the non-Microsoft camp by providing some of VB's rapid application development capabilities on non-Intel hardware. You must realize that until Java, the Unix operating system had nothing like VB—most development was in C and C++ (thus the syntax for Java). The idea that a modern programming language would need semicolons just so the parser can find the ends of the lines makes me shake my head in wonder.... Nevertheless, Java is important—primarily because it provides your easiest access to CORBA.

Microsoft's Component Object Model (COM) and the Common Object Request Broker Architecture (CORBA) are similar in concept. Both provide a means for objects developed without prior knowledge of one another to communicate with each other, and both provide a means of separating what an object does (the interface) from how it does it (the implementation). You can develop both COM and

CORBA objects with multiple programming languages and mix them together later without problems. Today CORBA provides a greater range of services, such as communication between remote objects, but you need to learn the interface definition language (IDL) to use it. COM provides fewer services, but anyone with a minimal knowledge of VB can create COM objects—you don't need to learn an interface definition language. In the near future, COM+ narrows the gap in capabilities considerably. Longer term, I expect that both will improve.

Unfortunately, the Java vendors support CORBA, whereas VB supports only COM. Microsoft's attempt to create a COM-based Java has failed. Without COM support, though, Java can't use VB objects. Without CORBA support, VB can't use Java objects. That leaves us poor developers stuck in the middle. My recommendation is to stay firmly in the middle. Learn them both. Java seems to be making inroads on the server level while COM has a firm grip on the desktop. While COM-to-CORBA (and vice versa) bridges are common and will become more so in the future, all bridges have a performance penalty. Maybe hardware advances will make such issues moot—but maybe not.

Java is a much more object-oriented language than VB. Of course, VB isn't really object oriented at all—it's interface oriented. Microsoft claims that interfaces are better than pure object inheritance, and they might be right, because both COM and CORBA focus on interfaces, not inheritance.

Large organizations keep tight control over both languages. Only Microsoft sells VB and a VB development environment. Java development environments are legion—some even free, but Sun Microsystems controls the Java language itself. That may be changing. Several other large organizations have announced (although not released) clean-room Java implementations. Sun may lose control of the language. If that happens, Java may splinter like C. The differing versions may become operating-system and/or machine-architecture dependent. But it doesn't matter much as long as CORBA, which is controlled by the Object Management Group, maintains its machine independence. The interface is the key, regardless of the language behind it.

As a VB programmer, you have access to the largest library of interfaces in the world—those built to COM specifications. However, remember that COM objects work under the Windows operating system almost exclusively (there are partial Unix implementations of COM). In contrast, CORBA works on virtually every operating system. Don't let the fact that Windows is on 90-plus percent of all computers affect your judgment—less than 50 percent of the Web servers in the world run Windows. Finally, don't let a few semicolons keep you from learning Java; you may need it.

# What about Database Technology?

Databases are as important to Web applications as files are to stand-alone applications. As applications become centralized, they need to put user-specific information somewhere. Files work well when you need only a few of them, but quickly become unwieldy when you work with thousands of them. Even desktop operating systems are likely to dispense with files as we know them now and begin storing content in a database instead.

There are two major trends in databases: keeping information in-memory, where applications can reach it faster, and changing the storage and technology so you store objects rather than data. You've seen both techniques in action in this book (although not with databases). Maintaining state via Session variables is similar to the idea of in-memory databases (IMDBs). Rather than write the information to disk, you cache it in RAM. Storing information in memory can speed up operations by several orders of magnitude. Similarly, when you use the PropertyBag to store binary object data, you can reconstitute the object itself from the stored information, not just the data. This technology should be commonplace already, but it's not.

Several IMDBs are available today. Microsoft provides a limited IMDB with Windows 2000 COM+ services. I think you'll find that the popularity of IMDBs rises as memory prices fall. Note that those costs are already low enough for the technology to be useful. In the future, you'll see massive databases that use disk storage only for backup—all database operations happen in memory. IMDBs are especially important to Web developers. In keeping with the theme of this book, you can get the data and get out more quickly than ever. Session variables become obsolete when you have an alternative that's just as fast *and* has the added advantage of permanence, with no extra coding. Consider this: If you can store state permanently, yet retrieve it nearly instantaneously, you don't need sessions. A user's "session" begins at registration and ends—well, never! At least, until you run out of memory. Seriously, you may need to retrieve a person's state from disk, but once retrieved, you can access it much as you do Session variables now.

Object databases are likely to become much more common. Today, you must either code repetitively or use modeling tools to get data out of databases and into objects. You must assign data to properties to re-instantiate objects, and you must assign properties to database fields to store objects. Consider an object with 15 or 20 properties (not an uncommon figure). Today in VB it takes roughly one line of code per property to save and retrieve the object. That's 30 to 40 lines of code! Wouldn't it be much more convenient to write code like the following instead?

```
Set myObject = "SELECT myObject FROM myObjects"
UPDATE myObjects WHERE myObjects.ID = myObject.ID
```

You'll be able to do that before too long—probably not with that exact syntax.

In the meantime, you might consider looking at XML databases. XML databases store not only data, but also the structure and relationships of that data. Relational databases also store data and relationships, but the relationships are separate from the data. Relational databases store structure as well, but in an extremely rigid manner: by imposing an artificial order or sequence for data. There's no particular reason why you should have to store a `LastName` value in column 1 and a `FirstName` value in column 2, except that relational databases enforce position as a means of capturing structure. In contrast, an XML database "knows" which item is the last name; the structure is part of the data. Columns become irrelevant. As XML becomes more common, so will XML databases.

You can already store ADO Recordsets to an XML file and re-instantiate them later. Code like that will make objects such as the CStoredRecordset obsolete as well. Sure, the ADO Recordset takes more resources, but it also provides more services. You can save an ADO Recordset onto a client, let the client modify the Recordset, then return the XML string to the server for centralized update. When Recordsets aren't too large, they can function as miniature, persistable databases. Today, we perform a tremendous amount of processing to put information into databases that are often mutually incompatible. It is relatively easy to foresee that keeping the information in XML form will be an advantage, both in portability and in processing power.

# What about XML?

Speaking of XML, it's hard to describe how important this idea is or how far-reaching its effects will be. If you haven't run across XML technology yet, here it is in a nutshell:

```
<person>
   <lastname>Doe</lastname>
   <firstname>John</firstname>
```

```
<phone>
    <type>home</type>
    <areacode>111</areacode>
    <number>2125938</number>
</phone>
<phone>
    <type>work</type>
    <areacode>111</areacode>
    <number>2126345</number>
</phone>
<address>
    <street>
      <number>1535</number>
      <name>Waldorf Place</name>
    </street>
    <city>New York</city>
    <state>New York</state>
    <zip>99284</zip>
</address>
</person>
```

You can read that file even if you've never seen XML before: *John Doe has two telephone numbers and lives at 1535 Waldorf Place, New York, New York, 99284*. XML, like HTML, contains both markup and content, but XML has a more consistent (and unfortunately, case-sensitive) syntax. Unlike HTML, each tag must have a terminating tag. Luckily, there are payoffs for the consistent syntax—speed and machine readability. Because XML has a consistent syntax, you can easily teach a computer to read XML files. The revolutionary idea here is that you have a data file where the *structure* of the data is part of the data file itself. XML files are called documents. Essentially, each XML document is a mini-database.

Until now, data files and the structure of the data have been separate. Sure, you've seen text files that include field names, but like relational databases, they're rigid. If John Doe had four telephone numbers instead of two, you'd have to either include fields for all four for everyone (a waste of space) or you'd have to tell John that he could have only two phone numbers. As programmers, we've seen both approaches many times. With the XML file, you would simply add two more telephone numbers to John's entry, no problem. The parser would still parse the file correctly. Queries via the XML parser would return John's four telephone numbers without complaint.

Now take this idea and apply it to programming. What is a programming language, after all, except a data file? Currently, languages produce syntactically specific data files—one or more types for each language. Consider VB. When you produce code, VB stores it in a text file. To the compiler, the text file contains only symbols and white space. The compiler parses the text file and expects to find specific symbols in a specific order. In the absence of other clues, the compiler treats all unrecognized symbols as variables unless Option Specific is in effect; then it treats all unrecognized symbols as errors. C++ and Java have a different syntax, produce different text (code) files, and have different compilers—but each language has nearly identical logical structures.

If you had an XML compiler instead (and I'm sure someone, somewhere, is already working on this), programming languages as we know them would become obsolete quickly. Instead of a version-specific text file targeted to a specific compiler, you would have a version-resistant text file usable by any XML compiler. Effectively, XML can provide the universal programming language, and your programming environment wouldn't even have to change. You could write and edit in VB—and a different person could write and edit in Java. Both languages would churn out XML code in the background. The next day, you could switch code files and keep working—still in your preferred environment.

This isn't a radical idea; it's a natural progression for all symbolic languages. Remember, it was only a few years ago that you couldn't transfer word processing files from one word processor to another. The lowest common denominator was the plain text file—but you lost all your formatting. With XML, the lowest common denominator is still a text file, but you get to keep all the formatting as well. Within the next few years, as programmers become comfortable with XML, proprietary file formats will begin to disappear. In the future, XML will become the common format for programming content, because it provides a competitive business advantage of storing code in a manner that won't become obsolete within a couple of years.

Programming languages are more alike than they are different. If you remove the barrier of syntax, they become nearly identical. For example, pseudocode is the same regardless of the eventual target language. Thus, the XML code generated by a future IDE might look something like this:

```
<object>
   <classid>{BA97FCA8-3037-11D3-B0D7-204C4F4F5020}</classid>
   <project>User</project>
   <classname>CUser</classname>
```

```xml
<properties>
 <public>
  <lastname>Doe</lastname>
  <firstname>John</firstname>
  <phone>
    <type>home</phone>
    <areacode>111</areacode>
    <number>2125938</number>
  </phone>
  <phone>
    <type>work</phone>
    <areacode>111</areacode>
    <number>2126345</number>
  </phone>
  <address>
     <street>
        <number>1535</number>
        <name>Waldorf Place</name>
     </street>
     <city>New York</city>
     <state>New York</state>
     <zip>99284</zip>
  </address>
 </public>
</properties>
<methods>
  <public>
    <getname/>
      <arguments></arguments>
      <returntype>string</returntype>
       <concatenate>
          <return>
             getlastname + ", " + _
             getfirstname
          </return>
        </concatenate>
      </return>
    </getname>
  </public>
</methods>
</object>
```

Does that look familiar? I believe you could translate that into any coding language. XML clearly illustrates the potential for a close relationship between objects, data, and code. Of course, you wouldn't write such code directly, just like you don't write .frm files, .dsr files, or Word files directly today—you use an editor. You'll work in a familiar or appropriate environment and the editor will create the XML output. The XML output is independent of the editor. Similarly, the specifics of translating the editor-generated XML files to machine code are independent of the code itself.

Until recently, XML has been used primarily for business-to-business data transfers. Office 2000 and Internet Explorer 5 are about to change that. Internet Explorer 5 comes with an XML parser, so it intrinsically "understands" the structure of XML. If you load an XML file into Explorer 5, it displays the file as an expandable tree structure, much like the directory view in Windows Explorer.

You've probably noticed that XML looks much like HTML. One difference is that XML is extensible, whereas HTML is fixed. You can add your own tags to XML, and they're just as valid as any other tags. XML doesn't contain any keyword tags. In addition, HTML is a layout language. It describes, very generally, how to display data. XML is a content language. It describes the meaning and function of the data, but not the layout. You can combine an XML document with an extensible stylesheet language (XSL) file to achieve fine control over display. The combination of the two is likely to replace HTML over the next few years.

The installation program for Internet Explorer 5 installs Microsoft's XML parser (`msxml.dll`) as well—and the XML parser is a COM object. You can use it from VB immediately. The parser exposes properties and methods that you can use to walk the structure of an XML document and to query that document about its content. If you have worked with IE's document object model (DOM) at all, you'll be able to use the parser with very little study.

You can instantiate an XML parser on the server, combine it with an XSL stylesheet, and deliver HTML to the client. That's similar to the concept behind IIS applications—the server does the work, so the applications are client independent. But you can also instantiate the XML parser on the client, via JScript or VBScript, and process XML files there. That means that you can send an XML document directly from the server, process it, and display the results by using client-side code. If you don't learn anything else this year, plan to learn XML.

# Conclusion

WebClasses are a necessary, but not sufficient, first step in extending Visual Basic to the Internet. The applications you write with VB today are not as powerful as C++, not as network aware or as portable as Java applications, and not as integrated with IIS as Active Server Pages. However, they do provide the most powerful debugging features ever delivered for Internet programming—and they do it without major changes to the most popular programming language ever invented.

WebClasses are infants, and infants have teething problems. But I think that Microsoft will continue to improve WebClasses—or at least the idea behind WebClasses—into the foreseeable future.

# INDEX

**Note to Reader**: In this index, **boldfaced** page numbers refer to primary discussions of the topic; *italics* page numbers refer to figures.

## SYMBOLS & NUMBERS

  (non-breaking space), 76
#INCLUDE FILE directive, 30
#INCLUDE VIRTUAL directive, 30
<% and %>, for server-side code, 32
<%@ LANGUAGE= %> directive, 31, 47

## A

Abandon method, of Session object, 17
AbsolutePosition property, of CStoredRecordset class, 226
Access. *See* Microsoft Access
access control list, adding default users to, 117
access denied, custom message for, 120
AccountHistory_Respond event, 183–185, *186*
AccountInfo project, **159–169**
    Account Options page, *181*
    AccountOptions_Respond event, 180, 181
    BalanceInquiry_Respond event, 182–183, *185*
    code to populate tables, 163–166
    createTransactionRecords function, 167–168, 169
    database structure, *161*
    field information, *162*
    findSignon function, 170–171
    flowchart, *160*
    getDateOffsetBy function, 168
    getRandomTime function, 169
    SelectAccount HTML template, 175–176
    SelectAccount page, *180*
    unauthorized access message, *187*
AccountOptions WebItem, 179
AccountOptions_Respond event, 181
    code, 180
Action parameter, for form tag, 41
Activate method, of ObjectControl interface, 326
Active Connection argument, of Recordset.Open method, 258
ActiveConnection property, for recordset, 275
ActiveDirectory services, 83
ActiveX DLLs, xvi
    accessing from WebClasses, **281–282**
    ObjectContext object, **282–284**
    testing, **284–290**
ActiveX objects
    ability to obtain references to other ASP objects, 21
    persisting, **290–297**
    to store state, 296
    storing, 222
        in Session variables, **290–294**
Add method, of Scripting.Dictionary object, 38

Add subroutine, in CStoredDictionary class, 228
AddHeader method, 200
   of Response object, 20
address bar of browser, URLData property information on, 179
adLockBatchOptimistic for database, 259–260
adLockOptimistic for database, 259–260
adLockPessimistic for database, 259–260
adLockReadOnly for database, 259–260
ADO (ActiveX Data Objects)
   basics, **252–253**
   for data retrieval, **256–273**
      with Command object, **261–265**
      Connection object, **256**
      cursor types, **256–257**
      record-locking options, **259–260**
      with Recordset object, **257–259**
   functions to simplify, **276–277**
   opening and closing connections, **254–255**
   Options argument, **260–261**
   Recordsets in XML file, 362
ADO object model, **253–255**
adOpenDynamic cursor, 257
adOpenForwardOnly cursor, 257
adOpenKeyset cursor, 257
adOpenStatic cursor, 257
adUseClient, 172
adUseServer, 172
anchor tag, href parameter in, 178
anonymous access, 120
   disabling, 118, 351
   IIS setup to allow, 116
AppendToLog method, of Response object, 20
appendToTextFile method, 110–111
Application Configuration dialog box, 137–138, *138*, 196, *196*
Application log
   error display in, 140–141, *141*
   MessageBox call in, 115

MTS error entry, *337*
   for permissions problems, 351
Application object, **15–16**
application state, 221
Application variables, for connection string for database, 213
App.Logpath property, 116
arrays, 173–174, 222
   as Command.Execute method argument, 265
ASP application
   code for providing fast access to table data, 58–63
   first, 41–42
   self-modifying, **42–51**
      code, 43–45
   structure of, **28–29**
ASP code
   request cycle, *23*
   vs. WebClasses, 66
ASP engine, to instantiate WebClass, 67
ASP files
   adding to package list, 346
   characteristics, 51
ASP object model, **13–22**
   Application object, **15–16**
   ObjectContext object, **22**, **282–284**, 285, 323
      and authentication problems, 289
   Request object, **18–19**
      and cookies, 198
   Response object, **19–21**, **19–21**, 128
      attempts to reference, 285–286
      and cookies, 198
      Status property, 120
   ScriptingContext object, **21–22**, 282, 283
   Server object, **14–15**
   Session object, **16–17**, **16–17**, 49
      cached data in, 194–195
      data saved in, 222
      hypothetical structure, *195*

ASP objects
    reference to, 283
        overusing in ActiveX classes, 289–290
ASP pages, 3, 12–13
    Browser Capabilities component in, 241
    calling object from, 287
    to display WebClass, 68
    On Error Resume Next in, 142
    to instantiate Browser Capabilities component, 242
    language independence in, **31–32**
    vs. WebClasses, advantages and disadvantages, **81–83**
ASPSESSIONID cookie, 34
associations, 15
AsVariant property, in CStoredDictionary class, 229
auditing, 351
authenticated user, object to represent, 300
authentication, 289. *See also* sign-on screen

# B

Back button in browser, 159
BalanceInquiry_Respond event, *185*
    code, 182–183
Base64 encoding scheme, 122
Basic Authentication, 120
BeginRequest event, 113–114, 205
beta testing, Web applications, **343–344**
binary compatibility, 330–331
BinaryCompare constant, 36–37
BinaryRead method, of Request object, 19
BinaryWrite method, of Response object, 20
<body>...</body> tag, 39
BOF property, of CStoredRecordset class, 226
bookmarks, error in Web applications from, 151

border, for empty table cells, 76
break mode, 139
breakpoints, in client-side scripts, 139
browscap.dll, 239
browscap.ini
    BrowserType object entry in, 239–241
    wildcard section in, 240
browser-based code repository, **297–310**
Browser Capabilities component, **241–243**
    ASP pages to instantiate, 242
BrowserCap object, Capabilities property of, 241
browsers
    closing to force new Session, 207
    code specific to, **244–248**
    determining type, **238–243**
    differences between, **236–238**
    History list, impact on counter, 218
    replaceable markers for pages specific to, **248**
    request process for files, **10–12**, *11*
    switching from debugger to, 101
    URLData information on address bar, 179
    View Source feature, hidden form variables and, 204
BrowserType object, 239–240
Buffer property, of Response object, 20, 47
business applications, Web applications as, 356–357

# C

C programming language, xv
CacheControl property, of Response object, 20
caching, **221–232**, 275
    data in Session object, 194–195
    in MTS, 315–316
    table data, **52–63**

Call statement, 131–132
CanBePooled method, of ObjectControl interface, 326
Capabilities property, of BrowserCap object, 241
cascading deletes, in Microsoft Access, 169
cascading style sheets, 236
    absolute positioning for graphic, 135
case-insensitive Dictionary object, function to return, 37
case sensitivity
    of Dictionary keys, 36, 37
    in HTML tags, 39
    of replacement tags, 96
CCode class, 299
central-data-to-client computing model, xv
centralized data, for IIS applications, 7
CGI (Common Gateway Interface) files, 12
Charset property, of Response object, 20
class files, adding to project, 230
class ID, and MTS, 331
Clear method, of Response object, 20
client-server applications, xv
    Web applications vs., **23–25**
client-side code, 32
    server-side code to write, **248–249**
    for window control, 303
client-side scripts
    breakpoints in, 139
    debugger for, **136–140**
        Internet Explorer as, 139–140
    on server, 138
    to submit form from link, 203–204
client-side state, unpredictability in, 204
ClientCertificate collection, of Request object, 19
clients
    refusal to accept cookies, 201
    storing information on, 198
CList class, 299
closing
    browser to force new Session, 207
    connections in ADO, **254–255**
CoCreateGUID32 API call, 219
code
    advantage of compiled, 82
    browser-based repository, **297–310**
    cleaning up, **341–342**
    executing on database server, 262–263
    MTS and reuse, 314
    optimizing, **77–81**
    separating display from programming, 72
    server-side vs. client-side, 32
    to write code, **248–249**
code base for IIS applications, 7
code reuse, xvi
    and Visual Basic, 5
CodePage property, of Session object, 17
CodeRepository project, **297–310**
    Administer Users page, 307, *307*
    Administration—Edit User page, *308*
    administrator access to user account information, 307
    Author/Administrator code view, *306*
    Code List page, *304*
    database structure, *298*
    Guest code view, *306*
    HTML templates in, 299
    menu and directions, *302*
    search page, 304, *305*
    separated layers, 299
    sign-on page, *300*
        redirection to, 299
    sign-ons, 299
collections, sizing and performance, 228
color, HTML and, 357–358
Column property, of CStoredRecordset class, 226
COM (Component Object Model), 3
COM specifications, for interfaces, 360

COM(+| z}, 314
comma-delimited string, for data inside Web-
    Class, 214
command-line interfaces, xv
Command object (ADO), 253–254, 275
    for data retrieval, **261–265**
commands, order of execution, 131
CommandText argument, impact of Options
    argument on, 260
comments, as markers for data placement,
    55–56
Common Gateway Interface (CGI) files, 12
Common Object Request Broker Architecture
    (CORBA), **359–360**
CompareMethod property, in CStoredDic-
    tionary class, 229
CompareMode property, of Scripting.Dictio-
    nary object, 36–37, 38
compiled code, advantage of, 82
compiled mode
    running WebClasses in, 117
    testing application in, **342**
compiling projects, **115–118**
Component Object Model (COM), 3
Component Wizard dialog, *332*, 332
components in MTS, 315
    changes in, 333
    client sharing of, 323
    data sharing between, 316
    updating, **320–321**
    using, **322–328**
computing model, central-data-to-client, xv
concatenating strings, 77, 275
    to create URL, 202
conditional statements, and include files,
    30–31
Connection object (ADO), 253, 254
    creating, 171
    CursorLocation property, 259
    for data retrieval, **256**

connection string to database source, Applica-
    tion variable for, 213
connections
    closing, 57
    for database access, 274–275
    to database source, DSN (Data Source
        Name) for, 211
    opening and closing in ADO, **254–255**
ConnectionString argument, for ADO Open
    method, 254–255
ConnectionString property, 171, 310
    of Connection object, 53
ConnectOptionEnum argument, for ADO
    Open method, 255
Contents collection
    of Application object, 16
    of Session object, 17
ContentType property, of Response object, 20
context object, in MTS, 323
context (Windows NT), 281
continuous scan for tag replacement, 95
cookies, **32–34**
    browser refusal of, 18
    GUID, 220
    maintaining state with, **198–201**, **208**
    maximum size, 199
    procedure for lost, 205
    size and server load, 23–24
Cookies collection
    of Request object, 19
    of Response object, 20, 33
CORBA (Common Object Request Broker
    Architecture), **359–360**
Count property
    in CStoredDictionary class, 229
    of Scripting.Dictionary object, 38
counter
    for database, 218
    persistent, 293
        code, 292

Counter WebItem screen, *207*
Counter_Respond event, 206–207
CPersistCounter object, 292
CPersistor class, 295, 300
crashing, 145
    MTS and, 316
    preventing, 152
Create New Data Source dialog box (ODBC), *212*
CreateInstance method of ObjectContext object, to create MTS object, 322–323
CreateObject method
    from ASP page, 287
    to create MTS object, 327
    for Server object, 14, 47–48, 284
        to create MTS object, 322
        to instantiate WebClass, 174
CreateParameter method, of Command object, 265
createTransactionRecords function, 167–168, 169
critical error handlers, 152
CStoredDictionary class, using, **230–232**
CStoredRecordset object, 224
    using, **230–232**
CursorLocation property, 258–259
    of Connection object, 53, 172
cursors
    in ADO, **256–257**
    server-side, 172
CursorType argument, of Recordset.Open method, 258
CursorType property, of Recordset object, 257
CUser class, 299
custom events, adding, *100*, **100–102**
custom message, for access denied, 120
custom tags, 71
Custom WebItem, to display message, 111–112

# D

Data Definition Language (DDL), 267
Data property, of CStoredRecordset class, 225
Data Source Name (DSN), for database, 211
database access component, changes for MTS, 324–326
database connectivity
    creating connection, 56
    opening connection, 53, 254
    for sign-on and password, 170
    as Web application requirement, 4
database counter, 218
database lookup, 181
    minimizing, 194–195
database server, executing code on, 262–263
DatabaseCompare constant, 36–37
databases
    code to populate tables, 163–166
    DSN (Data Source Name) for, 211
    locking, 259
    maintaining state, **204–205**
        with tables, **210–219**
    minimizing server resource use when accessing, 274–275
    portability, 358
    reversing parsing to update, 216
    rules for Web application access, 274–275
    trends, **361–362**
    WebClasses to access, **273–277**
DataCache project, 230–232
    Start Event results, *232*
dates, Format command for, 200
DCOM (distributed COM), for WebClass creation of external ActiveX DLL instance, 281
DCOM Machine Debug Manager Properties dialog, Security tab, *335*
dcomcnfg.exe, 281, *335*

DDL (Data Definition Language), 267
Deactivate method, of ObjectControl interface, 326
debugger, *129*
   for client-side script, **136–140**
   error logging and display, **140–144**
   for MTS components, 333
   refusal to step through WebClass code, 129
   switching to browser, 101
   in Visual Basic, 5, 126
DebugMode, for QueryString parameter, 143
Debug.Print statement, 128
default entry, in browscap.ini, 240
default IIS Web user, permissions assigned to, 116
default messages, overriding, 140
deferred execution, 132
deletes, cascading in Microsoft Access, 169
dependencies, in project files, 346
Depersist method, 295
design-time properties
   HTML templates, 95
   WebClasses, 90–91
development mode, running WebClasses in, 117
development server, 340
DHTML applications, Internet Information Server (IIS) applications vs., **6–7**
Dictionaries, 15
Dictionary object, 227. *See also* Scripting.Dictionary object
   adding colors to, 48
   to package database row, 172
   parsing string into, 214–215
directives, include, 30
directories
   for ASP application, 28–29
   for cookies, 200
   for HTML templates, 94
   for project files, 170

   for registration file, 119
   for SecuredSite project, *92*
   structure for ASP application, *28*
disconnected recordsets, **258–259**
display code, separating from programming code, 72
Distributed COM Configuration Properties dialog box, *335*
DLLs, replacing in IIS applications, **288**
documentation, for installation, 348
downloading, project code, xxi
drop-down list, 51
DSN (Data Source Name), for database, 211
.dsr files, 347
.dsx files, 347
dynamic HTML, 236
dynamic information, from Web applications, 4
dynamic-link library (DLL), runtime, 2
dynamic SQL, 172, 262

# E

empty recordset, error trapping for, **148**
Empty variant subtype, 99
encryption, for cookies, 201
End method, of Response object, 20
End-of-File (EOF) property, of recordset, 56
EndRequest method, 216
Enterprise Manager, in SQL Server, 267
EOF property, of CStoredRecordset class, 226
Error 91, "Object variable or With block variable not set", 140
error handling
   file overwritten by code for, 144
   generic, 153
error messages
   for ASP pages, 127
   overriding default, 140
error propagation, 152

Error property, of WebClass, 140
error trapping, **144–154**, 276–277
    for code creating WebClass, 142
    scenario, **146–154**
        empty recordset, **148**
        failure to obtain recordset, **147–148**
        missing critical data, **148–154**
    types of problems, 145
    in WriteTemplate method, 98
errors
    generating to test Web application, **342–343**
    logging and displaying, **140–144**
    unhandled in Visual Basic program, 115
    when running compiled DLL, 116
events, custom, *100*, **100–102**
Excel files, Internet Explorer display of, 237
executable file types, 12
Execute method, 56
    of Command object, 264–265
    of Connection object, 172
ExecuteSQL function, 277
execution order for commands, 131
Exists property
    in CStoredDictionary class, 229
    of Scripting.Dictionary object, 38
ExpandIncrement property, 228
    in CStoredDictionary class, 229
expiration date, to control data obsolescence, 221
Expires property
    of cookies, 199
    of Response object, 20, 68
ExpiresAbsolute property, of Response object, 20
eXtensible Markup Language (XML), 358, **362–366**
extensible stylesheet language (XSL), 366
external DLLs, 280
external errors, 153
    handling, 147
external resources, references to, 341

# F

familiarity, and Visual Basic, 5
FatalErrorEvent event, 98
    output from, *141*
FatalErrorResponse event, 140
Field object (ADO), 253
FieldCount property, of CStoredRecordset class, 225
FieldNumber property, of CStoredRecordset class, 225
fields in database, names vs. index numbers, 174
Fields property, of CStoredRecordset class, 225
File Auditing dialog, *352*
file extension associations, in Registry, 12
file formats, 357, 358
    proprietary, and XML, 364
files
    opening, 55
    request process for, **10–12**, *11*
FileSystemObject, 49
Filter property, of CStoredRecordset class, 225
Find function, of CStoredRecordset class, 225
FindRowNumbers property, of CStoredRecordset class, 225
findSignon function, 108, 170–171
    code, 109–110
firehose cursor, 257, 274
Flush method, of Response object, 20
fonts, HTML and, 357–358
For…Next structure
    for cookie handling, 199
    QueryString collection support for, 201
Form collection, of Request object, 19, 203
Format command, for dates, 200
Format constants, 109
<form>…</form> tag, 40, 203
forms in HTML, **39–42**
    testing whether user has posted, 48

forward-only recordset, 256
frames, 236
　problems with, 301
Franklin, Carl, 3
frmConcatenate.frm, code, 77–80

## G

Get method, 41
getAccountList subroutine, Recordset parameter for, 177–178
getBrowserCapabilities.asp file
　VBScript code, 242–243
　　output, *243*
GetChunk method, 173
getData method, 223
getDateOffsetBy function, 168–169
getGUID function, 220
getHTMLTemplate function, 106
getObjectContext method, 21, 22, 283, 324, 326–327
getProductSQL procedure, 273
getRandomInt function, 166
getRandomTime function, 169
getRows method, 222
getState function, 214
getStateValue function, 215
getString method, 222–223
global.asa file, 15
　adding to package list, 346
　editing on target server, 349
　external resources references in, 341
　initializations in Application_OnStart event procedure in, 16
　location of, 28
　to redirect browser, 29
　refusal to run, 46
　Session_OnEnd event, 218
　Session_OnStart event, 205, 213

graphics
　cascading style sheets for absolute positioning, 135
　HTML and, 357–358
Guest account, IUSR_MachineName and IWAM_MachineName as part of, 281
GUID (Globally Unique Identifier), 219–221
GUID cookie, 220

## H

hardware requirements for projects, xx–xxi
hash value, for user signon and password, 121
HasKeys property, of cookies, 198
HAVING clause (SQL), 263
<head>…</head> tag, 39
header information, Request object for, 18
hidden form variables, maintaining state with, **203–204**, 208, **209–210**
hidden input, 51
History list of browser, impact on counter, 218
href parameter, in anchor tag, 178
HTML, **39–42**, *40*
　adding Query String parameters to, 202
　browser display of, 236
　browser-specific from WebClass, **246–248**
　process for displaying file, 10, *11*
　without templates, **72–75**
　vs. XML, 366
HTML editor, xxi
　Visual Basic to launch, 104
HTML parser
　problems of, 96
　and replacement tag case, 134
HTML templates, **71–72**
　adding to package list, 346
　browser-specific, **244–246**
　and browser type, 238

case change of replacement tags by parser, 95, 96
in CodeRepository project, 299
creating, **92–99**
deleting unused, 341
design-time properties, 95
directories for, 94
editing, 104
for menus, 303
SelectAccount, code, 175–176
Visual Basic copying of, 94
WebItem as, 182
<html>...</html> tag, 39
HTMLEncode method, for Server object, 14
HTMLTableString property, 290
of CStoredRecordset class, 225
HTTP (Hypertext Transfer Protocol)
connections, 11
header information, 32–33
adding to page, 20
to tell browser to save cookie, 200
HTTP_USER_AGENT key, 238
searching, 243
hypertext, 158

# I

ID for current session, 17
"ideal" Web application, 83, *84*
IDL (interface definition language), 360
if...END structure, 30–31
IIS. *See* Internet Information Server (IIS)
IIS applications
MTS and, **317–319**
replacing DLLs in, **288**
request process for files, 10
IIS in-process components, *319*, 319
images, adding to package list, 346
<img> tags, 135

in-memory cookies, 33
in-memory databases, 361
COM+ support for, 317
include directive, 30
#INCLUDE FILE directive, 30
include (.inc) files, 28, **30–31**
#INCLUDE VIRTUAL directive, 30
index numbers, vs. names of fields, 174
information, invisible, 24
.ini file, 239
InitFromVariant subroutine, in CStoredDictionary class, 229
InitProperties event, 291
input controls, 50–51
installation. *See also* Web application deployment
installation package, creating, **345–347**
installation program, third-party vendors, 347
instance of object, method to return, 14
instantiation of WebClass objects, 66–67
Instr function, 228
interfaces
COM specifications vs. CORBA, 360
trends, 357
Internet Explorer
for debugging client-side scripts, 139–140
Enter Network Password dialog box, *120*
Netscape Navigator vs., 236, 237
response to 401 status, 121
version 4 for client-side debugging, 137
version 5 and XML, 366
Internet Information Server (IIS), 2
applications, vs. DHTML applications, **6–7**
Authentication settings, 120
permissions assigned to default Web user, 116
request handling on time-slice basis, 12
Virtual Directory properties, dialog box, 137, *137*
Internet Options dialog (IE), Advanced tab, *139*

Internet Server (ISAPI), 2
Internet Service Manager, **320–321**
    Authentication Methods dialog box, *118*
    Virtual Directory properties, 46, *46*
invisible information, 24
IP (Internet Protocol) address, 10
    shared, 32
ISAPI (Internet Server), 2
    default user, permissions assigned to, 116
IsClientConnected property, of Response object, 21
iSQL utility, 267
IsStoredRecordset property, of CStoredRecordset class, 225
Item property
    in CStoredDictionary class, 229
    of Scripting.Dictionary object, 38
IUSR_MachineName account, 117
    for file-based databases, 211
    launch permissions for, 336
    and permissions errors, 351
    permissions for, 281, 334
    testing, 349
IWAM_MachineName account, 116, 117
    for file-based databases, 211
    launch permissions for, 336
    and permissions errors, 351
    permissions for, 281, 334
    testing, 349

## J

Java, xvii, **359–360**
JavaScript, 31, 244
    Internet Explorer support of, 246
JScript, 31
    downloading, 140

## K

key fields, for updating disconnected records, 259
Key property
    in CStoredDictionary class, 229
    of Scripting.Dictionary object, 38
key-value associations
    for QueryString parameter, 201
    returning collection of, 16
Keys method, of Scripting.Dictionary object, 38
Keys property, in CStoredDictionary class, 229
Knowledge Base (Microsoft), 127

## L

<%@ LANGUAGE= %> directive, 31, 47
languages, xiv
    independence in ASP pages, **31–32**
launch permissions, for IUSR_MachineName and IWAM_MachineName, 336
LCID property, of Session object, 17
Library Package, 316
line breaks in HTML, 92
lists, interface for displaying large, 303
load balancing, on multiple servers, 197
local variables, 50
    reference to, 77
Lock method, of Application object, 16
locking, 274
LockType argument, of Recordset.Open method, 258
logging errors, **140–144**, 153–154
logic errors, 153
longConCat function, 81

# M

maintaining state, 192
  across sessions, 204
  with cookies, **198–201**, 208
  in database, **204–205**
  with database tables, **210–219**
  with hidden form variables, **203–204**, **209–210**
  MTS and, 316, 321–322
  with object persistence, **296–297**
  options for, **192–206**
  with QueryString variables, **201–203**, **208–209**
  with session variables, **194–198**, **206–207**
  summary, **232–233**
MapPath method, for Server object, 14, 49, 55
markers
  for browser-specific pages, **248**
  comments for, 55–56
  in HTML templates, 176
MaxKeyLength property, in CStoredDictionary class, 229
Me keyword, 97
memory allocation, 77
  Session variables requirements, 197–198
Menu template, 303
Menu_ProcessTag event, link creation, 303
MessageBox call, as Application log event, 115
messages
  Custom WebItem to display, 111–112
  customizing for denied access, 120
Method parameter, for form tag, 41
methodName variable, 147
Microsoft Access, xx
  cascading deletes in, 169
  database from Sybex Web site, 161
  limitations of, 252

queries, 262
stored procedures in, 263–264
for transactions, vs. SQL Server, 270–271
Microsoft Active Server Pages Object Library, 283
Microsoft Data Engine (MSDE), 252
Microsoft Distributed Transaction Coordinator service, 333–334, *334*
Microsoft Knowledge Base, 127
Microsoft Office 2000, and XML, 358, 366
Microsoft Office, Internet Explorer display of documents, 237
Microsoft Scripting Runtime Library, referencing, 47
Microsoft Transaction Server, 22
  Type Library, 283
MIME (Multipurpose Internet Mail Extensions), 11–12
Mode property, 53
  of Connection object, 255
Move subroutine, of CStoredRecordset class, 226
MoveFirst subroutine, of CStoredRecordset class, 226
MoveLast subroutine, of CStoredRecordset class, 226
MoveNext subroutine, of CStoredRecordset class, 226
MovePrevious subroutine, of CStoredRecordset class, 226
MoveTo subroutine, of CStoredRecordset class, 226
MSDE (Microsoft Data Engine), 252
MSDTC (Microsoft Distributed Transaction Coordinator service), 333–334, *334*
MSWC Browser Capabilities component, 239
mswcrun.dll file, 70, 127
msxml.dll, 366
MTS (Microsoft Transaction Server)
  component use, **322–328**

database access code as component, 274
Explorer, **317–319**, *318*, *320*
and IIS/Web application model, **317–319**
moving projects into, **328–336**
 code changes, **329**
 compiling project, **329–331**, *330*
 package creation and configuration, *331*, **331–332**
 permissions and, 336
 potential uses for, **321–322**
 running project, **333–334**
 to update component, **320–321**
 and WebClasses, 284
 what it is, **314–317**
MTS object, creating, 322
MTSTransactionMode property, 281, 315
Multipurpose Internet Mail Extensions (MIME), 11–12
multiuser applications, 358–359
multiuser environment, 68–69

# N

Name parameter, for form tag, 40
Name property
 of Field, 56
 for HTML templates, 95
 for WebClass, 90
NameInURL property, 90
names
 of fields, vs. index numbers, 174
 for variables, 99
nested loops, for filling table, 56–57
Netscape Navigator, vs. Internet Explorer, 236, 237
networks, xv
New keyword, 322, 328
 to access ActiveX DLL from WebClass, 288

New Project dialog (Visual Basic), 88, *89*
NextItem property
 impact on execute order, 132
 of WebClass, 75, 97, 103, 129, 130–131
no state management, 90
non-breaking space ( ), 76
NT Challenge/Response, 120
null value, and error handling, 150

# O

object databases, 361
Object Linking and Embedding Internet Server Application Programming Interface (OLEISAPI), 2
object variables, destroying, 76
ObjectContext object, **22**, **282–284**, 285, 323
 and authentication problems, 289
ObjectControl interface, 328
 advantage of implementing, 327
 methods for, 326
ObjectControl_CanBePooled method, 327
objects
 automating persistence and retrieval, **294–296**
 in memory, MTS maintenance, 321
 obtaining reference to, 48
obsolete data
 eliminating, **221**
 on state, deleting or archiving, 205
OCXs, xvi
ODBC Data Source Administrator program, 211, *212*
Office 2000
 Internet Explorer display of documents, 237
 and XML, 358, 366
OLEDB (Object Linking and Embedding Database) driver, 252

OLEISAPI (Object Linking and Embedding Internet Server Application Programming Interface), 2
On Error GoTo, 146
On Error Resume Next, 142, 146
OnEnd event
   of Application object, 16
   of Session object, 17
OnEndPage method, 69, 282, 283
OnStart event
   of Application object, 16
   of Session object, 17
OnStartPage method, 21, 69, 282
OnTransactionAbort event, of ObjectContext object, 22
OnTransactionCommit event, of ObjectContext object, 22
open database connectivity client cursors, 53
Open method
   of Connection object, 53, 254
   of Recordset object, 257–258
OpenConnection function, 276
opening connections, in ADO, **254–255**
OpenTextFile method, 108
optimizing code, **77–81**
Option Explicit command, 47
<option> tag, 51
Options argument, of Recordset.Open method, 258
Oracle, xx
output parameters, 275

# P

Package Wizard dialog, *331*
packages
   creating and configuring in MTS, *331*, **331–332**
   Transaction Explorer to list, 317, *318*
   using compiled WebClass in, 284
page requests, rerouting to sign-on screen, 88, *89*
.pak file, 349
parseStateString function, 214–215
parsing string
   into Dictionary object, 214–215
   reversing to update database, 216
Password argument, for ADO Open method, 255
passwords, 119
path, method to return, 14
Path property, for cookies, 200
performance. *See also* optimizing code
   dynamic SQL vs. stored procedures, 265
   persistence and, 297
Perl (Practical Extraction and Report Language), 31
permanent cookies, 18, 199
permission denied errors, 282
permissions
   assigned to default IIS Web user, 116
   for IUSR_MachineName and IWAM_MachineName, 281, 334, 336
   and Web application deployment, **350–353**
Persist method, 295
Persistable property, 291
persistence
   automating, **294–296**
   of object, to maintain state, **296–297**
   and performance, 297
persistent cookies, 33, 199
persisting ActiveX objects, **290–297**
PICS property, of Response object, 21
pointers. *See* cursors
pooling in MTS, 315–316
Post method, 41
   to submit form, 203
PowerPoint files, Internet Explorer display of, 237

presentation layer, WebClasses to manage, 106
ProcessNoStateInstance method, 69
ProcessRetainInstanceWebClass method, 69
ProcessTag event, 70, 71, 98–99, 132, 133
    TagName argument for, 134
program flow, **158–159**. *See also* AccountInfo project
    to include registration screen, *103*
    linear, 187–189, *188*
programming
    language trends, 358
    scope of, xiv
    separating code from display code, 72
    and XML, 364–366
project files, file locations stored in, 170
Project Properties dialog box
    Component tab, *330*
    Debugging tab, 129, *130*
    General tab, 115, *115*, *330*
    Virtual Directory tab, *137*
projects
    adding class files to, 230
    compiling, **115–118**
    dependencies in files, 346
    downloading code, xxi
    features for debugging, 343
    moving into MTS, **328–336**
        code changes, **329**
        compiling project, **329–331**, *330*
        name changes, 90
        running in MTS, **333–334**
Property Editor, design-time properties available, 90–91
PropertyBag object, 290, 293
    creating, 294
    storing multiple objects in, 296
proprietary file formats, and XML, 364
provider in ADO, 253
proxy server, for IP address sharing, 32

Public property, 90
pubs database, downloading, 52

## Q

queries, 172
    running multiple times, Connection object for, 262
    vs. stored procedures, 262
QueryString collection
    error handling, 151
    of Request object, 19
    and URLData, 186
QueryString variables, maintaining state with, **201–203, 208–209**

## R

read-only mode, opening connection in, 171–172
read-only recordset, 256
ReadAll method, 49
ReadProperties event, 291, 296
ReadProperty method, of PropertyBag object, 328
readTextFile function, 108
    code, 109
record locking, in ADO, **259–260**
RecordCount property, of CStoredRecordset class, 225
records
    stored procedures for retrieving, 271
    code, 272–273
RecordsAffected argument, of Command.Execute method, 264
Recordset object, 222–223, 253
    creating, 53

CursorLocation property, 259
   for data retrieval, **257–259**
   in Dictionary objects, 172
   retrieving data into, 256
   returned by Execute method of Connection object, 172
recordsets
   closing, 57
   disconnected, **258–259**, 275
   failure to obtain, error trapping for, **147–148**
   field names vs. index numbers, 174
   for getAccountList subroutine, 177–178
   as object property, 296
recordToDictionary routine, 172–173
Redirect method, of Response object, 21, 53
redirection, 53
   preventing endless loop, 301
   to sign-on page, in CodeRepository project, 299
   between WebClasses, 174–175
refreshing cached data, 52, 54–55
Register_Register event, 110
   code, 107–108
Register_Respond event, 104, 106
registration file
   directory for, 119
   security problems of, 117
Registry, 239
   file extension associations in, 12
   GUIDs in, 219
relational databases, 362
ReleaseInstance method, 193
Remote method, of Scripting.Dictionary object, 38
Remove subroutine, in CStoredDictionary class, 229
RemoveAll method, of Scripting.Dictionary object, 38
replace function, 55

replacement tags
   HTML parser and case of, 134
   placement of, 135
   in WebClasses, 95–96
reports
   sequence of conditions before displaying, 181–182
   WebItem for page, 179
RepositoryData ActiveX DLL, 308
repurposing
   vs. reusing, 170
   WebClasses, **170–174**
Request object, **18–19**
   and cookies, 198
request process, for files, **10–12**, *11*
ReScanReplacements property, 134–135
   for HTML templates, 95
   of WebItem, 132
resource errors, 149, 153
Respond event, 70, 97–98, 130
Response object, **19–21**, 128
   attempts to reference, 285–286
   and cookies, 198
   Status property, 120
REXX (Restructured Extended Executor), 31
RGB value for color, 48
role-based security, MTS and, 321
roles, in MTS.pak file, 350
routine, ConnectionString argument for, 310
Rows property, of CStoredRecordset class, 225
RowToDictionary function, of CStoredRecordset class, 226
run mode, 139
runat=server parameter, 32
runtime dynamic-link library (DLL), 2
runtime errors
   during HTML template processing, 98
   from mismatched tags, 96

## S

saveState function, code, 216–218
script code, in ASP files, 13
<script>...</script> tags, 31–32
scripting host, ASP engine as, 31
ScriptingContext object, **21–22**, 282, 283
Scripting.Dictionary object, **34–39**
    changing values of associations, 36
    determining key existence, 35
    methods and properties, 38
Scripting.FileSystemObject, 108
ScriptTimeout property, for Server object, 15
Secure attribute, for cookies, 201
security
    compiled code and, 82
    as Web application requirement, 4
security context, 116, 117
security for Web sites
    custom events, *100*, **100–102**
    custom WebItem, **103–113**
    how it works, **88**
    HTML template creation, **92–99**
    improving, **119**
    MTS and, 317
    program flow, *89*
    project creation, **88–91**
    project directory structure, *92*
    Register_Register event, code, 107–108
    registration screen, 102
        HTML code, 105
        program flow to include, *103*
    sign-on screen, *102*
    Signon_frmSignon method, 112–113
    testing, **113–114**
SelectAccount HTML template
    code, 175–176
    page, *180*
SelectAccount WebItem, 179
SelectAccount_ProcessTag event
    code, 176–177
    URLData property, 178–179
selected parameter, 51
<select>...</select> tag, 51
selectTable.asp file, 52, 58–60
SendTags argument, for ProcessTag event, 99
server applications, timeout by, 159
Server object, **14–15**
server-side code, 32
    to write client-side code, **248–249**
server-side cursor, 172
servers
    client-side scripts on, 138
    crashing, 145
    load balancing, 197
    Sessions on sites with multiple, 197
ServerVariables collection, 238
    of Request object, 19
Session cookie, and counters, 218
Session object, **16–17**, 49
    cached data in, 194–195
    data saved in, 222
    hypothetical structure, *195*
Session state, cookies to maintain, 32
Session variables, 48, 113, 181, 361
    assigning to local variables, 50
    maintaining state with, **194–198**, **206–207**
    to store WebClass, 193
    storing ActiveX objects in, **290–294**
    storing browser properties in, 242
    storing StoredRecordset as, 224
    testing, 294
session, what it is, **17–18**
SessionID cookie, 24, 214
    creation, 33
    request from browser without valid, 18
SessionID property, 34
    of Session object, 17
Session_OnEnd event, 205

Session_OnStart event, 205
   in global.asa file, 213
Sessions
   closing browser to force new, 207
   maintaining state across, 204
   storing state information across, **219–221**
SetAbort method, of ObjectContext object, 22
SetComplete method, of ObjectContext object, 22
setStateValue function, 215
Shared Property Manager, 316
shortConCat function, 81
showTable.asp file, 54, 60–63
showTable_Respond event, 76
   code, 74
sign-on screen, *102*
   HTML for, 92
      code, 93
   rerouting page requests to, 88, *89*
sign-ons, CodeRepository project, 299
Signon-ProcessTag event, 98–99
Signon_frmSignon method, code, 112–113
SmallTalk, 359
software requirements for projects, xx–xxi
Source argument, of Recordset.Open method, 258
speed, as Web application requirement, 4
SQL
   and error handling, 149
   field names vs. numbers in, 150
   vs. stored procedures, to populate database, **265–273**
SQL Server, xx
   to create stored procedure, 264
   Enterprise Manager, 267
   for transactions, vs. Access, 270–271
standards, xv
Start event, eliminating default code, 97
state. *See also* maintaining state
state data
   client-side, unpredictability in, 204
   deleting or archiving obsolete, 205
   and response time of application, 90
   storage location, 219
   storing across sessions, **219–221**
   storing in database, 205
state variable, functions to set and retrieve, 215
StateMaintenance property, of WebClass, 192–193
StateMaintenance.mdb Access database, 210
StateManagement property, 90
StaticObjects collection
   of Application object, 16
   of Session object, 17
Status property, of Response object, 21, 120
stored procedures, 275
   code for investigating, 267–270
   vs. dynamic SQL, 172
   vs. queries, 262
   vs. SQL, to populate database, **265–273**
   Transact SQL for, 263, 264
StoredDictionary class
   code, 230–231
   writing, **227–229**
StoredRecordset class
   code, 230–231
   writing, **223–227**
StoredRecordset object, 296–297
StoredRecordset property, of CStoredRecordset class, 224
StoreRecord subroutine, in CStoredDictionary class, 229
StoreRecordset subroutine, of CStoredRecordset class, 225
string handling, as Web application requirement, 4
string replacements, 55
StringConcatenation project, 77
StringFromGUID2 API call, 219–220

strings, 222
   concatenating, 77
   parsing into Dictionary object, 214–215
subkeys, in cookies, 198
Sun Microsystems, 360
Sybase, xx
Sybex Web site
   Access database from, 161
   downloading code from, 73
   downloading pubs database from, 52
System Audit Policy dialog, 351, *351*
System DSN, 211
System log, for permissions problems, 351

# T

table data, caching, **52–63**
TableName parameter, caching in local variable, 54
tables
   border for empty cells, 76
   releasing locks, 76
tag replacement, 132
   by mswcrun.dll, 127
tag replacement engine, 95
TagContents property, 99, 134, 135, 136
TagName argument, for ProcessTag event, 99, 134
TagName property, 136
TagPrefix property, 132, 136
   for HTML templates, 95
target server, determining configuration, **344–345**
<td>…</td> tags, 76
templates. *See* HTML templates
   HTML without, **72–75**
test server, 340
   screen captures of settings, 348
testing

ActiveX DLLs, **284–290**
   applications, 153
text files
   cookies as, 201
   opening and reading, 108
TextCompare constant, 36–37
TextStream object
   method to return, 49
   OpenTextFile method to return, 108–109
threads
   for compiled WebClasses, 340
   wcRetainInstance and, 193
timeout, by server applications, 159
Timeout property, of Session object, 17
<title>…</title> tag, 39
TotalBytes property, of Request object, 19
Transact SQL, for stored procedures, 263, 264
transactions, 10, 162, 166–167, 216
   inquiry record, 183
   MTS to manage, 314
   running or debugging components using, 333–334
   and SQL Server vs. Access, 270–271
   as Web application requirement, 5
   WebClasses and, 281
transient connection, to Web server, 11
transient cookies, 18
trapping. *See* error trapping
<tr>…</tr> tags, 76
trends, in Web applications, **356–359**

# U

unhandled errors, in Visual Basic program, 115
Unix operating system, 359
Unlock method, of Application object, 16
updating data, record locking and, 260
upgrades, and Web applications, 357

URL (Uniform Resource Locator)
    browser response to, 10
    and program flow control, 158–159
    relative, 341
    string concatenation to create, 202
    user access to, 187
    WebClass dynamic creation of, 106
URLData property
    information on browser address bar, 179
    QueryString collection and, 186
    in SelectAccount_ProcessTag event, 178–179
    for WebClass, 202–203, 208
URLEncode method, 203
    for Server object, 15
URLFor function, 106–107
URLFor method, 178
user input, Web applications and, 159
User Manager for Domains, 351
UserID argument, for ADO Open method, 255

## V

Value method, 173
Value property, of CStoredRecordset class, 225
variables
    forcing declaration before use, 47
    hidden form, maintaining state with, **203–204**
    names for, 99
    Session vs. local, 50
VB forms engine, 72
vbBinaryCompare constant (VBScript), 37
vbDatabaseCompare constant (VBScript), 37, 39
.vbp files, file locations stored in, 170
VBScript, 2, 31, 244
    downloading, 140
    function name to return values, 38
    Internet Explorer support of, 246
    vs. Visual Basic, 82
vbTextCompare constant (VBScript), 37
VBX-based control, xvi
version number, for program, 342
View Source feature of browser, hidden form variables and, 204
virtual directory, 196
    marking as Web application, 46
    set up, 349
virtual Web, Visual Basic creation of, 72
Visual Basic
    development, xiv
    limitations for Web programming, 2
    reasons to use for Web applications, **4–6**
    VBScript vs., 82
Visual InterDev, xxi, 126
    project setup in, 47
    to set breakpoints in client-side script, 139
visual programming, xv
Visual Studio Package and Deployment Wizard, 341
    Included Files list, *345*
    launching, 345
Visual Studio Service Pack 3, 127

## W

<WCImg>...</WCImg> tags, 135
WCMessage replacement tag, 95
<wcName> tag, 71
wcNoState, 90, 193
WCPassword replacement tag, 95
WCPersistence project, 291–294
    initial results, *293*
wcRetainInstance, 90, 193
WCSignon replacement tag, 95

&lt;WCTotal&gt; replacement tag, 135
Web application deployment
   permissions issues, **350–353**
   preparation, **340–345**
      beta testing, **343–344**
      code cleanup, **341–342**
      compiled mode testing, **342**
      generating likely errors, **342–343**
      target server configuration, **344–345**
      test server, **343**
   running installation, **348–350**
   target server, configuring, **347–350**
Web applications
   vs. client-server applications, **23–25**
   development, xvi–xvii
      model, xvii–xviii
   dynamic information from, 4
   reasons to use Visual Basic for, **4–6**
   requirements, 4–5
   testing, 153
   trends, **356–359**
   and user input, 159
   what it is, **3–4**
Web development environments, 46
Web farm, 197
Web pages, passing information between, 179
Web server, 2. *See also* Internet Information Server (IIS)
   file request to, 10–11
   isolation by MTS, 316
   lack of client information, 24
   loading DLLs directly into, 2
Web sites, 3
   for browscap.ini download, 239
   for JScript download, 140
   on MIME registered types, 12
   Sybex, 52, 73
   for VBScript download, 140
WebClass Designer, 73, *73*
   with sign-on template, *94*
   toolbar, *129*

WebClass event, **126–136**
WebClass object, 3
WebClass tags, 71
WebClass_BeginRequest event, code to write client-side script, 138–139
WebClass.dsr file, 97
WebClass_EndRequest event, 294
WebClasses, xvi, 66
   to access databases, **273–277**
   accessing ActiveX DLLs from, **281–282**
   adding function to, 109–110
   vs. ASP, advantages and disadvantages, **81–83**
   and ASP pages, 241
   browser specific HTML from, **246–248**
   and browsers, 237
   comma-delimited string for data inside, 214
   CreateObject method to instantiate, 174
   debugger refusal to step through code, 129
   design-time properties, 90–91
   error trapping for code creating, 142
   event sequence, *70*, **75–76**
   frames and requests to, 301
   as glue, **280**
   how they work, **66–70**
   impact of failure, 145
   and MTSTransactionMode property, 315
   redirection between, 174–175
   reference to, 97
   replacement tags, 95–96
   repurposing, **170–174**
   request cycle, *67*
   Retained in Memory option for, 115
   running in development mode, 117
   and ScriptingContext object, 286
   security risks, 82
   Sessions for, **196–198**
   vs. standard class, 69
   StateMaintenance property of, 192–193
   subroutine stub creation, 103

using multiple in application, **174–189**
VB-generated ASP page to display, 68
writing HTML inside, 72
WebClass_Initialize event, 69, 128, 142
    output, *143*
WebClassManager object, 69, 193, 280
WebClass_Start event, 69–70, 162, 246–247, 285, 287
    default response code, 97
WebClass_Terminate event, 128, 140
WebItem
    adding custom, **103–113**
    as HTML templates, 182
    for report page, 179
WHERE clause (SQL), 263
wildcard section, in browscap.ini, 240
Windows, xv
Windows NT
    audits, 352
    security, 119, **120–122**
Word files, Internet Explorer display of, 237
wrapper functions, 276
wrapper, ScriptingContext object as, 21
Write method, of Response object, 21, 77, 138
WriteProperties event, 291, 296
WriteTemplate method, 179, 202, 245
    trapping for errors in, 98

# X

XML (eXtensible Markup Language), 358, **362–366**
    databases, 362
XML parser, 366
XSL (eXtensible Stylesheet Language), 366

# GET MCSD CERTIFIED WITH SYBEX
## THE CERTIFICATION EXPERTS

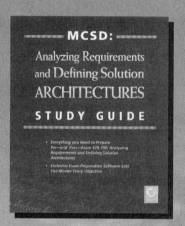

- Complete coverage of every Microsoft objective
- Hundreds of challenging review questions, in the book and on the CD
- Hands-on exercises that let you apply the concepts you've learned
- Page count: 592-752; Hardcover; Trim: 7½" x 9"; Price: $44.99; CD included

Ben Ezzell
ISBN 0-7821-2431-3

## Other MCSD Study Guides Available from Sybex:

MCSD: Visual Basic® 6 Desktop Applications Study Guide
Michael McKelvy
ISBN 0-7821-2438-0

MCSD: Visual Basic® 6 Distributed Applications Study Guide
Michael Lee with Clark Christensen
ISBN 0-7821-2433-X

MCSD: Access® 95 Study Guide
Peter Vogel & Helen Feddema
ISBN 0-7821-2282-5

MCSD: Windows® Architecture I Study Guide
Ben Ezzell
ISBN 0-7821-2271-X

MCSD: Windows® Architecture II Study Guide
Michael Lee & Kevin Wolford
ISBN 0-7821-2274-4
MCSD: SQL Server® 6.5 Database Design Study Guide
Kevin Hough
ISBN 0-7821-2269-8

MCSD: Visual Basic® 5 Study Guide
Mike McKelvy
ISBN 0-7821-2228-0

MCSE/MCSD: SQL Server® 7 Database Design Study Guide
Kevin Hough & Ed Larkin
ISBN 0-7821-2586-7

Available Summer '99:
MCSD Visual Basic® 6 Core Requirements Box
Michael McKelvy, Michael Lee with Clark Christensen & Ben Ezzell
ISBN 0-7821-2582-4
$109.97
**Contains:**
MCSD: Analyzing Requirements and Defining Solution Architectures Study Guide
MCSD: Visual Basic® 6 Desktop Applications Study Guide
MCSD: Visual Basic® 6 Distributed Applications Study Guide

**A savings of $25!**

www.sybex.com

# Access for Everyone
## FROM THE BEGINNER TO THE PROFESSIONAL DEVELOPER

ISBN 0-7821-2485-2
$24.99; 608 pages

ISBN 0-7821-2327-9
$44.99; 1104 pages; 1 CD

ISBN 0-7821-2326-0
$49.99; 1302 pages; Hardcover; 1 CD

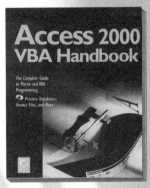

ISBN 0-7821-2324-4
$49.99; 1056 pages; 1 CD

ISBN 0-7821-2370-8
$54.99; 1008 pages; 1 CD

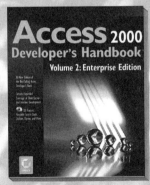

ISBN 0-7821-2372-4
$54.99; 1008 pages; 1 CD

ISBN 0-7821-2371-6
$89.99; 2200 pages; 2 CDs

SYBEX
www.sybex.com

# SYBEX BOOKS ON THE WEB

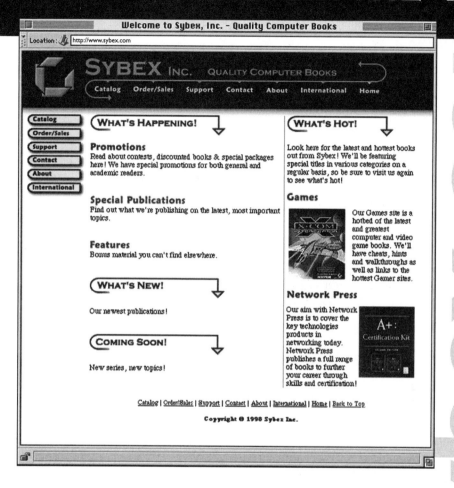

At the dynamic and informative Sybex Web site, you can:

- view our complete online catalog
- preview a book you're interested in
- access special book content
- order books online at special discount prices
- learn about Sybex

## www.sybex.com

SYBEX Inc. • 1151 Marina Village Parkway, Alameda, CA 94501 • 510-523-8233

# TAKE YOUR SKILLS TO THE NEXT LEVEL

## with Visual Basic Developer's Guides from Sybex

**VB Developer's Guide to ADO**
Mike Gunderloy
ISBN: 0-7821-2556-5 • 496pp
$39.99 • Fall '99

**VB Developer's Guide to ASP and IIS**
A. Russell Jones
ISBN: 0-7821-2557-3 • 448pp
$39.99 • Fall '99

www.sybex.com

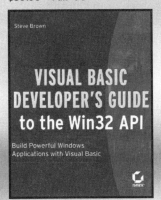

**VB Developer's Guide to COM and COM+**
Wayne Freeze
ISBN: 0-7821-2558-1 • 496pp
$39.99 • Fall '99

**VB Developer's Guide to the Win32 API**
Steve Brown
ISBN: 0-7821-2559-X • 496pp
$39.99 • Fall '99

**VB Developer's Guide to E-Commerce**
Noel Jerke
ISBN: 0-7821-2621-9 • 704pp
$49.99 • Winter '99

- Get the nuts-and-bolts information you need to develop industrial-strength enterprise applications.
- Dive deeply into topics that get only cursory coverage in the tomes claiming to be complete references.
- Focus on real-world issues, with code examples you can use in your own work.
- Learn from authors who are experienced Visual Basic developers.